CRITICAL *ACCLAIM*
FOR *TRAVELERS' TALES*

"The *Travelers' Tales* series is altogether remarkable."
— Jan Morris, author of *Journeys, Locations*, and *Hong Kong*

"For the thoughtful traveler, these books are an invaluable resource.
There's nothing like them on the market."
— Pico Iyer, author of *Video Night in Kathmandu*

"This is the stuff memories can be duplicated from."
— Karen Krebsbach, *Foreign Service Journal*

"I can't think of a better way to get comfortable with a destination
than by delving into *Travelers' Tales*...before reading a guidebook,
before seeing a travel agent. The series helps visitors refine their
interests and readies them to communicate with the peoples they
come in contact with...."
— Paul Glassman, Society of American Travel Writers

"*Travelers' Tales* is a valuable addition to any predeparture reading
list."
— Tony Wheeler, publisher, Lonely Planet Publications

"*Travelers' Tales* delivers something most guidebooks only promise:
a real sense of what a country is all about...."
— Steve Silk, *Hartford Courant*

"*Travelers' Tales* is a useful and enlightening addition to the travel
bookshelves...providing a real service for those who enjoy reading
first-person accounts of a destination before seeing it for themselves."
— Bill Newlin, publisher, Moon Publications

"The *Travelers' Tales* series should become required reading for anyone visiting a foreign country who wants to truly step off the tourist
track and experience another culture, another place, firsthand."
— Nancy Paradis, *St. Petersburg Times*

THE
GIFT *of*
RIVERS

*True Stories of Life
on the Water*

THE
GIFT *of*
RIVERS

True Stories of Life
on the Water

Edited by
PAMELA MICHAEL

Series Editors
JAMES O'REILLY AND LARRY HABEGGER

TRAVELERS' TALES · SAN FRANCISCO

Credits and copyright notices for the individual articles in this collection are given starting on page 269.

We have made every effort to trace the ownership of all copyrighted material and to secure permission from copyright holders. In the event of any question arising as to the ownership of any material, we will be pleased to make the necessary correction in future printings. Contact Travelers' Tales Inc., 330 Townsend Street, Suite 208, San Francisco, California 94107. www.travelerstales.com

Cover design: Michele Wetherbee
Interior design: Diana Howard
Cover photograph: From *The Hidden Canyon: A River Journey* © John Blaustein 1999 www.johnblaustein.com
Interior art: Kathryn Heflin. Watercolor painting of river rocks, Kings Canyon.
Page layout: Cynthia Lamb and Patty Holden using the fonts Cochin, Stuyvesant, and Castellar.

Distributed by Publishers Group West, 1700 Fourth Street, Berkeley, CA 94710.

Library of Congress Cataloging-in-Publication Data

The gift of rivers: true stories of life on the water/ edited by Pamela Michael.—1st ed.
    p. cm. — (Travelers' Tales)
    Includes bibliographical references (p. 249)
    ISBN 1-885211-42-2
    1. Rivers—Anecdotes. 2. Voyages and travels—Anecdotes. 3. Aquatic sports—Anecdotes. I. Michael, Pamela. II. Series.

GB1203.7 .G54 2000
910'.916'93—dc21   00-020272
                                                  CIP

First Edition
Printed in the United States of America
10 9 8 7 6 5 4 3 2

To trace the history of a river...is to trace the history of the soul, the history of the mind descending and arising in the body.

—GRETEL EHRLICH,
Islands, The Universe, Home

To Owen Lammers—
Pioneering champion of living, free-flowing rivers,
righteous foe to those who would dam them,
a man who may one day resurrect Glen Canyon from
its watery grave.
Go get 'em, O!

Table of Contents

PART III — *Streams of Consciousness*

PART IV — *Still Water*

Rivers and Stories: An Introduction

ROBERT HASS

This is a book of river stories, a wonderful book of river stories, and that would be enough to say by way of introduction, if it were not so interesting to think about rivers, and so urgent to think about them at this moment in the history of the human relation to the earth.

Wherever there is fresh water, there is abundant life. The mineral earth — with its dream shapes of mountain range and valley basin, desert and forest and taiga and prairie and butte and mesa, forged by the heat of the earth's core, scoured by the advance and retreat of glaciers, terminated by coastal cliffs and beaches of sand or shingle — is intricately veined with rivers. The story of our relationship to it begins, I suppose, with pieces of bone excavated along the Awash River in Ethiopia and a piece of a jaw excavated beside an ancient lake in Kenya. *Ardipithecus ramidus* and *Australopithecus anamenmsis:* they

are about 4.4 million years old. Almost 2 million years
ago, a welter of hominid species foraged the edges of the
same lake. Among them, most likely, were our ancestors.
Human life probably developed within easy reach of
rivers and lakes. Human civilization — along the Tigris
and Euphrates, the Ganges, the Yangtze, and the Nile —
certainly did.

Human beings must first have used rivers for drinking
and bathing and for food, fishing the shallows, and hunting the birds and mammals drawn to the banks for water.
It was probably fishing and hunting from floating logs
that led to boat-making, and boat-making must have
increased enormously the mobility of the species.

Agriculture developed in the rich deposits of the
floodplains, where sedentary tool-makers were soon har-
nessing the power of the water with mill wheels and
dams. Irrigation, as a technology, is about 3,000 years
old. It will tell you something about the stress human
beings have put on river systems in the last 100 years of
this history if you know that in 1900, 40 million hectares
of cropland were under irrigation worldwide. Forty million hectares in 3,000 years. By 1993, 248 million
hectares were under irrigation.

It's also a fact of the twentieth century that as a mode
of travel, for commerce and pleasure, rivers have been
largely displaced by highways, railways, and air travel. A
hundred and fifty years ago the epic stories of engineer-
ing had to do with canal building, connecting one river
system or one sea with another: Panama, Suez. The locks
of the Erie Canal and the extensive lock system of

English rivers belong now to a quaint and minor tourism. The stories of the twentieth century have had to do with nationalism and economic development and the prestige of massive dams. Rivers now supply 20 percent of the world's electrical power, most of it generated by large, economically destructive, often culturally destructive, dams. The still-to-be-completed Three Gorges Dam on the Yangtze is only the latest in a series of Faustian bargains technological culture has struck with the rivers of the earth.

Though the names are still magic—Amazon, Nile, Congo, Mississippi, Niger, Platte, Volga, Tiber, Seine, Ganges, Mekong, Rhine, Rhone, Colorado, Euphrates, Marne, Orinoco, Rio Grande—the rivers themselves have almost disappeared from consciousness in the modern world. Insofar as they exist in our imaginations, that existence is nostalgic. We have turned our memory of the Mississippi into a Mark Twain theme park at Disneyland.

Our railroads followed the contours of the rivers and then our highways followed the contours of the rail lines. Traveling, we move as a river moves, at two removes. Our children don't know where their electricity comes from. They don't know where the water they drink comes from, and in many places on the earth the turgid backwaters of our dammed rivers are inflicting epidemics of the old riverside diseases: dysentery and schistosomiasis, or "river blindness." Rivers and the river gods that defined our civilizations have become the sublimated symbols of everything we have done to the planet in the past 200 years. And the rivers themselves have come to function as trace memories of what we have repressed in the name of our technological mastery. They are the ecological unconscious.

So, of course, they show up in poetry.

"I do not know much about gods," T. S. Eliot—who grew up along the Mississippi in St. Louis—wrote, "but I think the river is a strong brown god."

"Under various names," Czeslaw Milosz—who grew up in Lithuania along the Nieman—wrote, "I have praised only you, rivers, You are milk and honey and love and death and dance."

I take this to be the first stirrings, even as our civilization did its damming and polluting, of the recognition of what we have lost and need to recover. When human populations were small enough, the cleansing flow of rivers and their fierce floods could create the illusion that our acts did not have consequences, vanished downstream. Now that is no longer true, and we are being compelled to reconsider the work of our hands. And, of course, we are too dependent on our own geographical origins to have lost our connection with rivers entirely.

Traveling in the world, even now, we confront, one way or another, the human history of rivers. Several times in the last few years I've arrived in a foreign city, gone to sleep in a hotel room, and awakened to look out the window at a river. The first time was in Budapest. The river was the Danube. I woke up just before sunrise, walked out onto a balcony, and in the cold air at first light, looked out across the Pest hills and the first glimmerings of day on the broad, mud-colored water. The smell of it was in the air. I realized that I didn't know much of its geography. I knew that it originated somewhere in the Alps, flowed east across southern Germany—the *Niebelungenlied* are Danube river tales—and south from Vienna through Hungary and then southeast again through Serbia, emptying into the Black Sea somewhere south of Odessa. I seemed to recall, vaguely, that the poet Ovid, after offending Caesar Augustus, had been exiled to a half-wild garrison town at the mouth of the Danube. And I knew that in the 1980s a particularly mindless plan to dam the river as it flowed across central Hungary had become so controversial that the government outlawed public discussion of the project by scientists.

The lights were going out on the bridges, I could make out the dim forms of a few barges on the river, and a voice drifted toward me on the wind. There must have existed and perished in 5,000 years whole dictionaries of river slang in half a dozen different languages, Magyar, and several German and Slavic dialects, and whatever hybrid Rumanian is. There must once have been a Romano-Serb or a Romano-Germanic river pidgen spoken by merchants and boatmen the whole length of it. And it may have been in Roman times that it acquired its common name, since the Romans were great makers of maps, though it had probably been, long before any legions marched along its banks, a local god in many different cultures, with many different names. I knew of one poem, by the Belgrade poet Vasko Popa, that addresses Father Danube in a sort of Serbian modernist prayer. Belgrade—*belo grad*—means "white city" in Serbian:

O great Lord Danube
the blood of the white town
Is flowing in your veins

If you love it get up a moment
From your bed of love—

Ride on the largest carp
Pierce the leaden clouds
And come visit your heavenly birthplace

Bring gifts to the white town
The fruits and birds and flowers of paradise

The bell towers will bow down to you
And the streets prostrate themselves
O great Lord Danube

I did not bow down. I found myself up to my neck in the comedy of consumer travel. I had called room service the moment I woke and ordered coffee. It arrived in a silver pitcher with a cream-colored china cup and a saucer with a fluted rim. I poured the coffee and then thought to check the bill. As near as I could tell, it was going to cost me $30.00, and this occasioned in me mild panic. The staff spoke English; I considered calling them and telling them there had been a mistake; I didn't require what the menu called a "morning beverage," after all. The problem turned out to be my arithmetic. The coffee was $3.00—

but I thought I was drinking a $30.00 pot of coffee when
I went back out onto the balcony and sipped the coffee,
which smelled like wine and unripe berries and dark
earth, very slowly, and watched the Danube turn silver
in the dawn. It was a kind of offering to the river god.

The second time I looked out such a window the river
I saw was the Whangpoo. I had also come into Shanghai
in the dark. This time I woke to a pearl-grey morning
hazy with river mist. The river itself was teeming with
traffic—barges, sometimes two or three together, linked
by thick cables, carrying lumber, sacks of cement, gird-
ers, building tiles; tankers low in the water, ploughing
against the current; tugs; packed ferries; a few sailboats;
other ancient and non-descript vessels. I counted eighty
going and coming before I stopped counting. The water
was grayish-brown, foaming against the embankments,
quays, warehouses, and docks. Just below me a crowd
of people and bicycles was queuing for one of the ferries.
Across the river was the Bund, the old commercial street
of the pre-World War II city, with its European-style
bank and insurance buildings and hotels in the shapes of
Greek and Roman temples, old coal-smoke-darkened
marble columns and domes.

Shanghai, I was to read later, is a relatively modern
city. The Bund, in the fourteenth century, had been a
tow-path for river barges above a reedy wetlands and a
small fishing village. The village became a town in the
sixteenth century. By the end of the nineteenth, it might
have been the commercial riverfront of any European
river city—Lyon or Glasgow or Amsterdam.

The street at dawn was already aswarm with the flow of human traffic and it seemed to mimic the movement on the crowded river. It was as if I were looking out not at another continent but another time. The river was a nineteenth-century river, thick with the traffic that had elsewhere in the world been transferred to trains and air-freight, and eighteen-wheel trucks. The Bund was a living memory of the forms of European piracy that came to be called the age of empire. I half-expected to see Joseph Conrad emerge from one of the buildings in his Edwardian beard, carrying a commission to captain a steamer up the Congo. But the scene also looked like a Chinese scroll painting, as if the jagged line of Maoist-era apartment buildings in the distance were mountains, and the river-mists the half-remembered forms of local and dynastic gods, and the river itself an allegory of human life: provision and supply, upriver struggle and downriver flow, and human crowds coming and going in a smudged and dreamy haze.

There was also something unsettling about the scene, and it was not until later in the day, as I was wandering around the city, that it dawned on me what I had seen. Or not seen. I turned abruptly around and traced my way back to the river, leaned against the embankment, and stared a long time. There were no birds. Not a single gull, no ducks, no herons or egrets. Not a cormorant or a grebe. There were not even sparrows or songbirds in the spindly trees in the riverside park. And there was not a fisherman in sight. The river, for all its human vitality, appeared dead.

The third river was the Nile. Even at night, from my room at the Semiramis in downtown Cairo, there was no mistaking it, though I couldn't make out that fabulous stream itself. Laughter, some of it good-natured, some of it hilarious, floated up to my window, and there were brilliant lights all along the riverside that seemed to be bridges and a promenade and open-air cafes. And there was the smell of it, even in the humidity and auto exhaust, green and cool.

My first glimpse came the next morning, in the unbelievable din of Cairo traffic—it seemed that not honking one's horn was the exception rather than the rule—and even in all that noise it looked peaceful. Greenish water, a strong, gentle current, reeds, palms, bankside banyans with their broad gleaming leaves, and, as if conjured from a late eighteenth-century watercolor, the red lanteen sails of the feluccas, skimming upriver in a following breeze.

Nilus is probably no older than any other of the discontinued river gods, but he is older in the human imagination, a fact that was demonstrated to me the next day when, quite unexpectedly, I ran into an old friend in the hotel lobby, an American woman living in London. She had one day in Cairo. She was about go have a look at the oldest synagogue in the city, which she needed to be able to describe in a novel she was working on. On an impulse I joined her.

The previous day had been an Islamic holiday, celebrated by a day-long fast, followed by the butchering of a live animal at sunset, goat or sheep, and a feast—to

commemorate, we had been told, the sheep sacrificed by
Abraham when the Lord God spared the life of his son
Isaac, once Abraham had established his willingness to
kill his own son for this deity. It meant that the corners
of Cairo streets were stacked with the still bloody pelts of
skinned animals, in which the flies were conducting their
own festival. The cobblestones were slick with reddish or
tea-colored puddles where the blood had been washed
from the streets. We made our way across the street gin-
gerly, wandered down an alley out of the novels of
Mahfouz, smelling of mint tea and applewood smoke
from tiny cafes, and came to the open courtyard of the
synagogue, which was closed.

My friend had to settle for a description of the exte-
rior of the building. A man rose from one of the cafe
tables across the square and approached us, gesturing
solemnly with two raised fingers for us to follow him,
which, somewhat hypnotized, we did. He took us
around to the other side of the building where, in a garden of palms and fuchsias, there was a well, covered
with ornate ironwork.

"Here," he said, "Moses was found in the bulrushes."
We both balked.

"Here?"

"Oh, yes," he said. "This was the old channel of the
river. It flowed straight through here. Moses was a Cairo
boy."

Within a few days I was to understand that the city
was full of these scholars of local legend. There was no
Cairo in Pharaonic times, but Memphis was just upriver,

and the river did once flow this way, so who was to argue the point?

Not far from the synagogue was a Roman wall of brick and rubble that had been given the name Persepolis, because a renegade band of Persian army deserters had established a settlement there which, later, in Trajan's time, served as the foundation of a Roman fort. And it was from this fort that the city of Cairo grew. Memphis and the Saqqarah pyramids were just twelve miles south. And if the infant of a Jewish slave had been placed in a basket made from the wicker of river reeds, it may very well have floated downriver to this spot.

The high Aswan Dam, constructed in the 1950s by the Nasser government as a monument to national independence, has had the unintended consequence of eating away the foundations of these old buildings. The dam has captured the flow of the nutrient-rich silt that created Egyptian civilization, making farmers dependent on chemical fertilizers. It has spread schistosomiasis through the communities of the Upper Nile, allowed the Mediterranean to wash away almost entirely the Nile delta and its lucrative fishery, and the diversion of water to marginally arable lands has forced the city of Cairo to draw down its freshwater aquifers. The result is that the salts underground are rising and eroding the foundations of Cairo's ancient mosques, churches, and some of the pyramids themselves.

Most of the planet's rivers are still alive, and of course, they are immensely resilient. It now seems possible that human civilization can begin to undo the damage it has done in this last century. U.S. Secretary of the Interior Bruce Babbitt, symbolically perhaps, has begun to decommission some American dams. The technology and the understanding of flood dynamics and of the need for water conservation have begun to make the twenty-first century work of river restoration a possibility. A starting place for this work would be to recover an elder imagination of the earth. That is one of the reasons why we need stories about rivers, and why this book has such intense resonance.

Rivers, of course, are *like* stories, and they are like stories that classical strictures on form would approve. They have a beginning, a middle, and an end. In between, they flow. Or would flow, if we let them. It's interesting to consider the fact that, in popular culture, what's happened to rivers has happened to stories. A dam is a commercial interruption in a river. A commercial is a dam impeding the flow of a story: it passes the human imagination through the turbine of a sales pitch to generate consumer lust. So it might be useful to remember, as you read this book and think about the rivers of the earth and about the task of reclaiming them that lies before us, that what you are reading are narratives without commercial interruptions—which is good for the health of rivers and good for narrative art.

———— ⌘ ————

Robert Hass is the author of several books of poems, including *Field Guide* and *Sun Under Wood*, and of a book of essays, *Twentieth Century Pleasures*. He served as Poet Laureate of the United States from 1995–1997, and is a member of the board of directors of International Rivers Network. With Pamela Michael, he co-founded River of Words, a children's environmental poetry and art project. He is professor of English at the University of California at Berkeley and lives in Northern California.

Preface

MY EARLIEST MEMORY IS OF A RIVER. For many years I thought it was just an odd remembered dream but my parents confirm that it actually happened on a tributary of the Des Plaines River when I was about eighteen months old. I was in a canoe between my panicked parents, who were paddling frantically through thick drifts of what turned out to be soap suds that rose well over our heads, obscuring all but occasional glimpses of blue sky above. The increasing roar of falls nearby all but muffled shouts and cries from a shore we couldn't see. (This memory, unfortunately, became the metaphor for the rest of my life at home. Up the you-know-where without a you-know-what.)

Eventually, moving toward the voices of the good Samaritans onshore, we found our way to the riverbank where we were met by concerned ladies in colonial garb who bustled us into a stone mill with a creaking water wheel and fed us hot chocolate and oatmeal. They told my parents, I later learned, that vandals had dumped a truckload of laundry detergent into the river, creating a surreal catastrophe that haunted me for years.

Not long ago, on a business trip to Chicago, I headed into the heartland in a borrowed a car and found that same childhood river and the mill, still operating as a "living museum," still staffed by costumed docents. I bought a sack of stoneground cornmeal for my parents and walked along the shore of what turned out to be no more than a creek, really. The falls seemed rather tame, too, and the countryside had been replaced by suburban lawns and cul-de-sacs that stretched almost to the water's edge.

I spent the day in a hazy kind of reverie, fluttering between nostalgia for a vanished wildness and childhood, and middle-aged delight at revisiting the site of such a vivid early remembrance. "I haven't been here for half a century," I blurted to a family out for a stroll. They scurried away down the waterside path nervously. A patrolling ranger was a bit friendlier, but then again, he was wearing a gun on his hip. Canoeing on the creek has been banned since the sixties, he told me; the water is too polluted. Today's children will have to look elsewhere for their future memories, I thought to myself.

My meanderings along the creek eventually led me to a more hopeful place—a newly opened nature center, abuzz with kids and families learning about their creek and the plants and animals that depend on it. I joined a group of children and naturalists for a guided nature walk and was struck by how passionate the children were about protecting the frogs, squirrels, robins, skunks, and butterflies they had come to see as something akin to neighbors. I watched as one little boy tenderly moved a slow-moving caterpillar out of harm's way on the busy footpath. He placed it in the crook of a tree, then returned with a handful of leaves for the lucky critter to munch on. Little Salt Creek's future suddenly seemed a bit brighter.

This creek and many other waterways, small and large, abused and neglected for decades, are finally receiving a lot of badly needed attention, much of it from schoolchildren. Around the world, young people are studying, monitoring, restoring, and caring for their local rivers and streams. This growing phenomenon of committed stewardship stems from a refound awareness of the importance of an intimate knowledge and experience of the water that flows through our lives and our communities, a relationship that was all but lost in the twentieth century. We enter the twenty-first with renewed understanding of the complex power of rivers to inspire, heal, cleanse, uncover, divide, move, remove, build, and destroy. Rivers have many stories to tell and we are once again learning to listen.

Perhaps, in the future, the rivers and streams of our childhoods will be a living, vital presence in our lives and not just the flimsy, unreliable stuff of memory. I hope, in some small way, that this book will contribute to that effort.

—Pamela Michael
Berkeley, California
Sacramento River Watershed
February, 2000

PART ONE

ESSENCE OF RIVERS

Spinning Down the River

JOHN CALDERAZZO

*A young man's river odyssey
becomes a lifelong journey.*

I'M FLOATING BACKWARDS DOWN THE RIVER in a canoe—backwards, sideways and around again, bow in the air, swirling dreamily on the mild current. The world rotates around me: shiny palmettos, floating clumps of hyacinth, ghost orchids, pygmy fringe trees, live oaks 100 feet wide exploding with resurrection ferns. A delirium of green! A single paddle stroke has set me off on this serenely idiotic waltz.

A young gator on a sand bar eyes me with alarm, then scrambles into the water and turns into pop-up eyes and a rippling tail. He flees upriver. My bow scrapes over a log from which turtles stacked like army helmets have just jumped for their lives.

I seem to have half the swamp on the run, and I see now that in my excitement to get going I forgot to shove my day pack and ice chest forward. That's why I'm aimed at the top

of cypress trees, as though with a couple of hard strokes I
could paddle off into the Florida sky.

It's easy to imagine that on the Hillsborough. Easy to
dream up almost anything on this gnarly river of mist so far
from the clear, thin air of my present home, the spare and
sensible foothills of the Colorado Rockies, gorgeous in their
own way. It's springtime there now, an endless brown season full of long vistas and wind.

Something scrapes my back and tips my straw hat into
my lap. A looped-down vine. It's as stiff and thick as my
wrist, as dark and fat as a water moccasin—hmmm—and I
watch it sway between sunlight and shade in the receding
distance.

And so downriver I go, round and round, snakes dripping from half the trees and who-knows-what is crouching
in the shadows. Is this any way to enter a wilderness? Well,
sure. Maybe the best way to slip into a dream is backwards.

I grew up in a forest fifteen miles from New York City.
It was my Long Island backyard, and it was shaded by giant
oaks with bark so thick I could work my fingers and sneak-
er tips into the ragged cracks and climb as high as my nerve
let me.

In the summer, when my mom called me in for lunch,
she'd sometimes look straight up. There I'd be, hanging bat-
like from a limb, studying an overturned world. I'd stare
down my skinny body at a sky I could fall into forever, then
up at a shaggy heaven of grass from which pine trees and
oaks full of squalling blue jays descended like chandeliers.
My mom, standing casually upside-down, would hold out a

ham sandwich and wave. Just thinking back on this now makes me dizzy.

A stream wandered through the edge of our acre and a half. Indians who drank milkweed and put acorns in their cereal lived there in invisible tepees. That's why we could never find them, my dad once told me. At one end of our place the stream flowed from a tangle of bushes; at the other it slid into a green wall of undergrowth. It smelled like black mud and sweet decay. I imagined that it started far away in snow-capped mountains, or maybe the center of the world.

I was getting just old enough to explore it alone when one morning a yellow tractor came grumbling and crunching upstream. The thing was huge and coughed up clouds of black smoke. A few weeks later, from a

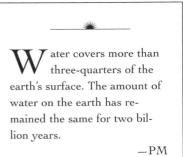

Water covers more than three-quarters of the earth's surface. The amount of water on the earth has remained the same for two billion years.

—PM

yard now half its old size, I stared through a barbed-wire-topped chain link fence at the moonscape of an irrigation ditch. My dad called it "a goddamn gift from the Army Corps of Engineers." It turned out that he and the neighbors had been fighting it in court for over a year.

The ditch ran straight as a ruler, and on the other side of it I could see half-built ranch houses and rolls of sod and dazzling white sidewalks where kids whom I was sure I'd hate would soon be riding tricycles and bikes. I know now that the ditch also ran back in time. It ran back through centuries of forests and twisting corridors of shadow and mist to the first, lost garden—a lush green world of not just innocence but imagination.

He reminded me of a heron. He was tall and bald with a stretched-out, strangled-looking neck and sinewy stick arms full of veins. His bony shoulders stuck out from a summer undershirt that might have been ventilated with a shotgun blast. He had little black bird eyes. He also had a rowboat I wanted to rent.

We were standing back from the Hillsborough under immense draperies of Spanish moss. He flicked his eyes at me. "Moved down from New York City, you say?"

"Just a small piece from it," I said as slowly as I could, trying to sound like a southerner, a Faulkner character maybe, a Snopes who'd come up in the world. What I probably really sounded like was a confused twenty-year-old. It was 1967 and I'd just dropped out of college. I'd been living in Tampa for a month.

He handed me two oars and a life preserver cushion. "Well, welcome to the Hillsborough River, son. The world's a more peaceful place down here."

We walked down to the water. The air was humid enough to soften a stone. In the river grass he bent down to flip over my boat, and then in dreamy slow motion he was flying backwards in a great soft arc, his arms flapping. He landed on his feet, lunged for a .22 that leaned against a tree, aimed and fired at something sliding into the river. The water thrashed. I rushed forward and saw a thick black snake pinwheeling on the surface, darkening the water with blood.

"Cottonmouth," he said. "And I just about stuck my big damn toe down its throat." He shook his head and with an oar lifted the snake's shuddering body out of the river. Its head looked as big as my fist.

I'd never seen a poisonous snake before. In fact, my last encounter with a wild animal may have been a stand-off I'd had with a snarling collie on my junior high school paper route. After the irrigation ditch had wiped out my private wilderness, anything more exotic than a squirrel had been hard to come by.

As I grew older, I'd found other woods and streams, but they always seemed like diminished things: fenced-in state parks, the bushes full of rock music and black-jacketed teen lovers, or rumpled men with nowhere else to sleep; strips of trees along whooshing highways.

When I asked my dad if he'd like to go camping, he said, "I did that already. It was called World War II." Later on I spent a few Julys at a Boy Scout camp, but I remember it mostly for water fights in clanking aluminum canoes and solemn Indian campfire rituals that I never understood.

And now I was standing knee-deep in a snaky Florida river I'd barely heard of. I climbed in the boat and began to pull myself upstream. The oars creaked. The man who looked like a heron waved and disappeared around a bend, and suddenly I was alone on the river.

I felt very small. Jungly walls slid by, and on the trunk of a cypress tree as wide as the boat I saw a spider the size of my outstretched hand. The undergrowth was outsized, too, so thick it could have hidden a Florida panther, a bright-winged parrot, an orangutan, a golden-spired temple, a

Vietcong sniper. Vietnam was heating up, and because I was drifting between definitions of myself and therefore jobs and colleges, I was bait for the draft. The sun beat down hard, and I hadn't thought to wear a hat. I leaned into the oars and tried to forget about my future, whatever it was. A warm river smell of sweet decay and black mud came to me. In almost zero current I let the boat glide.

Then I noticed a vague hum. At first I thought it had something to do with the sun or the blue, double-winged dragonflies flitting around the oars and landing on my knees. Then I realized that I wasn't hearing some faint brushstroke of sound. I was hearing no sound at all—no music in the bushes or distant hum of traffic, no outboard motor ratcheting a mile downriver. For the first time in my life I became aware of silence in the world—and the way a river could turn into a state of mind, a kind of feeling.

Everything's shipshape now, ice chest up front, canoe aimed downriver, young gators and turtles waiting me out somewhere in the cool muck of the bottom. I sip foam from a sweating can of Bud, then practically drop it when a wild turkey explodes from a branch overhead. After all these years on the river, it's the first turkey I've come across and easily the biggest bird I've seen move so fast anywhere.

Last week I brought my friend Richard out here. He's a former teacher of mine from graduate school in Ohio, a gentle soul whose much-younger wife recently left him. At the airport, his face had looked the color of fog, the color of northwest Ohio, and he spoke in bruises. On the river, I took the stern and paddled, and he turned around to face me and talk. Soon he was lounging back in the liquid light, looking up at the undersides of trees, their dark bones. A heron floated over us on cloud-white wings. Richard's thin frame began to droop between the struts. He closed his eyes. He closed them the way I sometimes did during my first year or two in Tampa, when I was desperate for someone to talk to—for a girlfriend, mainly. I was a quiet guy, far too unsure of myself to approach even the women who smiled at me when I finally took some classes at the University of South Florida. So now and then, lonely and bored and probably full of self-pity, I'd jump into a canoe and head upriver.

Somewhere into a six-pack of beer, I'd close my eyes and construct myself a girlfriend. She was a kind of river wraith, gorgeous, of course, and a composite of the women I'd most wanted to talk to on campus. She always wore jeans and one of those light denim work shirts tied in front to show off her waist. Usually she'd be sitting on a sandbar past a bend in the river, waiting for me. Who knew how she got there? All that mattered was that the brush of her hand on mine would crack open my husk of solitude. When I opened my eyes to find nobody, at least I had the river.

As Richard and I lazed along, patterns of sunlight and shade slid over his skin. At the airport he'd looked so tired, translucent with despair. Now his eyes opened a little. He gave me a smile, some color drifting into his cheeks.

Logs, I told myself as the rowboat drifted into a muddy cove on that long-ago first afternoon on the Hillsborough. Gray-black logs. Too still to be alive. Too big.…

Besides, fresh from New York, I only half believed that

alligators existed outside of zoos or the Manhattan sewer system or old Tarzan movies. So I edged up close until the rough bark on the logs turned into leathery scales, and suddenly two snaggle-toothed gators blew past me like rockets. They actually leaped clear of the water! With a whipping of prehistoric tails, they disappeared into the deep part of the river. My heart booming, I yanked on the oars and fell backwards, clonking my head. The boat bumped into a bank. I got up, looked around, and laughed.

The gators had been unbelievably fast. And huge, longer than the twelve-foot boat. Was that possible?

"Behold him rushing forth from the flags and reeds," wrote William Bartram of an alligator he saw on another Florida river more than two centuries ago. "His enormous body swells...the waters like a cataract descend from his opening jaws. Clouds of smoke issue from his dilated nostrils. The earth trembles with his thunder."

That was a Florida that shimmered with flamingos and clouds of green-gold parakeets and passenger pigeons, where wolf packs still loped through the palmettos, where eighteen-foot gators—real eighteen-footers—hadn't yet been shot off by the handbag industry, where pelicans had not yet been slaughtered for their throat bags, which were turned into tobacco pouches. Bartram was a botanist, a trained observer of tropical plants, yet his alligator description reveals little of the cool eye of science. His *Travels* reads like a book of wonders. When I first picked it up, that puzzled me. But then I came to see that his fire-breathing gator and my two monsters rushed forth from a shared inner landscape that dates back past the Book of Job.

"Who can open the doors of his face," the Lord asks rhetorically about Leviathan, a crocodile-like creature. "Round about his teeth is terror…Out of his burning nostrils comes forth smoke, as from a boiling pot.…"

For all their size and lightning strength, and despite the fact that I once heard a big gator hiss like a flared-out cobra, gators and crocs aren't dragons. So Bartram obviously picked up a thing or two from the hyperbole and literary style of Job.

And passed them on: his descriptions of gushing azure springs—which are concentrated in Florida like nowhere else on earth—inspired Coleridge to write of Kubla Kahn's "sacred river" that ran through caverns "measureless to man."

And so I wonder what stories boatmen and traders told the Old Testament poets about their river beasts. What did they think swam in the misty headwaters of the Jordan or the Nile?

Writers and storytellers always seem to have known that fabulous landscapes live inside of us as much as we live in them. Dante's dark wood hides the entrance to our worst imaginings. The thick forests of the Brothers Grimm, Hawthorne, and Faulkner shelter gnomes and devils, enormous bears, and our own murky souls.

And so as I get older I keep coming back to forests and swamps, which inform so many of my *best* imaginings. In a world of too many maps, I like my terra incognita right in front of my nose.

Time to watch out. The river's forgetting itself, wandering off into shallow channels, crooked luminous-green corridors

with almost no current. Which do I take? As I think about
it over a Cuban sandwich from the cooler, I bump among
cypress knees that stick out of the water like dark melting
candles, swampy stalagmites. A musk of sweet death and
wild ripening drops over me.

A slightly creepy smell, yet it's something I often miss in
my reasonable middle age, a source of daydreams and the
body, an almost erotic reminder of travels I've made to raucous green places, steamy anarchies of swift growth and
decay, the life cycle on fast forward.

Over the years, I've floated down the Mekong in south
China, watched boulder-sized hippos break the glassy surface of Kenya's Lake Victoria, poled a dugout canoe in
Ecuador's Oriente. I've hiked through squishy rain forests
in Dominica and Thailand (where I learned that cobras do
indeed hiss, and loudly). Each of those trips owed something to the luxuriant possibilities of my childhood wilderness in New York and especially to the Hillsborough. None
of those places were prettier than parts of this river.

The channels rebraid and coax me back into a sort of forest lagoon that looks like the place I tried to explore once on
a ridiculously hot day with my friend Frank. I was in my
mid-twenties, no longer lonely for girlfriends—whenever I
brought somebody new out to the river, her eyes looked
bright green—and thanks to the draft lottery, Vietnam had
raged on without me. But suddenly I seemed to have found
a way to die much closer to home: Frank and I had got completely lost.

We were sunburned and bugbit and flushed from the
heat, couldn't see more than ten or fifteen yards ahead, yet

had to slog waist-deep in clinging muck and shoulder the canoe over fallen trees. The water felt cool and dangerous.

But today the lagoon seems to be just a lagoon, and soon it turns back into a river loafing along at about the speed of nostalgia. Over its length of fifty-four miles it drops just eighty feet. I watch an osprey zoom low over the water, snap open its claws, and hook a big, twisting fish with barely a ripple. An armadillo snuffling along the ferny bank rears up like an ancient tiny horse to sniff at my passing.

The river bends left, right, eases me past a big cypress tree growing out of a tremendous stump—a sign of the fabulous forest that covered 27 million acres of Florida until the turn of the century. For all my talk of jungle walls, I'm not fooling myself about the condition of the river. It's not really the Amazon. But then, nowadays, neither is the Amazon.

If I could actually paddle myself into the sky, here's what I'd see: the Green Swamp—the river's source—a great swatch of hardwood forest and swampland so thick that local hunters fear getting lost. It's only a few miles west of Disneyworld, but nobody I know outside of Florida has ever heard of it.

The Swamp percolates with 70 percent of the state's drinking water, but cut into its edges are circuit-board patterns of bright-roofed retirement homes and RV parks— chunks of swamp drained and scraped raw with names like Scandinavia USA and Gem o' the Hills. Of course, there are no hills.

Out of the swamp rolls the blue-green river, root beer tinged in places from tannic acid. It squiggles along inside a fuzzy green ribbon that bulges for various parks, an enormous old ranch, a hunting reserve.

On all sides stretches the Florida that most of us know, a mauled landscape of cow fields and orange groves giving way to golf courses, theme parks, freeways, miles of new homes. A *malled* landscape, too, with sunblasted parking lots the size of European republics.

The Hillsborough rolls through it all, then past Sulphur Springs, where escaped chimps from old jungle movies once jabbered in the trees. It winds through the red-brick streets of Tampa's Cuban neighborhoods, past tin-roofed cigar factories, under rusting drawbridges. Finally, downtown, the river widens and slides by postmodern glass skyscrapers into Hillsborough Bay.

If you're lucky, you might spot the pudgy silhouettes of West Indian manatees swimming upriver from the bay. One afternoon a veteran downtown bridgekeeper told me that he'd never seen any. When I told him that seemed strange, since manatees were always surfacing upriver, he looked at me as if to say, You think so, eh?

He'd developed a theory. Florida, he said, is riddled with subterranean channels that even scientists don't know about. Thanks to those, plus the secret language of animals, manatees and river otters and water moccasins and all sorts of fabulous creatures are able to swim from one place to another without being seen. "Hell," he said, nodding gravely, "upriver, ain't nobody knows what's really up there."

I wish there were such channels—caverns measureless to man, swarming with animals that maybe whisper about us. Tampa's so crowded now that biologists have had to start identifying manatees by the propeller slash marks on their backs.

Yet from where I sit in my canoe in the shade of a live oak, this noisy, overwrought world seems far away. Thanks to people who love the Hillsborough and have learned to fight for it, it's hanging on, changed but in lots of ways cleaner and more protected than it was 30 or 100 years ago.

"God is in the river," says Sister Mary McNally, a leader in the struggle to preserve the Hillsborough. She heads the Franciscan Convent Center, a lovely shaded retreat along the river in the middle of Tampa. It's a good place to stroll in the evenings and contemplate the ineffable.

The most famous preacher in the world thought so, too. In 1937, blond and square-jawed Billy Graham came from North Carolina to study at the Tampa Bible College in Temple Terrace, ten miles upstream from the Franciscan Center. Billy had bronchitis, and his parents thought Florida's climate might help.

He took to the river, swimming and canoeing on weekends, and he wrote home that he'd never felt so close to God. He practiced his first awkward sermons along its banks, preaching to whomever would listen, including the gators. Spanish moss from live oaks trailed in the water, and on one moonlit, other-worldly evening, the future advisor to presidents had his first visions of big stadiums, big meetings.

I'm not much like Billy Graham. But I've come to realize that lots of my spiritual life swirls along the Hillsborough and its interpenetrations of moss and air and water, entanglements of roots and clouds, dark mud and sweet decay.

Four years ago, I practiced walking meditation for the first time. Each step became a source of wonder. I was far from Florida and nowhere near a river, but as I walked and breathed I felt a twining of the physical and the metaphysical that was like my first long-ago moment on the Hillsborough.

Or like the first time I saw a roseate spoonbill flying over my canoe, just this spring. Flocks of them had once flashed up and down the river, but I thought they'd been gone for decades, hunkered down in what's left of the Everglades.

Suddenly, though, one came floating out of the trees—an impossible bird, loony and beautiful and fabulously pink. It landed on a nearby branch and gazed calmly out over the water. Then it looked upriver toward the trees it had flown out of.

I looked, too. Tangled silence, a delirium of green. I felt so happy about myself and the world, and so full of hope.

———— ∞∞∞ ————

John Calderazzo has floated down rivers in China, Thailand, and Ecuador as well as in the U.S. Lately, he's been climbing around burning rocks as research for a new book, *Where The Earth Begins: Volcanoes and Our Inner Lives*. His nature and other essays have appeared in numerous publications, including *Audubon, Orion, Ohio, Georgia Review*, and *American Nature Writing*. He frequently writes a "Science and the Shore" column for *Coastal Living* magazine, and teaches literary nonfiction workshops at Colorado State University.

A Room on a River

JAN MORRIS

*From the wheelhouse of a moored steamboat,
a foreign correspondent watches
the world float by.*

NOT COUNTING THE ROOM I AM WRITING in today, the room that has meant most to me in life is, I am glad to say, one that no longer exists. I would hate to think of other people using it now, fouling it with tobacco smoke or debasing it with trendy furniture. I want my rooms to be always Me, or Us anyway, so I am pleased to know that this particular chamber saved itself from alien tastes by sinking to the bottom of the river Nile.

To get to it from the center of Cairo you took the big Kasr-el-Nil bridge to the suburb-island of El Gezira, and crossing to the other side, where the western branch of the river flows, walked down an avenue of luscious bougainvillea, purple against the almost invariably cloudless sky. Beneath a trellised gateway, over a gangplank, and you found yourself upon the deck of a superannuated steamboat, alleged by some romantics to have taken part, long before, in Kitchener's campaign to revenge the death

of Gordon. It was now permanently moored beside the
riverbank but was still ineffably nautical — tall raked funnel
amidships, engines shrouded down below, awnings everywhere against the sun and wheelhouse high above. It had a
galley and a saloon, like any proper steamboat; it had state-
rooms and deck cabins and a big shady poop; and well forward on its upper deck, square, windowed all round, white-
painted but a little blistered by the heat, in the days when I
commanded the retired paddle steamer *Saphir*, in the early
1950s, stood my workroom — the most glamorous room, the
most suggestive and the most unforgettable that I have ever
occupied.

I was a newspaper correspondent then, covering the Middle East from this unconventional headquarters in Egypt, and
my cabin up there above the river was essentially function-
al. It had no space for frills, because as the former wheelhouse it was walled largely in glass. Also I had crammed it
with the usual paraphernalia of the foreign correspondent's
calling, the maps and telephones and typewriters and piles
of official handouts and stacks of newspapers and service
cables from head office — pinned to the wall if laudatory,
crumpled under the table if not.

But I never thought of it as an office. It was far more
than that. Such wall space as it offered sustained the small
hopeful library of my youth — the couple of hundred volumes which represented, so to speak, the state of my mind
so far. The record player beside the door (radiogram, as we
called it then) was almost always playing Mozart. And there
seeped perpetually through its windows an intoxicating
assortment of sensual stimuli.

There was the dry dazzling light of Egyptian sunshine. There were the rippling reflections on my white ceiling of the majestic river outside. There were exotic smells—of cooking oil, of wood fires, of earthy water, of gasoline. Best of all there were sounds, wonderful sounds—the muffled roar and hooting of the city streets, of course, but also the creaking of timbers, the banging of copper pots and pans, the chanting of the blind Koran singer who sat all day on his wicker chair alongside the road, and three times a day the call to prayer from the mosque across the river, eddying hauntingly over the water and through the trees, and answered as in echo from countless minarets near and far across the capital.

All round me the life of the river proceeded, intimately near, so that as I sat there among my books I felt truly a part of it. Huge, brownish, deep in the water the feluccas came lurching downstream or urgently tacking up, so close that I could hear the grunts and phlegmatic coughing of their crews, and sometimes looked up to see a prickly face grinning back at me through my window only a few feet away. When some especially heavy cargo was being poled upstream, the sailors might break into a sonorous river song, and hour after hour I would hear it, slow and lugubrious, over and over again, fainter and fainter as they heaved their way toward the equator.

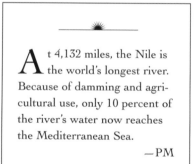

At 4,132 miles, the Nile is the world's longest river. Because of damming and agricultural use, only 10 percent of the river's water now reaches the Mediterranean Sea.

—PM

Then there was the presence of the other houseboats moored along the bank. This was mostly raffish. Plain-clothes policemen paid frequent visits to our neighborhood, and agreeable suggestions of low life often reached me in my room—high prurient laughter, sudden screams or shoutings, splashes that I took to be the jettisoning of in-criminating evidence, all diffused in the general sense of live-and-let-live which, especially in the glorious dog-hours of the Egyptian afternoon, also ruled the responses of my room on the upper deck.

Our own shipboard life proceeded leisurely enough. Often and again my steward Abdu would appear at the open door of my room with a silver coffeepot upon a silver tray, a jug of buffalo milk and a plate of Playbox biscuits. Now and then the cook shambled by, returning to his quar-ters after a hubble-bubble of hashish in the privacy of the rope-locker. Slowly, purposefully, methodically about his business went Idris the deckhand, an aged sailor in a long brown *galabiyyah* topped in cold weather by a blue maritime sweater. His task it was, at the end of a long riverine career, to keep the old steamer afloat and shipshape—rolling and unrolling the awnings, touching up the paintwork, and most important of all, shifting our moorings according to the sea-sonal rise and fall of the water, which sometimes raised my room high above the street and its trees, and sometimes left us cowering in the lee of the bank.

Idris often sloped past the windows of my room, but somehow he seldom caught my eye. He moved with a pre-occupied air, as though he resented what had happened to the ship, forever tied up there, its paddles never to churn again, its engines always silent.

It saddened me, too. I thought it an unworthy fate for the little vessel, even if in fact it had never run the gauntlet of the cataracts with Lord Kitchener; and I was not at all unhappy when, returning to Cairo many years later, and finding only an empty space at our mooring beneath the bougainvillea, I was told the *Saphir* had sunk. Idris, Abdu and the half-stoned cook had gone elsewhere, and only the trellised gateway remained to show where my ship had lain—that and a snatch of Mozart, I fancied, still drifting blithe but wistful across the muddy water.

Welsh essayist Jan Morris is the author of more than thirty books, including *Hong Kong: Epilogue to an Empire*, *The World of Venice*, *Long Ago in France*, and *Pleasures of a Tangled Life*, from which this story was excerpted.

Northwest Passage

DAVID JAMES DUNCAN

Two boys, a school of coho, and a river struggle to find their way.

W HEN I WAS SIXTEEN AND HATED HIGH school, one of the things I did to get through a school day was rip pictures out of magazines. I did this in the school library, and the magazines belonged to the school: the ripping was a deliberate act of vandalism. But I only stole photos I loved. And I felt that, in taking them home to my bedroom, I was stealing them away to a better life than the one they'd led in the library.

I had festooned my bedroom—floor, walls and ceiling— with blankets, cheap imported tapestries, wooden crates and sheepskins. It looked more like the interior of a desert Bedouin's tent than the generic sheetrocked cubicle it was. When I'd get my stolen photos into my "tent" I'd prop them like books in front of me, light candles or kerosene lanterns before them, stare at them till they swallowed me, and virtually worship the daydreams, wanderlust and longings these makeshift icons allowed me to feel.

One such photo, plundered from a *National Geographic,* was of the confluence of the Ganges and Jumna rivers in India. It depicted a barren, boulder-strewn plateau beneath a range of mountains. You could see white water churning in the background. But the place was stripped of vegetation, desolate, and would have held no photographic interest at all if the rocky plain along the river hadn't been strewn with huts. *Hundreds* of huts. Maybe a thousand of them. Crude, leaky, diminutive hovels no red-blooded American would dream of keeping a lawnmower in. Yet in these, men were living. "Holy men," the caption called them. In any case long-bearded, huge-eyed, emaciated men, just existing on the rocks by the river there. And the reason they chose to do this, so the caption maintained, was that "the *rishis* of ancient India considered the confluence of two or more rivers to be a sacred place."

I couldn't have explained why I found this riverside ghetto so appealing. Trying to hone in on my feelings with the help of a dictionary, I looked up the word *holy* and in the margins of the photo wrote, "1. hallowed by association with the divine, hence deserving of reverence; 2. inviolable; not to be profaned." But weeks passed and understanding did not deepen. I was still in a kind of love with the confluence-dwelling holy men and still unable to say why, when an old friend named Jered asked me to go fishing.

It was early on a school day, in mid-October. Jered's plan was to try for jack and silver salmon that very afternoon—which we'd lengthen slightly by cutting our last class. Jered and I had been fishing buddies as kids, inseparable for a season or two. In the years between I prided

myself on having changed completely, while Jered prided
himself on not having changed at all. I'd become a hippie;
Jered still had a crew cut; I aspired (with no success) to
vegetarianism; Jered was still shooting, cleaning and happily devouring scores of the indigenous mammals and birds
of the Northwest; I was trying to piece together some sort
of crazy-quilt bhakti/Wishram/Buddhistic/ball-playing mysti-
cism to live by; Jered was your basic working-class, Consciousness One, Huntin'-'n'-Fishin' type guy. But I said yes
for three reasons. The first was that we shared a respect,
despite all differences, based on the fact that we each considered the other to be the best fisherman we knew. The second was that he had enough boraxed salmon roe for both of
us, and the fishing had been in his rudimentary but reliable
diction, "hot." And the third reason, the decisive one, was
that the place he proposed to fish was one the *rishis* of
ancient India held sacred; a joining of rivers—this one in
downtown Camas, Washington, where Lacamas Creek and
the Washougal River both meet the Columbia, and the
Crown Zellerbach papermill met them all.

I knew, before going, that this confluence would be a
place I would hate. I'd lived within sight and smell of the
Crown Z mill, directly across the Columbia, all my life. My
plan for the day, though—having read of the ancient
rishis—was to see whether it might be possible to love what
I also hate.

To get to our confluence we drove half an hour down the
Oregon side of the Columbia, half an hour back up the
Washington side, then parked in the Crown Z visitors' lot.
Ignoring the NO TRESPASSING, HIGH VOLTAGE and DANGER

signs, we passed through a hole in a cyclone fence, detoured around a gigantic mill building, crossed disused railroad tracks and bulldozed fields, reached the Washougal's last riffle. We clambered downstream through brambles and scrub willow. We eased alongside another huge mill wall, in front of which lay a kind of bay. The confluence proper— the exact spot where the crystal-clear Washougal blended with the complicated greens of the Columbia—turned out to be a slow, fishy-looking glide directly below the mill wall, just at the neck of the bay.

The riverbank there was interesting: it was made of hard-packed clay; bare rock; spilled oil; logging cable; shards of every kind and color of pop, beer and booze bottle; flood-crushed car and appliance parts; slabs of broken concrete with rebar sticking out of them; driftwood; drift Styrofoam; drift tires and reject mill parts—huge reject mill parts.

We found a rusted sprocket the size of a merry-go-round and sat on it. Our legs fit perfectly between the teeth.

We had come, I felt in my very center, to a joining of everything that created, sustained and warped us. The question was: Was it a viable home? Was it still somehow holy? Or was I, with my Bedouin bedroom and stolen Oriental photos, right to long only for escape?

We began setting up the odd tackle we'd together come to prefer: a stiff fiberglass fly rod and light spinning reel (mine open-faced, his closed); monofilament line a third the test of that used by most salmon fishermen (to increase casting distance). There wasn't a holy man in sight. There wasn't any kind of human in sight. The mill rumbled behind us like an insatiable stomach; tugs dragged log rafts up Crown

Z's own private slough; a dredge worked the slough a half-mile downriver; trucks and cars whished along the jettied highway across the bay; ships and barges plowed the Columbia beyond. It was the machines you saw and heard, though, not the people inside them. Industrial men, not holy ones. Them's the kind we grew in these parts.

Yet it was still beautiful at the confluence. We could see east to the Cascade foothills, west clear to the Coast Range, and an enormous piece of Oregon lay across the river to the south. There is a Gangian majesty to the lower Columbia, and something awesome, if not holy, in knowing its currents are made of the glaciers, springs, desert seeps and dark industrial secrets of two Canadian provinces and six American states. When I kept my eyes on distant vistas, or on the two waters blending at our feet, I could even imagine some kind of "association with the divine" here.

Snaking out of the Canadian Rockies with tremendous power, the Columbia River is over 1,200 miles long. Ten miles wide where it meets the Pacific, the river's massive force pushes a finger of freshwater 400 miles out to sea.

—PM

Though I'd no faith in the wisdom of the resident machine operators, I could picture Indians, the American kind, watching these same mountains while awaiting these same fish, some of them maybe knowing what the *rishis* knew.

But when I turned, as I had known I must, to the third waterway, things immediately began to break down. I knew, from studying maps, that a creek named Lacamas — a genuine little river — entered the Crown Zellerbach mill on the opposite side from us. I knew this creek headed in the mountains north of Camas, and that it'd had its own run of salmon once. But the mill-used fluid that shot from the flume just downstream from our sprocket bore no resemblance to water. It looked like hot pancake batter, gushing forth in a quantity so vast that part of me found it laughable. It looked like Satan's own nostril risen from hell, blowing out an infinite, scalding booger. But it was a steaming, poisonous, killing joke that shot across the Washougal's drought-shriveled mouth in a yellow-gray scythe, curved downstream and coated the Columbia's north shore with what looked like dead human skin for miles. And maybe a *rishi* could have pondered it and still felt equanimity. All I could feel, though, just as I feared, was fury and impotence and sickness. I said nothing to Jered — who'd merely pinched his nose, said, "Pyoo!" and set about fishing. I just squeezed my eyes shut, tried the same with my brain and waited for my friend to take us elsewhere. But I couldn't help but hear the flume's diarrheal gushing. And then, over the gushing, a strange double splash.

The first half of the splash was a bright coho salmon. The second half was its echo, bouncing so hard off the mill wall behind us that I turned to the sound, half-expecting to see yet another river running through the rubble and broken glass.

"Look!" Jared whispered as a second bright coho leapt high in the evening light, fell back in the river — and again the loud, clean echo. Then another one leapt, and another, all amazingly high, all in the same place—a point in mid-river, just upstream from the toxic scythe.

My first impulse, lip-service vegetarianism and all, was to grab my rod. A big school of silvers was clearly moving in. But Jered, the unabashed carnivore, had stopped fishing, he just stood watching and listening now. I would not have done the same if he hadn't set the example, but I too grew satisfied to watch: for those salmon leaps were language. They were the salmon people's legend, enacted before our eyes. And though we'd heard the old story a thousand times, thought we knew it by rote, there was a twist, at this confluence, that we two sons of the same troubled waters needed to sit still and hear.

The familiar part of the story, the rote chorus, told how these unlikely creatures had been born way up this mountain river, had grown strong in it, then had left it for the Pacific; yet some impression of their birthplace, some memory or scent touched them years and leagues later in that vastness, brought them schooling in off the Columbia's mouth, forced them to run the gauntlet of nets, hooks and predators, search the big river's murky greens, solve the riddle and enter again the waters of their fatal, yet life-giving home. Then came the twist—in the shape of the scythe.

Salmon are not stupid. They grow tentative in rivers. They know when to spook, and when to wait quietly; when to leap, when to hide, when to fight for their lives. As these coho entered the confluence and tasted the scythe they must surely have tried everything—must have hesitated, sought another channel, circled back out into the Columbia, come round again and again, waiting for the pain of the thing to diminish, for rain to fall, for rivers to rise, for industries to die. But salmon have no choice: their great speed and long journeys, like ours, create an illusion of freedom, but to live as a race they must finally become as much a

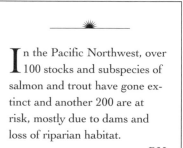

In the Pacific Northwest, over 100 stocks and subspecies of salmon and trout have gone extinct and another 200 are at risk, mostly due to dams and loss of riparian habitat.

—PM

part of their river as its water and its stones. So in the end, they entered. With eyes that can't close and breath that can't be held they darted straight into this confounding of the vast, the pure and the insane. And the slashing leaps that now shattered the river's surface were each the coho word for their cold, primordial rage against whatever it was that maimed them—and their equally cold primordial joy at having reached the waters of their home.

So we never did fish that day, Jered and I. We just sat like a couple of Ganges River hut-jockeys on a reject mill sprocket, watching salmon leap as the day grew dark. Yet after each leap my breath caught as the splash resounded, impossibly loud, against the walls of the mill, and the surface rings tripled, at least for an instant, the two dimensions of the killing scythe. Feeling a frail hope welling, feeling a need to memorize, for life, this same wild leap and passage, I suddenly began to dread my old fishing partner—or to dread, at least, the Consciousness One, Huntin'-'n'-Fishin' type summary I expected him to make at any moment, thus crew-cutting the beauty off all that we were seeing.

But when I finally did turn to my stick-in-the-mud friend, he didn't even notice me, and in his eyes, which were brimming, I saw nothing but that same cold anger, and that same wild joy. Jered was not watching the fish jump. He was raging and exulting in the coho as if they were our people; as if ours were the ancient instincts that had sorted the Columbia's countless strands, ours the unclosing eye the scythe betrayed and blinded, ours the bright bodies leaping and falling back into the home waters—falling just to burst them apart; just to force them to receive, even now, our gleaming silver sides.

David James Duncan is the author of *The River Why* and *The Brothers K*. He lives (and fishes) in western Montana, where he is at work on his next novel. This story was excerpted from his book, *River Teeth: Stories and Writings*.

River Rising

WENDELL BERRY

*A meditation on what it means
to "ride on a river."*

W E PUT THE CANOE IN ABOUT SIX MILES
up the Kentucky River from my house. There,
at the mouth of Drennon Creek, is a little
colony of summer camps. We knew we could get down to
the water there with some ease. And it proved easier than
we expected. The river was up maybe twenty feet, and we
found a path slanting down the grassy slope in front of one
of the cabins. It went right into the water, as perfect for
launching the canoe and getting in as if it had been worn
there by canoeists.

To me that is the excitement of a rise: the unexpected-
ness, always, of the change it makes. What was difficult
becomes easy. What was easy becomes difficult. By water,
what was distant becomes near. By land, what was near
becomes distant. At the waterline, when a rise is on, the
world is changing. There is an irresistible sense of adventure in the difference. Once the river is out of its banks, a

vertical few inches of rise may widen the surface by many
feet over the bottomland. A sizable lagoon will appear in the
middle of a cornfield. A drain in a pasture will become a
canal. Stands of beech and oak will take on the look of a
cypress swamp. There is something Venetian about it. There
is a strange excitement in going in a boat where one would
ordinarily go on foot—or where, ordinarily, birds would be
flying. And so the first excitement of our trip was that little
path; where it might go in a time of low water was unimaginable. Now it went down to the river.

Because of the offset in the shore at the creek mouth,
there was a large eddy turning in the river where we put in,
and we began our drift downstream by drifting upstream.
We went up inside the row of shore trees, whose tops now
waved in the current, until we found an opening among the
branches, and then turned out along the channel. The current took us. We were still settling ourselves as if in prepa-
ration, but our starting place was already diminishing
behind us.

There is something ominously like life in that. One would
always like to settle oneself, get braced, say "Now I am
going to begin"—and then begin. But as the necessary quiet
seems about to descend, a hand is felt at one's back, shoving.
And that is the way with the river when a current is running: once the connection with the shore is broken, the journey has begun.

We were, of course, already at work with the paddles. But
we were ahead of ourselves. I think that no matter how delib-
erately one moved from the shore into the sudden violence of
a river on the rise, there would be bound to be several uneasy

minutes of transition. It is another world, which means that one's senses and reflexes must begin to live another kind of life. Sounds and movements that from the standpoint of the shore might have come to seem even familiar now make a new urgent demand on the attention. There is everything to get used to, from a wholly new perspective. And from the outset one has the currents to deal with.

It is easy to think, before one has ever tried it, that nothing could be easier than to drift down the river in a canoe on a strong current. That is because when one thinks of a river one is apt to think of *one* thing—a great singular flowing that one puts one's boat into and lets go. But it is not like that at all, not after the water is up and the current swift. It is not one current, but a braiding together of several, some going at different speeds, some even in different directions. Of course, one *could* just let go, let the boat be taken into the continuous mat of drift—leaves, logs, whole trees, cornstalks, cans, bottles, and such—in the channel, and turn and twist in the eddies there. But one does not have to do that long in order to sense the helplessness of a light canoe when it is sideways to the current. It is out of control then, and endangered. Stuck in the mat of drift, it can't be maneuvered. It would turn over easily; one senses that by a sort of ache in the nerves, the way bad footing is sensed. And so we stayed busy, keeping the canoe between the line of half-submerged shore trees and the line of drift that marked the channel. We weren't trying to hurry—the currents were carrying us as fast as we wanted to go—but it took considerable labor just to keep straight. It was like riding a spirited horse not fully bridle-wise. We kept our direction by *intention*; there could be no dependence on habit or inertia; when our minds wandered, the river took over and turned us according to inclinations of its own. It bore us like a consciousness, acutely wakeful, filling perfectly the lapses in our own.

But we did grow used to it, and accepted our being on it as one of the probabilities, and began to take the mechanics of it for granted. The necessary sixth sense had come to us, and we began to notice more than we had to.

There is an exhilaration in being *accustomed* to a boat on dangerous water. It is though into one's consciousness of the dark violence of the depths at one's feet there rises the idea of the boat, the buoyancy of it. It is always with a sort of triumph that the boat is realized—that it goes *on top of the water*, between breathing and drowning. It is an ancient-feeling triumph; it must have been one of the first ecstasies. The analogy of riding a spirited horse is fairly satisfactory; it is mastery over something resistant—a buoyancy that is not natural and inert like that of a log, but desired and vital and to one's credit. Once the boat has fully entered the consciousness it becomes an intimate extension of the self; one feels as competently amphibious as a duck. And once we felt accustomed and secure in the boat, the day and the river began to come clear to us.

It was a gray, cold Sunday in the middle of December. In the woods on the north slopes above us we could see the black trunks and branches just faintly traced with snow, which gave them a silvery, delicate look—the look of impossibly fine handwork that nature sometimes has. And they looked cold. The wind was coming straight up the river into our faces. But we were dressed warmly, and the wind didn't matter much, at least not yet. The force that mattered, that surrounded us, and inundated us with its sounds, and pulled at or shook or carried everything around us, was the river.

To one standing on the bank, floodwater will seem to be flowing at a terrific rate. People who are not used to it will commonly believe it is going three or four times as fast as it really is. It is so all of a piece, and so continuous. To one drifting along in a boat this exaggerated impression of speed does not occur; one is going the same speed as the river then and is not fooled. In the Kentucky when the water is high a current of four or five miles an hour is about usual, I would say, and there are times in a canoe that make that seem plenty fast.

What the canoeist gets, instead of an impression of the river's speed, is an impression of its power. Or, more exactly, an impression of the *voluminousness* of its power. The sense of the volume alone has come to me when, swimming in the summertime, I have submerged mouth and nose so that the plane of the water spread away from the lower eyelid; the awareness of its bigness that comes then is almost intolerable; one feels how falsely assuring it is to look down on the river, as we usually do. The sense of the power of it came to me one day in my boyhood when I attempted to swim ashore in a swift current, pulling an overturned rowboat. To check the downstream course of the boat I tried grabbing hold of the partly submerged willows along the shore with my free hand, and was repeatedly pulled under as the willows bent, and then torn loose. My arms stretched between the boat and the willow branch might have been sewing threads for all the holding they could do. It was the first time I realized that there could be circumstances in which my life would count for nothing, absolutely nothing—and I have never needed to learn that again.

Sitting in a canoe, riding the back of the flooding river as it flows down into a bend, and turns, the currents racing and crashing among the trees along the outside shore, and flows on, one senses the volume and the power all together. The sophistications of our age do not mitigate the impression. To some degree it remains unimaginable, as is suggested by the memory's recurrent failure to hold on to it. It can never be remembered as wild as it is, and so each new experience of it bears some of the shock of surprise. It would take the mind of a god to watch it as it changes and not be surprised.

These long views that one gets coming down it, show it to move majestically. It is stately. It has something of the stylized grandeur and awesomeness of royalty in Sophoclean tragedy. But as one watches, there emanates

---

When European explorers arrived in the New World in the 1600s, they discovered the canoe to be the primary mode of transportation for native peoples to maintain their hunting and gathering lifestyles. The original canoe—a dugout, or hollowed log boat—had given way to the bark canoe developed by woodland Indians and animal-skin boats developed by the northern Inuit. These lighter, more versatile craft enabled natives and newcomers to easily use the interconnected waterways of North America's interior.

—Laurie Gullion, *Canoeing*

from it too, an insinuation of darkness, implacability, horror. And the nearer look tends to confirm this. Contained and borne in the singular large movements are hundreds of smaller ones: eddies and whirlpools, turnings this way and that, crosscurrents rushing out from the shores into the channel. One must simplify it in order to speak of it. One probably simplifies it in some way in order to look at it.

There is something deeply horrifying about it, roused. Not, I think, because it is inhuman, alien to us; some of us at least must feel a kinship with it, or we would not loiter around it for pleasure. The horror must come from our sense that, so long as it remains what it is, it is not subject. To say that it is indifferent would be wrong. That would imply a malevolence, as if it could be aware of us if only it wanted to. It is more remote from our concerns than indifference. It is serenely and silently not subject—to us or to anything else except the other natural forces that are also beyond our control. And it is apt to stand for and represent to us all in nature and in the universe that is not subject. That is horror. We can make use of it. We can ride on its back in boats. But it won't stop to let us get on and off. It is not a passenger train. And if we make a mistake, or risk ourselves too far to it, why then it will suffer a little wrinkle on its surface, and go on as before.

———— ∞∞ ————

Wendell Berry is a conservationist, farmer, essayist, novelist, professor of English, and poet. He was born and lives in Kentucky. Among his many published works are *Another Turn of the Crank*, *A Timbered Choir*, and *Recollected Essays 1965–1980*, from which this story was excerpted.

The Amazon Queen

ISABEL ALLENDE

*Seeking a remedy for writer's block, an author
is healed in the Brazilian jungle.*

A POWERFUL DREAM LED ME TO THE AMAZON. For three years I had been blocked, unable to write, with the feeling that the torrent of stories waiting to be told, which once had seemed inexhaustible, had dried up.

Then one night I dreamed of four naked Indians emerging from the heart of South America carrying a large box, a gift for a conquistador. And as they crossed jungles, rivers, mountains and villages, the box absorbed every sound, leaving the world in silence. The song of the birds, the murmuring of the wind, human stories, all were swallowed up. I awakened with the conviction that I must go there to look for that voracious box, where perhaps I could find voices to nourish my inspiration. It took a year to realize that wondrous journey.

How shall I describe the Amazon? From the airplane, it is a vast green world. Below, on the ground, it is the kingdom of water, vapor, rain, rivers broad as oceans, sweat. It is not Tarzan's jungle, but it is still a mysterious and fascinating land. The Amazon occupies 60 percent of Brazil — an area larger than India — and extends into Venezuela, Colombia and Peru.

In some areas, as in the Atalaia do Norte triangle, the "law of the jungle" rules. Bandits and traffickers in drugs, gold, wood and exotic animals murder one another and exterminate the Indians. In other places, like Pico de Neblina, there are marvelous national parks where one can take demanding, but relatively secure, tours. In the Valle de Yavari, one still finds isolated tribes. It is estimated that some 250,000 Indians live there. Despite the irrational exploitation of resources, official Brazilian figures maintain that only a small fraction of the enormous potential of the Amazon has been destroyed. Ecologists, on the other hand, are alarmed: 500,000 square kilometers have been deforested, and the process continues.

I approached the Amazon through Manaos. The city is far from the Atlantic coast, and appears on the map as solid jungle. I imagined a village on stilts, ruled over by an anachronistic baroque theater. I had been told that during the height of the rubber boom, the city was so prosperous that its ladies sent their clothing to Paris to be laundered, but probably such tales were only legend.

It was a surprise to land in an effervescent city of a million inhabitants, a free port, a center of a broad spectrum of businesses and trafficking, both legal and suspect. A wall of heat struck me in the face. The taxi took me along a highway bordered with luxuriant vegetation, then turned into twisting little streets where the homes of the poor and the middle class were democratically interspersed, both far from the neighborhoods of the wealthy who live in luxurious fortresses under heavy guard.

The famous opera theater, remodeled, is still the major tourist attraction. During the last century, Europe's most famous opera stars traveled to Manaos to delight the rubber barons. The surrounding streets are paved with a mixture of stone and rubber to mute the wheels and horses' hooves during performances.

My first meal was pirarucú, the best freshwater fish in the world—delicious, but horrifying in appearance—served on a terrace in the port facing the incredible river, which in times of flood stretched out like an ocean. I stayed in Manaos only a couple of days, eager to leave civilization behind. To gain a sense of that strange region, one needs to plunge many kilometers inland along its great rivers and their tributaries, and to pass some time among the jungle dwellers, the *caboclos*.

From Manaos, I set out on a boat with a powerful outboard motor. For an hour we traveled upstream at a suicidal pace, following the Rio Negro to an eco-hotel constructed in the treetops. The hotel consists of several towers connected by passageways open to monkeys, parrots, coatis and every insect known to man. Chicken wire everywhere prevents animals from coming into the rooms, especially monkeys, which can wreak as much destruction as an elephant.

Easy, comfortable tours can be booked from the hotel. The more adventurous find a guide and go farther upstream in a boat, or deep into the jungle in a private plane. No one even considers land travel.

I took a walk through the thick undergrowth, led by a young *caboclo* guide. It seemed to me that we walked for an eternity, but afterward I realized that the walk had been ridiculously short. At last I understood the meaning of the last line of a famous Latin American novel: "He was swallowed up by the jungle." Compasses are useless there, and one can wander in circles forever.

The jungle is never silent; you hear birds, the screeching of animals, stealthy footfalls. It smells of moss, of moistness, and sometimes you catch the waft of a sweet odor like rotted fruit. The heat is exhausting, but beneath the dark canopy of the trees you can at least breathe. Out on the river the sun beats down unmercifully, although as long as the boat is moving, there is a breeze.

To inexpert eyes, everything is uniformly green, but for the native the jungle is a diverse and endlessly rich world. The guide pointed out vines that collect pure water to drink, bark that relieves fevers, leaves used to treat diabetes, resins that close wounds, the sap of a tree that cures a cough, rubber for affixing points on arrows. There are more than 30,000 species of insects, and the forest is the largest biogenetic preserve on the planet.

The Indians use a biodegradable plant poison they throw into the water to stun the fish. They collect them when they rise to the surface, then eat them without effect because the poison quickly degrades.

Hospitals and doctors are beyond the reach of the *caboclos*, but they have a pharmacy in the forest vegetation. It is calculated that we have identified barely 10 percent of the enormous variety of medicinal plants in the forest. Some with poetic names are sold in the hotel: *mulateiro*, for beautiful skin, *breuzinho*, to improve memory and facilitate concentration during meditation; *guarana*, to combat fatigue and hardness of heart; *macaranduba*, for coughs, weakness and lugubrious chest.

But as the *caboclos* lose their indigenous oral traditions and the old shamans die, this ancestral medicine is disappearing. It is feared that the exploitation of the forest is destroying thousands of plants and animals before they can be classified. Finally, after several decades of turning a deaf ear to the clamor of the scientists, the government of Brazil has adopted a conservationist policy in regard to the Amazon, but it is difficult to enforce in this enormous territory of vaguely defined boundaries....

We went to a native village which was in fact the habitat of a single extended family. These were Sateré Maue Indians, who had been evicted from their land and forced to emigrate to the city, where they ended up in a *favela*, or slum, dying of hunger. The owner of our hotel had given them some land where they could return to living in harmony with their traditions.

We arrived at their village late one afternoon by boat, at the hour of the mosquitoes. We climbed a muddy hill to the clearing in the forest where, beneath a single palm roof, a bonfire blazed and a few hammocks were strung. One of the Indians spoke a little Portuguese, and he explained that they had planted manioc and soon they would have the necessary tools to process it. From the root they make flour, tapioca, and bread—even a liquor....

I walked over to the fire to see what was cooking, and

found an alligator about a meter in length, quartered like a
chicken, with claws, teeth, eyes and hide intact, sadly roast-
ing. Two piranhas were strung on a hook, along with something that resembled a muskrat. Later, after I got a good
look at the skin, I saw it was a porcupine. I tried everything:
The alligator tasted like dried and reconstituted codfish, the
piranhas like smoke and the porcupine like petrified pig.
The Indians were selling the modest crafts they make from
seeds, sticks, and feathers. Also a long badly cured boa skin,
brittle and pathetic.

The *caboclos* are Indians with European or African blood,
a mixing of races that began during the sixteenth century.
Some are so poor that they don't use money; they live from
fishing and a few crops, trading for fuel, coffee, sugar, flour,
matches and other indispensable supplies.

There are a few villages on land, but as the water rises
more than fifty feet during the annual floods, submerging
thousands of acres, people prefer to build houses on stilts or
live in floating huts. The dwellings are not divided into
rooms, as the *caboclos* do not share the white man's urge for
privacy. They have few possessions, barely what is needed
for survival.

All communication and transportation is by river. The
radio reaches where mail could never go. Telegrams replace
the telephone, a nonexistent luxury, but one sees television
sets in the most unexpected places, and people gather to
watch the soccer matches and soap operas.

The majority of inhabitants of the Amazon do not
appear in the census or government statistics; there is no
justice system, no law, no progress. For the *caboclos*, time is

measured in days by boat; life, in rainy seasons. The incentive of acquisition is unknown; people fish or hunt for the day's needs, because anything more than that spoils. The tacit law is respected despite the fact that some *caboclos* now have electric generators and refrigerators. Sometimes, if they catch more than their daily quota, they keep the live fish in bamboo baskets in the water.

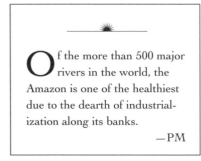

Of the more than 500 major rivers in the world, the Amazon is one of the healthiest due to the dearth of industrialization along its banks.

— PM

News can take weeks to travel by word of mouth to the nearest radio, where it awaits its turn to be transmitted in the form of a telegram. As a result, the death of a family member may be learned a year after the fact, and birth when the child is already walking. So what sense is there in rushing? Life, like the river, goes nowhere. The whole point is to keep afloat, paddling through an unchanging landscape.

A few months ago on the Alto Yavari river, on the border between Peru and Brazil, they discovered a tribe that never had any contact with white civilization. To record that first encounter, airplanes and helicopters laden with television cameras filled the air, while on the ground the Indians, surprised in the midst of the Stone Age, readied their arrows....

One morning we left before dawn to see the sun rising on the red horizon and to watch the frolicking of rosy dolphins. Dolphins are among the few Amazonian creatures that are not eaten; the flesh tastes terrible and the skin is unusable.

The Indians, nonetheless, still harpoon them to rip out their eyes and genitals to make amulets for virility and fertility.

In the same river where the water is as warm as a soup, where the previous afternoon we had watched some German tourists catch dozens of piranhas with a pole, a string and bare hook, I had swum naked. Piranhas are edible—very tasty, in fact—but the Germans were catching them for sport and, after photographing them, throwing them back into the water. Some fish had taken the hook so many times their mouths were raw and bleeding. Like us humans, who keep tripping over the same stone in our path, they never learned. Normally piranhas do not attack people; like the caymans, they fulfill the useful function of cleaning the water. Like birds of prey, they eat carrion.

That night we went out in a canoe with a huge, battery-powered spotlight to look at the alligators. The light blinded the fish, and in their terror some leaped into the boat. Knowing they were piranhas, we took them carefully by the tail and threw them back into the water, not wanting to lose a chunk of flesh to those horrifying jaws. We saw bats and huge butterflies flying in the darkness.

The boatman, an adolescent *caboclo* who spoke little English and laughed openly at our discomfort, would beam his light into the tree roots when he spotted a pair of red eyes and jump into the water. We would hear a great thrashing, and soon he would reemerge holding an alligator by the neck in his bare hand if it was small, and with a cord around its muzzle if it was larger. We saw photographs of one they had caught the week before: it was longer than the boat. There are more than thirty species of manta rays in those same waters, all very dangerous. And to think I had swum there!

After ten days we had to leave. I did not find the four naked Indians with their magic box, but when I returned home I carried some bit of that vast greenness within me, like a treasure. For the sake of discipline, and because of superstition, I begin all my books on January 8. On January 8, 1997, I finally ended the three-year block I had suffered and I was able to write again. My dream of the jungle was not without its reward.

Born in Peru, raised in Chile, and currently living in Northern California, Isabel Allende is the author of *Daughter of Fortune*, *The House of the Spirits*, *Eva Luna*, *Aphrodite*, and a number of other novels.

Vessel of Last Resort

JEFFREY TAYLER

*One of the few tourists who had preceded the author
up the Congo River had arrived,
but dead of malaria.*

J OSEPH CONRAD TRAVELED 1,100 MILES UP THE
Congo River to find the heart of darkness; I was sure
I had seen it at mile one. I stood on the rusty, urine-
stained deck of a cargo barge watching Kinshasa, the capital
of Democratic Republic of Congo, formerly Zaire, recede
into a humid gray haze. The city that from Brazzaville had
looked so prosperous, with its skyscrapers and dock cranes,
turned out up close to be a farrago of squalor and raucous
mayhem: troops of beggars limping on pretzeled legs
clogged the multilane Boulevard du 30 Juin; fires smoldered
in refuse heaps alive with the ulcerous, emaciated bodies of
those too weak to beg; silver Mercedes rocketed through the
rubble, scattering crowds, carrying their owners to hush-
hush diamond deals in posh Gombe. And outside the con-
fines of the modern district, in the old Cité and beyond,
gangs of youths armed with guns and knives patrolled slums
4 million strong. Someone must have gone mad here to let

all this happen: If present-day Kinshasa wasn't Kurtz's "Inner Station," I didn't know what was.

With our barge cabled to its bow, the white-and-blue *pousseur*, or pusher boat, headed out toward mid-river, and we were free of Kinshasa's stench. It was evening; the day's heat was abating. Ahead, toward the equator, the sky and water dissolved into a mist of luminous azure.

Travel on the Congo River has never been easy, and with the chaos prevailing in the country since 1990, it has become more difficult than ever. The national transportation company has gone bankrupt, only rarely sending upriver its one functioning Congo barge—actually a floating slum of some half a dozen barges lashed to an ailing pusher boat. As a result, merchants have turned to private barges for transport and to conduct trade with the interior, where most of Zaire's 45 million people live, and where roads, if they exist at all, are truck-swallowing quagmires for most of the year. But the barges lack even the skeletal amenities (rat-infested cabins, clogged toilets, starchy food) that the ONATRA boats offered, and travel is brutally basic. For the equivalent of thirty dollars you get a space on a rusty steel deck and no more. That will have to suffice for two to six weeks of floating through some of the steamiest terrain on earth. Congolese wondered what misfortune could have driven me to take the barge, and every expatriate I met in Kinshasa said that such crafts were not for non-Congolese. "When cholera breaks out on board," an American missionary warned me, "people just die and they throw the bodies overboard." A British expat said that the last tourist to take a barge to Kisangani had arrived, but dead of malaria.

I was no old Africa hand, no seasoned veteran of tropical travel. In fact, I had spent the three previous years in Russia, and a desire to escape the cold and break out of the gray-bureaucracy syndrome I suffered from there had a lot to do with my thoughts running equatorward at every idle moment that winter. When, in February, I came upon the British explorer Henry Morton Stanley's account of his voyage down the Congo, I was mesmerized. The desire seized me, *possessed* me, to quit the northland and travel this greatest of all subSaharan Africa's rivers, no matter what the risks or discomforts. I was not a missionary or a naturalist, nor was I a vacationer expecting the civilized pleasures of an all-inclusive Kenyan game-park safari; rather, I was a northerner gripped by a monomania for the primal truth of the Congo, and the only cure would be a crucible on its muddy waters.

The deck was empty save for a few crew members and a pimpled pastor from Lukolela engrossed in a Jimmy Swaggart tract. But our solitude was not to last: we were drawing toward the port at Selza, a suburb of Kinshasa, where a crowd was scrimmaging on the pier. Even before we docked, people started casting aboard foam mattresses and baskets and bales of cloth, leaping over the watery divide onto our deck. Gendarmes thrashed at the crowd with rope whips, but in vain: by the time we moored, every square inch was occupied. Tinny Congolese pop blared forth from the barge's loudspeakers. The floating river fête had begun.

The boat's owner, Nguma, had taken pity on me and assigned me a crew member's cabin; but with a loudspeaker

over the door and no windows, it turned out to be a noisy
oven. I gathered up my mosquito net and sheets and billeted
myself in solitude above the bridge on the *pousseur*. Feeling
nauseated with shock from the crowds, the heat, and the
excitement of the trip, I lay down on my foam mattress and
peered through the gauze at the stars, thinking back on the
history of this enormous river, the second longest in Africa.
Stanley had fought his way down it from Nyangwe in 1876
and 1877, losing many of the members of his expedition to disease, to drowning, and to battles with the tribes that live on
the middle and upper banks even today. My trip, tame as it
was by comparison, still seemed an impossible feat: this
cramped floating crate of steel had to chug up 1,100 miles of
jungle river. If I got sick, if anyone got sick, if we broke down,
there was nothing to be done about it but hope that
Providence, so clearly unmoved by the tableau of mass suffering in Congo, might decide to make a gesture of divine
benevolence toward us. Many merchants, I was to learn, had
had friends die on the river, from cholera or malaria or other
nameless fevers—a fate I hoped to avoid with half a dozen
vaccines and a satchel stuffed full of the malaria prophylaxes
commonly prescribed in Congo. The commencement of every
voyage up the Congo was thus attended by fervent prayers for
Godspeed, by whispered supplications to fetishes, by wailing
farewells from relatives on shore. Our voyage was no exception. No one was certain who would arrive alive in Kisangani.

Dawn found us coursing past grassy flatland marked
here and there by trees whose majestic canopies spread like
giant green mushroom caps. I climbed down the ladder from
the upper deck.

"Would you like to bathe?" asked Jean, the lean, neat, green-eyed chief accountant. "My room has the only bath on the barge."

He led me around the *pousseur* and through his quarters to the "bathroom"—a slimy metallic cubicle with a hole in the floor—and handed me a bucket filled with unctuous green water, bath-warm with a frothy head, drawn as it was straight from the Congo's hot currents. As I scrubbed and rinsed with it, I had the sensation that it was an organic fluid. It felt viscous, sebaceous; I seemed to be bathing in plasma. It stung my eyes, and I wondered how river blindness was transmitted (not like this, it turns out).

Everywhere on deck straw mats lay strewn with bolts of cloth, sacks of sugar and salt, malaria pills in white boxes, batteries, needles and thread and scissors, cookie tins, Bic pens, school notebooks with green covers. The merchants—who were the majority of the barge's passengers—laughed and bantered among themselves in Lingala, the language most widely spoken along the river, interrupting their discourse to shout, "*Ey, mondele!* [white man] *Bonjour!*" as I walked by. Mothers scrubbed down two-year-olds, skillets sizzled with onions and chunks of fish in palm oil, thump-thump-thumps resounded as women in rainbow robes pounded plantains into mash with carved mallets. A congregation led by the pastor from Lukolela chanted Lingala spirituals at the stern.

I chatted, in French, as I walked around. Among the merchants there were high hopes for the income this voyage might bring, as well as fear. A twenty-five-year-old man originally from Bandundu said to me, "I was a tailor in Kin, but when the *pillages* began, in 1991, I lost my business, so I took to the barges. I have a fiancée—she'll leave me if I can't buy her dresses and jewelry. So here I am, risking this voyage. People get diarrhea and dysentery on these trips, and sometimes the boats sink. Man proposes, but God disposes."

Those who have taken to the barges confront head-on the timeless, primal phenomena of sun, rain, wind, and heat, and engage in a pattern of trade millennia old. All day they sell their basically urban merchandise to villagers paddling up in dugout canoes, immediately using their profits to buy the manioc root, smoked fish, monkey, crocodile, and antelope offered by these same villagers. The merchants then hawk these foodstuffs in the huge markets of Kisangani after the ascent of the river or Kinshasa after the descent. Even crew members stockpile smoked fish or monkey for their families at home. Everyone aboard becomes a *debrouillard*—a master at getting by—or doesn't last.

Day three found us amid whitecapped waters and buffeting winds. We chugged ahead into rushing rafts of water hyacinth, through the part of the river known as le Chenal, a narrow strait paralleled by low mountains. The sky was lowering and iron-gray, with lightning flickering from the equator ahead. No pirogues came out to meet us; villages were few. But the first signs of a great jungle were appearing: on ridges stood massive, broad-boughed trees, and the savanna's underbrush gathered into higher and denser clumps.

The next day began with a flurry of shouts in rainy fog. Loaded with pineapples and manioc tubers, pirogues in V-shaped formations of three and four were shooting toward us through the mizzle and docking at our sides. I stood at the railing composing shots on my Nikon.

"*Nina*! *Nina*!" someone shouted. "*Nina*!" An excited murmur arose on deck. A man with "*Nina*" on his lips forced his way through the crowd and hurled himself overboard, just missing a pirogue. Thirty feet from the barge floated a fish the size of an inner tube, dead and belly-up in the choppy gray waters.

"An electric catfish, a *nina*!" a boy next to me shouted. "What a prize! It will bring him ten dollars." But the man missed it, it floated past, and then the drama for those on deck became whether he could catch up with the barge again. He thrashed the water in a sloppy crawl, landing near the *pousseur* at the stern, and hoisted himself aboard. A hero for the entertainment he had provided, he raised his arms to general applause.

The heat in the Kinshasa region had been bearable, but my travel mates warned me that after Bolobo, which we had just passed, the climate would turn equatorial. The next dawn dragonflies and fat, sluggish moths covered my mosquito net. The river had become a sheet of glass spreading to infinity around us, overhung by a suffocating mist; the air had turned heavy, gone sour with tropical rot. No banks were visible, although the occasional island—a ragged outcropping of black tree silhouettes—drifted by in the steam. Noon brought white heat and steely white light; the Congo became a lifeless, utterly still lake of glare, ten miles wide, all colors reduced to black and gray against the white of water and sky. The barge's surfaces became untouchably hot, and shade diminished as the incandescent ball of the sun rose directly overhead. The merchants erected tarps up and down the deck and lay prostrate under them, torpid with the heat.

Dusk came. We were a spearhead slicing into an azure river-and-sky melange, seemingly released from the bounds of earth, floating in a blue domain. Astern, to the west, the river was bankless, tinctured lilac, bleeding red, running into cool purple with the sun's descent.

Recovered from the day's heat, I sat under the light behind the owner's cabin trying to read V. S. Naipaul, a futile endeavor given the moths and cicadas swirling around me. Then something golf-ball-sized slammed into my temple. I looked down and saw a huge armored beetle writhing at my feet. Djili, the freight manager, came over and picked it up. "We eat these beetles, you know. Come over and answer a few questions." He led me to a circle of palm-wine drinkers at the bow. Marijuana, called *bangi* in Lingala, was being smoked on the deck, and its pungently sweet aroma perfumed the air. The drinkers were chasing their wine with fat, white, fried palm grubs that they selected from a bowl at their feet.

"Your country is supposed to stand for human rights, but what about the rights of a man?" Djili asked, biting off the head of a grub and chewing it lustily a few inches from my face. "Have a grub. I hear that your government would forbid me to have more than one wife. I should be able to have as many wives as I choose—that's my right as a man. But your government would forbid it. *C'est pas juste.*"

Fearfully tasting my grub, and finding it chewy and

squirting hot palm oil, I muttered something about polygamy being unChristian, but this only provoked a tirade. *I am eating a larva*, I said to myself.

"UnChristian? Polygamy goes back to Jesus's day! It's your government that's unChristian, allowing pornography in the streets and forbidding me my basic rights as a man! Here, try a caterpillar." Djili held out a bowl of the brown squirming things. Still inwardly reeling from the grub, I had to refuse, but a little girl, looking at me wide-eyed, took one of the living creatures and chomped it to pieces, swallowing it with a gulp. We talked, or I should say Djili raved, until night fell and the mosquitoes drove me off the bow.

The ninth day found us hugging the bank close to the great jungle, a tangled mass of green lucent in its nearest reaches with sunlight pouring in from above, but dark and gloomy farther in. Occasionally a monkey would scream and bound branch to branch back into the trees, or red-and-gray parrots would squawk and take flight. Huge, gangly birds that the locals call *kulokoko* screeched at the sight of us, like pterodactyls horrified to discover men trespassing in their prehistoric domain, and *wuff-wuffed* away in heavy-winged flight. Once, I caught sight of a cobra, some fifteen feet long and black, swimming along the hyacinth, its emblematic curved head and neck slicing the coffee-brown water. We were deep in the midst of an Africa many would have thought vanished centuries ago, an Africa as eternal as the dugout canoes and the blood-red sunsets.

One day a villager paddled up with a five-foot-long live crocodile, its jaws roped shut, in the bottom of his pirogue;

it was bought by Maurice, a merchant from Kinshasa. "I'll smoke this and sell it," he said. "It'll pay for my return ticket." He and the villager struggled to get the thrashing black reptile out of the pirogue without receiving a blow from its tail or dropping it into the water; several bystanders helped, but the croc still whacked one boy in the face with its tail. When they had dragged it away from the edge of the deck, Maurice took to pounding in its skull with the handle of a machete until it ceased struggling, its emerald eyes slit with black and staring fiercely, even in death.

At night the specters of great trees loomed black against the Milky Way's lustrous wash of stardust. With our spotlight probing the waters in front of us, searching for shoals, illuminating swirling beetles and crow-sized bats, with mosquitoes showing like a fine mist in their millions, we threaded our way through a dark labyrinth of isles. Drumbeats announcing our arrival resounded from villages ahead; 700 miles into the jungle we were still beset by pirogues, many carrying stacks of monkey carcasses, blackened, their eyes and mouths wide open as if they had been smoked alive in stark terror. Some paddlers were bare-breasted women, others men in loincloths. Once we ran over a pirogue, occasioning loss of property but not of life: its occupants jumped free in time. All night there were shouts, drumbeats, armadas of canoes laden with bush meat streaming toward us.

Late the next evening I was watching a dispute between the barge's security chief, Augustin, and a couple of drunken fishermen when the barge lurched. I grabbed the rail; others fell flailing into their merchandise. The engine sputtered, and crew members raced toward the *pousseur*, jumping over cooking pots and sacks of salt. The engine roared, coughed. Behind the propellers the spotlight showed fulminating clouds of sand in the water. We had run aground so violently that one of our two rudders had been severed and an engine incapacitated.

I was exhausted. Almost three weeks of heat and crowd and hassle on the barge seemed to have drained the life out of me. Nze, the chief mechanic, said that this was a serious accident that could delay us by three days at least. We were already a week late. I wanted to scream. To the south, over the forest, lightning flared silently at first, and then with rumbles of thunder. We sat still, with the Congo's warm fluids rushing past our motionless bow in a rippling V.

In despair I retired to my spot above the bridge. A full moon hung over the silhouettes of trees on the distant bank and dappled the waters below with its orange glow. Nevertheless rain came that night, soft and slight in the beginning, and then hot, copious, and pummeling. I gathered up my net and retreated to the awning under the bridge. Until dawn I watched the lightning flare up and show the vast river around us. I shuddered at the crash of thunderbolts that seemed aimed at our craft on the open water.

After a long repair session on a sandbar the next morning, during which the mechanics detached the broken rudder and then placed the good rudder next to the engine that worked, we started up again and moved on toward the black-clouded horizon, past five-story-tall, broad-canopied trees guarding the entrance to the jungle like jealous sentinels.

At noon we began drawing near a stretch of sandy shore.

Villagers, mainly young men in rags, came whooping and hollering out of their huts. They leaped into their pirogues and paddled furiously toward us. Augustin whistled in alarm. The owner emerged onto the bridge platform bearing an automatic rifle. The villagers let loose what sounded like a war cry, and Augustin yelled to them not to dock, but some tried anyway. At this the owner brandished his rifle and began firing shots into the air, and the villagers abandoned the barge, with one pirogue capsizing in our violent, single-engine wake.

"It is dangerous here," the owner said. "These people are cannibals. They will see you and say, 'Ah, the flesh of the *mondele* is like sugar!'" He laughed uproariously. "This is a dangerous area for robbers and murderers. The deep jungle is wild in people as well as beasts."

A boy on the bank made a motion with his arms as if machine-gunning me, and soon all his little pals imitated him. Desi, a merchant from Lokutu, turned to me. "You see, they fear you, the *mondele*," he said. "White people to them are murderers, villains. The children hear how the Belgians used to eat little boys and girls, and they think you, any white, is a Belgian. For them to kill you would be an act of self-defense."

Eleven hundred miles and twenty-one days after leaving Kinshasa we pulled into Kisangani, in the very heart of equatorial Africa. The merchants, though they complained that business had been bad on this run and that they would barely break even, laughed and shouted jokes to one another as they struggled to haul their smoked fish and bush meat to the huge market. Here Conrad's Marlow alighted to find

a spiritually diseased and languishing Kurtz, but here I was
to disembark into mainstream modern African life, with no
ceremony, no commentary ready to deliver on the malaise of
twentieth-century humanity's soul. Dazed with fatigue, disoriented, I followed the merchants off the barge and began
making my way up toward the dusty main street, with its
placarded hotels and diamond traders, with the bells of the
city's broad white cathedral chiming over the din of the
crowds.

Jeffrey Tayler is a freelance writer and traveler based in Moscow. He has
written on Transylvania, Siberia, and Congo (Zaire) for *The Atlantic Monthly*,
and contributes regularly to *Atlantic Abroad*.

River of Light

MORT ROSENBLUM

*If Paris is the heart of France,
the Seine is the aorta.*

A GLANCE AT THE RIVER IN PARIS TELLS YOU what is going on in France. If it is not slopping over its stone quais at the new year, farmers had a bad time with drought. When it runs fast, high, and cocoa brown in April, the skiing was terrific; keepers had to drop the sluice gates on the Marne to drain off melting snow. When France is happiest, for a bicentennial celebration of the revolution or on Bastille Day, barges and barks jam the Seine on their way to the fireworks.

You can gauge the crop of tourists by counting heads hanging over the rails of *bateaux-mouches*. When barges are so heavy with gravel that water splashes over their gunwales, construction is booming. Seine watchers knew France was hooked on American television when the police began blasting past in hot little patrol boats, driver erect at the wheel, bound for lunch à la *Miami Vice*.

And downstream past Rouen, that glance at the Seine

can tell you the state of the world. Long before most people got their lips around a new household word, *perestroika*, Jacques Mevel knew the curtain was coming down. A river pilot, he travels the world each day without leaving the Seine. He noticed that Soviet sea captains suddenly started smiling and talking to strangers.

From the beginning, the French soul has bobbed in the waters of the Seine. On its bridges, love blooms; beneath them, lives end. Hardly anyone can tell you exactly where the river starts, or much else about it, but it flows through every romantic's spirit. It nourished Maupassant's pen and watered Monet's lily pond.

Paris was the City of Light long before there were switches to flip. The *rayonnement,* that radiance which the French have always beamed to the less enlightened, emanates from the pinks and oranges and sparkling flashes of the sun sinking into the Seine. When Baudelaire wrote that all around was nothing but *"ordre et beauté; luxe, calme et volupté,"* he was looking at the river off the Ile Saint-Louis.

A few generations ago, Guillaume Apollinaire mused:

Beneath the Pont Mirabeau flows the Seine
And our love...
While passes beneath the bridge of our arms
The eternal gaze of the sultry waves.

But the river is not always as the poets would have it, voluptuous and unchanging. In late winter, its mood shifts. When only slightly aroused, it floods the fast lanes along the Left Bank, gridlocking traffic from Saint-Michel to the Eiffel Tower. In 1910, hell-bent on mayhem, it went knee-deep into the fancy shops off the Champs-Elysées. A century ago, by the placid banks of a Normandy village, the current swallowed Victor Hugo's daughter Léopoldine, who toppled from a boat and sank in her Sunday best.

For 2,000 years, the Seine was alimentary canal to a nation that took its nourishment seriously. Grain moved upriver, passing cargoes of wine headed downstream. Most food travels by road and rail these days, but a look at the Seine suggests that it is still at least France's digestive tract. By the time it reaches Paris, the river carries enough detritus of civilization to sicken your average sewer rat. This, of course, does not deter the swimmers who race periodically from Notre-Dame toward Neuilly, emerging undissolved. The Seine will confound you every time.

Visitors have never gotten enough of the river. Gertrude Stein ran her dogs by the Seine. Henry Miller walked off his excesses along it; in a houseboat, Anaïs Nin took hers to new levels. Fish was the first course of Hemingway's moveable feast; he loved to watch the anglers along the Pont des Arts footbridge: "It was easier to think...seeing people doing something they understood." The idea of Seine sushi is pretty revolting, but the old guys are still there in late spring when fishing is best.

Today's generation, if less lost than Hemingway's, still comes to the Seine in summer to shed inhibitions. Parisians strip down to nothing and sunbathe on its warm stone banks. They hide their wine in brown bags only when embarrassed by the label. On certain stretches of the quaiside, Paris is gay. On others, kids and dogs frolic. Aging pigeon feeders occupy the benches by day, but lovers claim them at night.

Even its small mysteries intrigue. One evening a black wingtip shoe floated past my boat, dry inside, sole flat on the surface. Enough Parisians insist they can walk on water; would one of them shortly stride past? My upstream neighbor, Pierre Richard, did well as the lead in a film called *The Tall Blond Man with One Black Shoe.* Who knows?

People mark their history with memories of the Seine. One night in 1958, my friend Jo Menell stood on the Pont-Neuf and watched mysterious loglike shapes bobbing by the dozen in the swift current. France was at war to keep Algeria under her wing, and the shapes were Algerians murdered by French zealots who countered terror in Algiers with terror in Paris. Bodies, as tradition demanded, were dumped in the river.

Politics changed, but the eternal waves flowed on. A few years after Jo stood on the Pont-Neuf, Algeria and most other French colonies went free, and people of two dozen cultures crowded into the *métropole.* By 1993, France decided it was no longer a land of asylum. On that same bridge, police stopped an African and demanded his papers for a routine identity check. He flung himself over the stone parapet and drowned in the Seine.

"The Seine is the great receptacle which first receives the victims of assassination or despair," wrote Fanny Trollope in 1836. "But they are not long permitted to elude the vigilance of the Parisian police; a huge net, stretched across the river at Saint-Cloud, receives and retains whatever the stream brings down; and anything that retains a trace of human form which is found amidst the product of

the fearful drought is daily conveyed to La Morgue;—
DAILY; for rarely does it chance that for four-and-twenty
hours its melancholy biers remain unoccupied; often do
eight, ten, a dozen corpses at a time arrive by the frightful
caravan from *'les filets de Saint-Cloud.'*"

These days, the number is down. During 1992, Paris
police recovered thirteen bodies from the Seine. They res-
cued another twenty-three people who had fallen in, acci-
dentally or on purpose. And they extracted nine cars. It was
an average year.

The net at Saint-Cloud is also down. Today, God knows
what would shred it, or fill it, in minutes. When the current
is fast, huge trees are hurled downstream, like battering
rams. Other items, smaller than trees and sometimes
unspeakable, also float down the Seine. Here, for example,
is a brief sampling from the log of a young visitor to *La Vieille*
[the author's boat and home] who watched for half an hour:
one mattress, countless Styrofoam containers, a bloated pig,
several condoms, dead fish, live ducks, a television set,
someone's jacket, someone else's trousers, many people's
lunch—at one stage or another....

In no time at all, the river bewitched me. Most likely, it happened that July morning when I was wakened by a mother
duck giving hell to eight fuzzy ducklings. With a fresh cup
of coffee, I sat on deck to survey my new neighborhood. The
Seine was calm but by 8 A.M. *La Vieille* was rocking gently,
like a cradle. The air bore a pleasant nip and fresh river
scent. The bridge statues gleamed gold. Suddenly, sweet
notes of music wafted down to the deck. Up in the trees,

masked by leaves, I saw a bandsman in blue and red with shiny brass buttons tuning a French horn.

On balmy summer nights, we sat on deck until the Eiffel Tower blinked off at 1 A.M. Then we drank wine and giggled, forgetting to go to bed, until it was time for sunrise and the duck serenade.

Soon, I started talking funny. When I remarked to a normal person, "I've got dry rot in my head," he nodded in agreement, not aware that I was referring to the bathroom ceiling. At the time, the world was in turmoil, and my job as a reporter kept me nearer the Volga, the Vltava, and Victoria Falls. But every time I came home, the Seine had a new surprise. I decided I had to learn more about this magical river and the people who live on it.

The books lined up in *La Vieille*'s saloon were of some help. Mostly, they confirmed a single bit of nautical knowledge: deck leaks make pages stick together. Within a year I had hired storage space for a library that would have capsized the boat: old musings in heavy leather, mildewed maps and slim volumes of verse. I spent afternoons gazing at paintings to see what had captivated the impressionists. I studied the river's moods, attuned to rising currents and falling barometers. With the help of Captain Jacques, I got *La Vieille* ready to roll, and we snooped into the river's innermost secrets. The more I realized that the depths were unfathomable, the more I loved the mission.

Looking around, I found the river's rich history bubbled regularly to the surface, refusing to lie dead in books. One morning I returned to Paris to find a Viking longboat—gargoyles, oars and all—docked at the visitors' quai. This being the Seine, it would not have surprised me to find it full of hairy Norwegians in animal skins and pointy helmets looking for loot after a thousand-year time warp. It was a replica, part of an exhibition at the Grand Palais.

Since Roman times, the Seine was an Old World thoroughfare. Norsemen routinely plundered riverside abbeys and towns until Charles the Simple bought off King Rollo in 911 with a spare daughter and Normandy. The Vikings turned their energies into taming the river; their channels and dikes lasted ten centuries. On the Seine, William the Conqueror put together the flotilla that invaded England. He chased his cousins back to Scandinavia, and they have yet to return, except for Wimbledon.

Among the old stones of Paris are traces of walls built to repel the Vikings and remnants of later medieval forts that Napoléon III blasted away last century to let the river run free. By Notre-Dame, for instance, the Petit Pont has been around in one form or another since the birth of Christ. It was once flanked by wooden buildings, but they went in 1718, in a Parisian precursor to the Mrs. O'Leary cow incident. When things got lost in the Seine, back then, people went to a local convent for a hunk of bread blessed with a prayer to St. Nicolas. This, balanced on a plank along with a lighted candle, was placed in the river. Wherever the candle went out was the spot to look. A widow who lost her only son in the current launched a plank to find his body. The candle did not go out. It ignited a hay barge which struck the bridge, setting a three-day fire. Twenty-two houses burned to the pilings.

As the French went from monarchy to republic to empire

to monarchy to empire to republic, the Seine remained their centerpiece. I had not only a river to explore but also a few thousand years of the soul of France.

The Seine that is synonymous with Paris is actually 482 miles long. In a straight line, it travels only 250 miles, but the Seine is in no hurry. It wells up from three cracks at the foot of a limestone hill in a forest glade in the Côte d'Or province of Burgundy, 30 miles northwest of Dijon. The Gauls, knowing magic when they saw it, built a temple at the source to the river goddess, Sequana, whose name was later smoothed out into Seine. Until the fourth century A.D., when German invaders destroyed the temple, pagan Perrier cured ancient ailments. A few believers remain convinced.

For the first mile or so, you can pop a cork across the Seine while *déjeunering sur l'herbe.* By the time it reaches Le Havre, after twenty-five locks in all, the river has broadened to an estuary hardly distinguishable from the English Channel beyond. From source to mouth, the Seine drops only 1,600 feet. At its widest, it can be dead calm, translucent in deep green hues. Or it can look like café au lait on the boil.

"La Seine" is sanctified by a signboard on an old stone bridge in the village of Billy-les-Chanceaux, eight miles from the source. The water beneath is crystal clear and hardly deep enough to drown a dwarf. It twists and turns, picking up the odd stream, until it reaches the bottom of Champagne country. By then, its banks are dotted with the remains of wooden wheels that once ground flour or cranked up a few watts of electricity.

Châtillon-sur-Seine is a miniature Paris, Seine-wise; its oldest part nestles between two branches of the river. But neither branch is wider than ten yards or more than a yard deep. Navigation starts at Marcilly, 120 miles from the source. River traffic once reached the medieval port at Troyes via canal, but the grand waterway ordered by Napoléon was closed less than a century after it opened, one more casualty of a vanishing way of life.

At Montereau, the Seine gets significant. The Yonne joins in, doubling the flow and adding traffic from canals and rivers that reach the Mediterranean. Farther on, at the impressionists' paradise of Moret, there is the Loing. Soon after, the Essonne. Then the Marne empties in, bringing water from the mountains of the Vosges and barges from beyond the Rhine, as far away as the Black Sea. The Seine is swift and murky and ready for Paris.

From the City of Light, the Seine winds into the heart of darkness. Past the abandoned hulk of a Renault factory on the Ile Séguin outside Paris, the riverside homes peter out. Suddenly, it is as if you are on Conrad's steamer among mangrove swamps on the Congo. And then, just as abruptly, the river turns and you sense the luminosity that inspired so many painters.

The Oise comes in below Paris, and the Eure and others. Long past the wrought-iron terrace of La Fournaise, where Renoir painted the luncheon clientele and Maupassant scribbled on the walls, it passes near the village near Rouen where Flaubert's Emma Bovary learned home economics the hard way. Plaques along the way mark where battered Englishmen went home after their Hundred

Years' War and where, a long time later, the English helped run off Germans. A little tower marks the spot where Napoléon's ashes came ashore, for a carriage ride to Paris, after sailing up the Seine in a frigate painted black.

On a map of Normandy, Sequana looks like an earthworm with stomach cramps. The river snakes among spectacular castles and abbeys, set against a backdrop of plunging white escarpments and thick woods. In spring, its lazy loops are flanked in the shocking pink of cherry orchards. It changes again and again, meandering through history and humdrum, on toward open waters.

No statesman has missed the significance of this varied thoroughfare. "Le Havre, Rouen, and Paris are a single town," Napoléon said, "and the Seine is Main Street." He planned to build canals so that boats from lesser states to the east could visit the capital of Europe by inland waterway.

The Rhône, wild and wide, was once a Roman freeway. The Loire, lovely and long, winds among sumptuous châteaux. Next to either, the Seine is a stream. Its normal flow, 400 cubic meters a second, is a fifth of the Rhône's and a sixth of the Danube's. But the Seine and its tributaries water an area totaling 78,878 square kilometers, 15 percent of France. Seventeen million inhabitants, almost a third of the French population, live within its reach. More than half of France's heavy industry, 60 percent of the phosphoric acid plants, 37 percent of the petroleum works, and a pair of nuclear reactors flank the greater Seine. The port of Paris handles 26 million tons of freight a year, equal to a million truckloads.

With all that, the people who live and work on the Seine

reject the geographers' term *fleuve*, the French word for a
river that feeds into the sea. Instead, the Seine is *la rivière*,
which is supposed to apply only to gentle inland waterways.
Sequana was a lady, Seine people insist, and so is their river.

As the lyricists have it, Paris makes love to the Seine. At
least, the city embraces its waterways like nowhere else on
earth. New York ignores two rivers. London turns its back
on the Thames. Comparisons with Venice are more than
hyperbole. The Canal Saint-Martin loops deep into the Right
Bank, carrying barges past chestnut trees and dramatic old
landmarks to the Ourcq and Saint-Denis canals. From these,
you see a Paris that most Parisians would swear vanished
decades ago. There is the hulking Grands Moulins de Paris,
which made the flour for bread no one could match. And the
Hôtel du Nord, which gave its name to another film classic.
When Arletty leaned from a bridge and rasped to Louis
Jouvet, *"Atmosphère, atmosphère…,"* Parisians cried a river.
The city's Grand Canal, the Seine itself, winds among parks
and fancy mansions you reach by crossing water.

Venetian waterways are public thoroughfares, but their
edges are jealously guarded. *Vaporettos* carry gawkers past
private landings and closed wooden doors. But you can get
off a Parisian Bat-O-Bus at any stop and walk along like
you own the quai. On the upper level, *les bouquinistes* offer
bestsellers from the 1930s and travelogues of Timbuktu
from open-air stalls. Down below, you can converse ami-
ably with corn-fed tourists off the bus or play AIDS
roulette with the rough trade. You'll hear French and
English and Japanese, but also Catalan and Lapp and Dari.

On the Ile St-Louis or the Ile de la Cité, you can walk by the river and peer into mysterious worlds when someone swings open any of those massive double doors. At 17 Quai d'Anjou, for instance, Baudelaire and the *club des hashishins* — a play on *assassins* — met to smoke dope and plot the discomfiture of stuffy citizens. Rilke and Wagner and Delacroix were regulars; Hugo took a few hits and dropped off to sleep. Balzac didn't inhale.

Today's bohemians still gravitate to the river. So do most other Parisians. If most moored boats are people's homes or cargo haulers, and you approach uninvited on pain of death, others are there to be visited. Floating restaurants offer everything from tempura to tacos. By Notre-Dame, the *Metamorphosis* has been transformed from a sand barge to an Italian-style magic theater.

Down any quai, you can let your imagination run wild. Ask a few questions, and people are likely to misinform you about neighbors they hardly know. They guess by default; etiquette frowns on their prying in any obvious manner. Also, affairs are seldom as they seem. The Doges' Venice was straightforward as a Boy Scout troop next to a Seine-side boat community. People on the river by and large treasure their status as characters.

Mort Rosenblum is the former editor-in-chief of the *International Herald Tribune* and the author of *Mission to Civilize, Back Home,* and *Who Stole the News.* This story was excerpted from his book, *The Secret Life of the Seine.*

A Gathering of
River Rats

JOHN MADSON

*How does a game warden like his
fish prepared? Poached!*

THE TRUE QUALITY OF A DISH CAN BE ENTIRELY
obscured by a keen appetite, of course, and I had a
powerful case of hungries at the time, but even with
that qualification I believe one of the best meals I've ever
eaten was a fish chowder created on an autumn island in the
Upper Mississippi by a hard-used old river rat named
Charley Gibbs.

We had left his boat landing just after sunup, and the
work and savor of the chilly morning had me thinking of
lunch not long after breakfast. By noon, when the last of
the skin ice had melted from sheltered pools off the
Butterfly Chute, we had already been on the river for nearly
five hours, running and resetting fyke nets and basket
traps. Then we pulled into a quiet slough, secured the
loaded johnboat to a snag and waded ashore to a little clearing in the willows.

While I rustled dry driftwood, Charley took off his rub-

72

ber apron, broke out a blackened Dutch oven and a sack of provisions, and carefully selected a solid, fresh-caught buffalofish from the bin amidships. With the fire working, he set the kettle in place and dropped in a half-pound of snowy leaf lard. As this melted he swiftly "sided" the fish with a thin-bladed, very sharp knife and cubed the fillets into chunks. The lard was melted, smoking hot. He dropped in the chunks of fish and turned to his grubsack again, producing potatoes and onions that he diced into the pot.

With a pothook he moved the Dutch oven to the edge of the fire and we sat on the driftwood log, smoking and talking about the morning's catch and the business of the River. After a while, Charley went over to the boat and returned with a water tin, pouring a half-gallon of spring water into the steaming kettle, with a half-pound of butter as an afterthought. He added a handful of mixed salt and pepper, several dashes of Tabasco sauce, and then sat down again to solemnly regard the fire. A lean, tempered river man with a long and somewhat horsy cast to his face, Charley Gibbs always wore a faintly mournful expression even when things were going fine, even as the fish were beginning their fall run and the chowder was coming done.

He straightened slightly and looked beyond me.

"Hear that?"

Somewhere behind us a bent branch had scraped against canvas. A moment passed, and Gibbs spoke to the willows: "Noisy as you are, how do you ever ketch anybody?"

A short, weathered man in an old hunting coat parted the screen of willows and scowled fiercely.

"Well, what we got here?" said Three-Finger George

Kaufman. "A fat young violator and a skinny old violator cooking the evidence, huh? By God, I'll just have to confiscate some of that!"

Gibbs looked into the fire, more mournful than ever. "How come us poor working fishermen always got to feed old game wardens?"

"Maybe it's because they can't catch their own fish," I offered. "You ever known Kaufman to catch a fish?"

"Never have," replied Charley. "Never caught a fish. Never shot a duck. Lives on what he can confiscate, like a gull."

"Damn right!" said Kaufman. "I'm pure predator. Right up there at the point of the food pyramid. I hunt the hunters, and I caught you bastards red-handed. When is that contraband gonna be ready?"

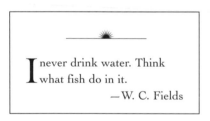

I never drink water. Think what fish do in it.
—W. C. Fields

So we sat together and swapped river gossip and all the while the smell from that Dutch oven was enough to break a hungry man's heart. Lansing fish chowder, smoking hot, its savory essence riding the autumn wind to bait a hungry old game warden. There was some more ritual cussing, but not even Three-Finger George Kaufman, senior officer of the Fish and Game Division, could scowl and bristle when the chowder was ready on a crisp, blue-and-gold October noon on the Upper River.

My two companions were classics: Charley Gibbs, archetypal Upper Mississippi commercial fisherman, and George Kaufman, the archetypal river warden.

Charley's work world was the labyrinth of running sloughs, chutes, channels, lakes, and pools that lay between Channel Dam 9, near Harper's Ferry, and the Iowa-Minnesota border. It is, to be charitable, a mess. I once tried to count the islands in that twenty-six-mile stretch of river and gave up at around 300. There are many more than that — some not much more than mud bars and sand shoals, others, like Battle Island, enduring landmarks. Within this maze of islets and islands are the convoluted sloughs that may wander back into hidden ponds out on mud flats. Few men know those waters well, and one of them was the late Charles Gibbs, third generation of his family to fish for a living out of Lansing, Iowa.

I first met him about thirty years ago, when he was fifty-three and had been a professional fisherman for over forty years. A quiet man, as men of his kind are likely to be, but not taciturn. A pragmatic man as well, as a river professional must be, and not given to any romantic illusions where his Mississippi was concerned. If he were ever awestruck by any of the sudden revelations of beauty and grandeur that had so often come his way during all those years on the river, he was not likely to bruit it about — which isn't to say he was unaware of such things, even though a lifetime on the Mississippi might make them commonplace. On that particular autumn day he had been in the act of casting his grabhook when he suddenly paused and looked back at me, saying: "I don't a s'pose a tree can do much better than that, no matter where you go," pointing with his chin at a rock maple on the steep ground above the slough, a tree in its full, vivid, October crimson. It stood by itself with no other maple in view, set off by a pair of brilliantly yellow hickories in a burst of ruby and gold just below the wall of buff limestone. Then the grabhook was cast and dragged for the tail line of a basket trap, the old fisherman again seeming to be oblivious of the autumn pageant that blazed around us.

John Madson is well known in the fields of ecology and the outdoors. His articles appear regularly in such national publications as *National Geographic* and *Audubon*. His book, *Where the Sky Began*, was cited as one of the "most notable books" of 1982 by *The New York Times*. This story was excerpted from his book, *Up on the River: An Upper Mississippi Chronicle*.

PART TWO

AGAINST THE CURRENT

Time Bandits

RICHARD BANGS

*An eighteen-year-old's summer job
as a river guide inspires
a lifelong obsession.*

A FLOAT DOWN THE COLORADO THROUGH the Grand Canyon is a stark descent through light and density and time. From the soft sandstone and flamingo limestones of the Kaibab Plateau, exposed at river level Lees Ferry, the Colorado cuts through rock that progressively ages, hardens and darkens. It plunges through the eons and the strata, through shales, conglomerates, and basalts, residues of primordial seas and cataclysmic eruptions and upheavals. Until, at last, in the Inner Gorge, in the deepest corridor of the canyon, the river washes against the oldest, blackest, and hardest rock of all: Vishnu schist. Dark as Dante's Inferno, almost 2 billion years old, the rock is a relic of a time when the earth's molten center disturbed its surface, imposing unfathomable heat and presses that recrystallized sediments into new minerals. So dark it seems to swallow light, Vishnu schist is named for the Hindu deity worshiped as the protector, a syncretic personality composed of many lesser cult figures and associated with the sun. The rock, like depictions of the god, is dark-skinned and noble. From sandstone to schist, the voyage down the Colorado is one of dramatic change, a metamorphic journey. And like the peels of stone that compose the walls, the people who pass through the Grand Canyon change with each mile. They grow darker, harder, older. And some make the apotheosis to Vishnu himself.

I cozened my way onto the Colorado. Like any eighteen-year-old, I was searching for the fantasy summer job during college, and when I learned people could get paid to raft tourists down the Colorado, I knew that was for me, my lack of big-water boating notwithstanding. So, I drew up a résumé featuring my experience on the Potomac, Shenandoah, and other Eastern Seaboard rivers, but also listing some of the classic Western rivers as intimates, although I had never seen them beyond a book or a slide show. My cover letter was as colorful a piece of creative sophistry as ever penned: rafted twenty-two major rivers, guided professionally for three years, knew all the ropes (when, in fact, I couldn't even tie a decent bowline).

In 1968, the rafting business was barely that, but rapid growth was just around the corner. Bobby Kennedy had floated the Colorado with Hatch River Expeditions, the company to which I applied, and through the wizardry of Press Secretary Pierre Salinger, the story was a worldwide pickup. Between 1869, when John Wesley Powell made his exploratory voyage, and 1949, a grand total of 100 people had floated through the Grand Canyon. By 1965 some 547 people had rafted the Colorado; in the summer of 1972 the numbers had swelled to 16,432, and the Park Service stepped in and froze the use at that level. But in the late 1960s and early 1970s the wave of popularity was becoming tidal, and the few concessionaires servicing the budding industry had to find guides to meet the growing demand. My timing couldn't have been better, and Ted Hatch, the largest outfitter on the Colorado, hired me for the following season the day he received my missive. It was Halloween, 1968. I encouraged John Yost, who had become my best friend, to apply as well, but he had an even sexier opportunity. His father was a Foreign Service officer at the State Department and was just posted to Ethiopia as DCM (deputy chief of mission, or vice-ambassador). So, while I was to go rafting, John was going to visit his parents in Africa, at the U.S. government's expense, and explore exotic landscapes. I knew nothing whatsoever about Ethiopia, but asked John to look around and see if there might be any rivers worth rafting.

Six months later, I was circling over the Glen Canyon Dam, the 710-foot-high plug that creates the 186-mile-long Lake Powell, before we began our descent into Page, Arizona, a town erected in the red dust of nothingness to accommodate dam workers. Within minutes I was standing in the parking lot of the Page Boy Motel, where I met Ted Hatch, scion to rafting royalty (his father, Bus, had pioneered many rafting runs in Utah and Colorado in the 1930s and 1940s). Ted extended a puffy, freckled hand in greeting, but he couldn't mask his disappointment as my skinny hand met his. Here he had hired a gangly, pale Atlantic Seaboarder who appeared as guidelike as Ichabod Crane. But he rolled with it.

"You're swamping tomorrow's trip. We have the Four Corners Geological Society, 110 people, ten rafts. Drive the winch truck down to the ferry as soon as you change out of that blazer and try and help the boatmen rig. Welcome aboard, kid. You'll be a good swamper."

"Ahhh, one question, Mr. Hatch."

"Call me Ted. Now, what's your question?"

"What's a swamper?"

Ted reared his Cabbage Patch doll head in laughter before explaining. "You dig the toilet hole at camp, help the boatmen cook, wash the dishes, bail the rafts. And assist the guides in every way. Now, get on it."

He handed me the keys and pointed to the truck. When I sidled into the cab, I knew I was in trouble—it was a stick shift. I'd grown up in an automatic suburb. I'd never even been in a manual. I studied the diagram on the knob.

Holding my breath, I turned the key. It hummed. Fine. toeing the clutch, I maneuvered the stick to first position and the truck eased forward. Beautiful. I finessed across the parking lot, then headed down the motel driveway, a wave of pride washing over me. I slipped into second. No problem. Then, a thunderclap and plastic shrapnel sprayed the windshield as the truck jerked to a halt and stalled. Leaping from the cab, I ran for cover, finally looking back to survey the scene. I had driven the winch, which stood a good five feet above the truck roof, smack into the middle of the Page Boy Motel sign hanging above the driveway. The motel owner, with Hatch in tow, bolted to my side, issuing obscenities at floodgate rate.

"Can you take it out of my pay?" I meekly asked my new boss.

"Forget it, kid. I'll cover it. But don't screw up again."

That was the beginning of a miraculous metamorphosis from sandstone to schist, boy to boatman, river ingenue to river god. And it took its toll.

Somehow I managed to negotiate the truck down the 50-mile route to Lees Ferry. One of the only access sites for the length of the canyon, it was named for John Doyle Lee, a Mormon fugitive who had ferried passersby across the river, after being implicated in the Mountain Meadow massacre of 1857 in which 123 non-Mormon pioneers were mysteriously murdered in southwest Utah. Lee was one of the first known non-Indians to find a new identity here, far from the persecution of Salt Lake City and civilization. Or so he thought. He was tracked down and arrested in 1874, apparently a scapegoat for the massacre, and executed in 1877. Perhaps progenitor to the waves of river guides who would come a century later, Lee was a man who had found his place in the sun on the river and was finally eclipsed because of it. He was also the Anglo embodiment of the fate of hundreds of Native Americans over the centuries— Havasupai, Hopi, Hualapai, Navajo, and Paiute—who had sought sanctuary and new lives in the rarified environs of the Grand Canyon, far from rival tribes, conquistadors, marauding white settlers, and Colonel Kit Carson.

Lees Ferry is now designated Mile Zero of the 277-mile Grand Canyon experience, launching pad for all river trips. It was here, in April of 1969, I took my assigned spot on the pontoon raft and held on tight as we pushed into the Kool-Aid green that passes for the Colorado, so colored since the silt settles out in the reservoir 15.5 miles upstream and the remaining microplankton refract their dominate hue. In the first mile I spun my head around frantically, taking in a view as otherworldly as a landscape out of a Frank Herbert novel.

As we passed into the buff-colored, cross-bedded cliffs of the Coconino sandstone and into the gates of Marble Canyon (not yet officially part of the Grand Canyon; that would come in 1975), propelled by a 20 hp Mercury outboard attached to the orange transom of our baloney boat, I desperately gripped a line, fearful that if I let go I'd be flung back to reality. We slipped into the soft red-and-maroon walls known as Hermit shale, clifftops soaring two thousand feet on either side. The din of a rapid, sonorous and deep in timbre, thickened as we eased toward Badger Creek, named for the mammal shot by Mormon explorer Jacob Hamblin.

This was thrilling. After six months of anticipation, of poring over picture books, I was on the lip of a major rapid of the Colorado. Glancing to the stern, where Dave Bledsoe controlled the tiller, I saw nonchalance unrivaled, a face fairly dancing with the aplomb of a centurion. As we slid down the coconut-butter tongue into the yaw of Badger Rapid, the crisp 47-degree water slapped me, and the pontoon pranced like a dolphin in flight. It was over in ten seconds and we pulled to shore to set up camp.

As we went about our tasks, erecting tables, filling buckets, clearing the beach of tamarisk (a loathsome weedlike tree encroaching on the beaches since the dam closed its gates in 1964, gates that denied the annual spring floods that once washed away such nonsense), Dave Bledsoe made a discovery—there were no paper plates. His veneer of pluck seemed to crack ever so slightly as he rifled the commissary boxes for a second look. "This is terrible," his words floated up the walls. "How can we serve 110 geologists without plates? We need plates." Seeing we were camped at the mouth of a tributary canyon (Jackass Creek), I asked Dave if it exited to a road, and if so, then perhaps I could hike out and fetch some plates. He thought the canyon emerged somewhere near Highway 89A, connecting Flagstaff and the North Rim. He figured I could hike out, hitch to the Hatch warehouse near Lees Ferry, hire a jetboat capable of traveling down to the lip of Badger and back to the Ferry, and get the plates to camp by dinner. So, with canteen filled, I took off up the twisting side canyon.

After an hour's hiking, the mazelike canyon divided into passages of equal size. Flipping a mental coin, I took heads, the left route, and continued. It divided again and again and again. By the time I pulled myself up onto the flat plateau, I was completely disoriented, utterly lost. I could only guess the direction the highway passed. Kicking the red dust, passing a few Engelmann prickly pear cacti, I started east, away from the sun. But after half a mile I came to a sheer defile 100 feet deep. Turning north, I came to another steep cut in the tableland. West, the same. It was Sartre-esque; no exit. Finally, toward the south, a spit of level ground streaked between two gorges, and led to the shimmering asphalt of 89A.

On the climb out I had ripped my shorts, leaving a slightly obscene appearance, which didn't help the hitchhiking cause. It also didn't help that even in rush hour this highway served less than a car every quarter hour. Despite my frantic waves, the first four autos, all crammed with vacationing families, passed me by. Salvation came in the fifth, a Navajo in a pickup who delivered me to the warehouse, where I found several cartons of paper plates. I tracked down Fred Burke, who operated the Park Service jetboat, and in the waning light, we surged downstream.

As we approached Badger, I caught a queer sight on the right bank. On the spit of a sandbar, backed by a vertical limestone wall, a solitary man was hysterically waving his overshorts at us. Fred spun the boat around and picked up the marooned man, who was on a few inches of dry land that was disappearing as the river rose. This Daniel Defoe character was part of the Four Corners expedition. Several hours earlier when the group had stopped for lunch on what was then a broad beach, this Canyon Crusoe had decided to take a quick snooze behind a rock. He awoke hours later to find the cold Colorado nipping at his toes and the rest of the party gone. As one of the consequences of progress, the Colorado would rise and fall many vertical feet each day in an artificial tide created by the diurnal differences in electrical demands, flushing the four turbines that spin in the belly of one of the world's highest dams, Glen Canyon. In another hour, Crusoe would have had no place to stand, no place to go, save downstream, without a life jacket.

Reunited, just after soup, we passed out the plates in time for the salad and entrée. I was treated like a hero for my derring-do hike, and for the first time I had a sense of how it felt to be a river guide. The marooned client settled into the group little worse for wear, and I took my first repast in the canyon.

I remember little of the next few days. As is not uncommon to first-timers on the river, I picked up a bug and spent much of my time heaving over the gunwales or in delirium, collapsed on the duffel as we caromed through rapids, swept past unconformities, synclines, and other geological anarchy. At trip's end, I expected to be fired. I thought I had been a lousy swamper—sick for the majority of the passage, sluggish in my chores, not used to the harsh sun and physically demanding days.

But Hatch, in a moment of leniency, kept me on. He assigned me to the boat-patching detail at Marble Canyon Lodge, a ramshackle motel near Navajo Bridge. For a month I lived the life of a desert rat, filling my days with Barge cement and neoprene patching material, and reading old adventure magazines like *Argosy* and *Saga*. Every few days another trip went out, and I stood aching at the Lees Ferry ramp, waving as the rafts dipped into the Paria Riffle just downstream. Out of boredom and desperation one afternoon, after uncovering a supply box filled with cartons of rotten eggs left from a previous trip, I drove down the Lees Ferry road and plastered each road sign with a battery of omelets. Waiting at road's end was John Chapman, the ranger, who promptly sent me retracing my yellow trail with wire brush and soap and water. It took me two days to clean the baked-on eggs off the metal signs.

Finally, miraculously, a trip was departing that was short on help, and Dave Bledsoe requested me. This was my big chance and I hustled at every turn. I watched Dave's every move; I hung on his every word. He was fatherly to me in a way my own had never been. Where my dad was cerebral and couldn't fix a broken widget, Dave was a doer and could take apart a Mercury outboard while floating through a rapid; while my dad was governed by a keen morality, Dave was expedient and bent the rules to get things done. While my father was a quiet soul, Dave was an artful story-teller. His lecture hall filled with stories of hermits such as Louis Boucher, who operated a copper mine from 1891 to 1912, and of prevaricators such as "Captain" John Hance, who claimed to have crossed the dense clouds from the South Rim to the North on snowshoes. But the lesson that sunk in deepest was the history in the making, the story of river guides.

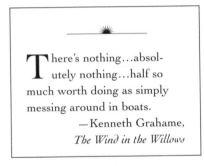

There's nothing...absol-utely nothing...half so much worth doing as simply messing around in boats.
    —Kenneth Grahame,
      The Wind in the Willows

My ascension up the Hatch hierarchy was not mercurial. I swamped seven trips the summer of 1969—a record, I believe, before being made river guide. Some newcom-ers—Perry Owens, Jim Ernst—were piloting by their third trip. I wasn't disappointed, though. I loved the river. I lived for each trip and socked away my $20-per-day earnings while on the river.

At last, on my eighth descent, I was given my badge and my own boat to steer. I was a river guide. Now, peculiar things happened to me. My tan deepened, my chest filled out, my hair grew lighter and more lustrous. But beyond that, a heretofore unplumbed confidence surfaced and I found people reacting to me in an entirely different manner. At Northwestern, where I was attending undergraduate studies in winters, I was undistinguished academically, athletically, socially. I was painfully shy with women and had never dared venture alone into a bar. But, on the river, everything changed. I brandished the rudder through the rapids, affecting the stern, purposeful look I'd picked up from Bledsoe. I lectured eruditely about the likes of John Wesley Powell and other explorers, and about the deltaic sedimentary Hermit shale. I stirred Dutch ovens over the campfire like an outdoor Julia Child. People looked to me for guidance, wisdom, direction, political opinions, even sex.

My second year, the summer of 1970, I guided the president of MGM, a celebrated political journalist, the editor of the Chicago *Sun-Times*, writers from *Newsweek*, and *The New York Times*, Broadway actors, television stars, successful professionals of every sort. I was in awe of these folks. I would never be able to speak with these people in the winter months, let alone eat, laugh, and play with them. But here, they were in awe of me, kowtowing, following my every direction, hanging on my every word. It was sobering, unbelievable. When the president of MGM sheepishly asked me to help him set up his tent (he couldn't figure it out), I felt like the roaring lion in the famous logo.

And this was happening to every other guide on the river, every country-roughneck-cowboy-Vietnam-vet-farmhand who somehow backeddied into this nouveau elite club. At night, women—single, coupled, married—sneaked over to the guides' sleeping bags under the cover of darkness. River romances were as common and flighty and full of trills as canyon wrens. Back at Northwestern, I couldn't get a date to save my life. But on the river, I couldn't find an

evening alone. Klutzy romantics in December transformed
to lusty Don Juans in June, and egos soared.

Most boatmen were quick to capitalize on this center
stage and let loose bottled histrionics, and I was no exception. We sang off-key before appreciative audiences, told
bad jokes that sent laughter reverberating between the
Supai sandstone, played rudimentary recorder as passengers swayed. Every guide took advantage of the rapids, all
161 of them. Those pieces of effervescence in the long, emerald band of the river were chances to shine, to showcase
mettle and stuff, to enhance the legend of dauntless river
guide. Of course, we boatmen would never admit to the
rapids' tendency toward impunity to visitors. We could flip,
wrap, broach, jackknife, catch a crab, lose an oar, tubestand,
endo, and swim the rapids and be relatively assured of
emerging intact in the calm water below. But that was classified information.

All this theater was heightened in 1970 with the motor-
driven pontoon raft. Nobody had yet figured out how to get
through Lava Falls—the Colorado's biggest rapid and one
of the last on the trip—with the engine running. The few
attempts ended in broken shear pins, bent shafts, or outright
loss of outboards, as the propeller invariably hit a rock soon
after entry. So, two sets of twelve-foot oars, desuetude on a
typical trip, were lifted from their straps on the sides of the
raft and mounted on the thoe pins marking the orange frame
that gridded the pontoon's center. Then, the outboard was
lifted and tied flat, like a roped calf, to the stern floorboard.

All the passengers then walked around the rapid (Ted
Hatch deemed the run too dangerous in those days) and

watched and photographed in horror as two boatmen, one seated behind the other, entered the rapid, madly pumping the huge oars while being pitched and folded like laundry in a spin cycle. Then, as the last roostertail was broached on the back side of the crest, the rear captain had to leap to the stern and, in a genuinely risky maneuver, pull out a knife, cut the ropes binding the outboard, pull the eight-pound motor up, slide it onto the transom mount, clamp it down, and pull the starter cord.

Time allowed just three or four chances to kick the engine to life (and it was a sometimes too swamped to catch) in order to power the raft to a wisp of an eddy at the mouth of Prospect Canyon, where the passengers could reboard. If the engine didn't start in those few seconds, the raft would dive into the next rapid, Lower Lava, which was walled by a 75-foot cliff on the south bank that prevented passengers from hiking farther downstream. They would have to wait for the next raft and crowd onto it as it taxied them down to their own carrier, bobbing in a large eddy a mile downstream on the north bank. If the last raft in the party didn't make the critical landing or if all the boats on a trip were swept into Lower Lava—and this happened occasionally—the passengers would have to hike a half mile upstream, swim across the cold river, knowing that if they cramped they could be sucked into Lava, and then hike a primitive path down the north bank to the waiting rafts. Or they could wait for the next rafting company to come by.

All this action made a great spectacle for those on shore. What I soon learned was that rowing through Lava was really nothing more than a show. No matter what you did with the oars, be it snapping hard strokes throughout or freezing the blades in place, the results would most often be the same. It was, more than anything else, a piece of theater, and I learned to play it with Kabuki-like stagecraft.

This dashing, somewhat pretentious rowing ritual was also employed, at some water levels, at the two other rapids rated 9-10 (the Grand Canyon has its own 1-10 classification scale for rapids): Hance and Crystal. A new addition to the fold, Crystal was created in December 1966 when a massive flood bulldozed a boulder-debris fan into the river at Mile 98. But at the cusp of the 1970s, motor routes were being pioneered, many by Hatch honcho Dennis Massey, regarded by some as King of the River, the man who could make his raft dance in any wave, hole, or eddy on the Colorado.

Whether Massey, or guides named Brick, Snake, Whale, or Bear, once below The Rapid, the boatmen would be feted as heroes, hailed as Galahads, Lindberghs, champions charged with extraordinary backbone and bravery. Prior to my guiding, my only work experience was as a bellboy and carhop, and that didn't quite prepare me for idolatry. The river guides, me included, were exalted. The problem was some began to believe it, creating a duality in personality and self-perception, an almost schizophrenic state that was not easy to cope with or resolve. We were walking, rowing oxymorons. All of us relished those moments of Canyon adulation, but reality always returned at summer's end. Some turned to the slopes, some to carpentry or other crafts or service jobs. I went back to school. Still others dipped

into their black books of summer clients, those, who tugged
from the beach after lingering embraces, said through tear-
stained smiles, "Whenever you're in town, you must look
me up. Come stay with me..." Following those words, many
boatmen roamed from client home to home, reliving the
summer through slides, scrapbooks, and Super-8 movies,
and wearing out welcomes. But wherever we wandered,
whatever we did, it seemed mundane by comparison to our
summer work and identities.

The Colorado irrevocably changed me, as it does everyone. It fanned a false ego, then doused the fire. The boatman subculture was a strong one, a brotherhood bond
formed in the summer months, and we kept in touch in the
off-season, compared notes. Everyone seemed to suffer the
same fate and searched in vain for a winter's equivalent of
the astral light that caressed us in the Canyon. But few
found it. One bleak winter Dennis Massey, King of the
River, was driving a pizza delivery truck, and he shot himself in the head. Years later, Whale, a ski-lift operator, did
the same, on the eve of a boatmen reunion party. These
were the extremes. Sometimes, though, the spool rolled the
other way. Some people who were undistinguished in their
normal lives, perhaps shy, or living with untapped potential,
found an unplumbed confidence while guiding, and that
allowed them to stretch, assert, and experiment, and sometimes become extraordinary in ways they otherwise might
never have been. A few guides went on to become celebrated
photographers, film directors, businessmen, politicians, and
one, perhaps the most envied, became the road manager for
The Grateful Dead. And there was one who went on a

quarter-century global quest to find the perfect river, and the endless summer.

For the 1971 rafting season I convinced high school Raft Club friend John Kramer to come out to the Colorado and be my swamper, with intent to graduate to guide under my tutelage. He proved a quick study, becoming a lead guide in near record time. I had also tried to recruit John Yost, but he was heading back to Africa, with his own ambitions of setting up an import business. I also met a kindred spirit in Bart Henderson, from Vernal, Utah, where Ted Hatch lived. Bart came from river-running royalty (his Christian name was Royal), and was finally breaking into the Colorado. His uncle was with Bus Hatch in 1938 on the famous first descent of the Green River, a trip sometimes cited as the birth of modern river running. His father bought a pile of surplus ten-man rafts in the early '50s and started river running, often taking his young son on the water. Bart was guiding by the time he was thirteen. An artful athlete blessed with chiseled good looks and a lion's mane of blond hair, Bart was a great guy, and the first boatman I had met who would consistently beat me in chess. I taught Bart the ropes, but within a month he surpassed his teacher with sheer native ability and smarts, and ended the season as one of the finest guides on the river.

By the end of the summer, my third as a river coxswain, I came to realize a common current ran through all those who drifted into the life of a guide on the Colorado River — it was the knowledge that the cosmos could be reduced to a cool, wrapping white wave, to the pull of an oar or the twist of a tiller, to the crest of a wave—and at that moment, the top of the world was reached, all magic was white, and all was good and great.

Once that knowledge soaked in, every guide, no matter how far his pursuits carried him, came back to the river.

———⟨≈≈≈⟩———

Award-winning author and river explorer Richard Bangs pioneered river rafting on more than thirty-five remote waterways. Among his many books are *Riding the Dragon's Back, Rivergods: Rafting the World's Great Rivers,* and *The Lost River: A Memoir of Life, Death, and Transformation on Wild Water,* from which this story was excerpted.

Grabbing the Loop

DAVID QUAMMEN

*A journalist learns the meaning of wild
on a South American river.*

A T THE SOUTHERN END OF THE ANDES,
coming out of the highlands of Argentina and
down across southwestern Chile, flows a little-
known river called the Futaleufu. From a continental perspective it's just a tiny hydrological squiggle that doesn't
show up on the less-detailed maps. Even the people of Chile
have scarcely heard of it. The river is short, about fifty miles
in length, and the valley through which it winds is remote.
So you might take this for a backwater place. But no, the
waters of the Futaleufu are decidedly forward.

Chile itself is a land of climatic and topographical
extremes—tilted steeply east-west from the Andean cordillera to the sea and, along its north-south axis, ranging
from the breathless aridity of the Atacama Desert to the
glaciers and cold storms of Chilean Patagonia. About five
hundred miles south of its capital, Santiago, is the Región de
los Lagos, the Lake District, a zone of snow-capped volca-

noes, verdant national parks, glacial lakes left behind by the
retreat of the Pleistocene ice, gentle pastures, fertile fields
of grain, timber and fishery operations, and an old-fash-
ioned agricultural economy, all of which cause urban
Chileans to view it with roughly the same ambivalent attitude—romantic yearning vitiated by condescension—that
New Yorkers direct toward Montana. The *huaso*, country
bumpkin, is a half-affectionate Chilean stereotype often
associated with the region. Toward the south end of the
Lake District, beyond where the vacationers from Santiago
and the tourists from Miami generally go, beyond the
provincial capital of Puerto Montt, you come into a harder,
more edgy realm that feels genuinely like frontier. From
there, catch a boat or a small plane onward to the little port
town of Chaitén, then start driving into the mountains.
After a few hours of bumping along, with the valley walls
rising on each side, you'll enter the thrall of the Futaleufu.

From the Pacific coast to the Argentine border, there are
just a few villages along the valley, and the road is unpaved.
Campesino homesteads are scattered sparsely, many reach-
able only along dirt paths. Heavy loads travel the paths by
oxcart, and the personal vehicle of choice is a horse. Fences
and gates are hand-hewn from split logs. The little farms are
hardscrabble, low tech, and diversified. The people face the
same life-and-death struggles faced by country people in
harsh climates everywhere—keeping the crops and the animals alive despite drought or blizzard, stretching stored
food through the winter, enduring childbirth and disease
with little or no doctoring, doing the sort of hard, risky
labor that turns young bodies quickly old. The landscape

they inhabit is graced with jagged volcanic peaks, forested mountain slopes, Andean condors soaring on thermals above the deep slot of the river, and a sense of time gently arrested in a matrix of pioneer virtues. Central to everything, like a big moody god, is the river.

The Futaleufu has its source in Argentina, draining out of the shadows of the majestic, sequoia-like *alerce* trees of Parque Nacional Los Alerces. Crossing the border, it picks up tributaries, speed, and heft. By the time it passes near the village that shares its name, it's too deep to ford and too fast for a ferry. Local folk treat it respectfully, staying out of its grasp, whereas thrill-hungry river rats from three continents come to toy with it. The name itself, Futaleufu, reportedly means "big river" in one of the languages of the Mapuche Indians. In certain stretches the Futaleufu is so limpid and sleek that though sliding along swiftly, it looks like a slab of buffed jade. But don't be fooled. Elsewhere, around the next bend, it explodes fearsomely into foam.

Some knowledgeable people will tell you that the Futaleufu is the greatest whitewater river in the world. That's what they've told me, and that's why I'm here. God help the middle-aged journalist who thinks he can handle a kayak.

Of course *greatest* is an insupportable adjective as applied to rivers, which are infinitely various. If the Futaleufu is in some sense superlative, is the Zambezi of southern Africa secondary? Not hardly. What about the Colorado where it roars through the Grand Canyon, or the upper Pacuare in Costa Rica, or Devil's Gorge on the Susitna in Alaska? Each of those rivers has its own unique balance of menace and charm, capable of gladdening any traveler who hankers for a soul-rinsing immersion in wild water. Whether the balance in a given case leans toward the sheer difficulty of the rapids, or the grandeur of the scenery, or the exotic flavor of the locale, never mind. My point is merely this: The Futaleufu belongs in that class.

It has the difficulty, it has the grandeur, it has the flavor. It has rock walls and dense mossy forests, meadows punctuated by clumps of bamboo, snowy mountains, cool breezes, solitude along its scarier reaches, friendly people on the byways round about. It has blasting summer sunshine in January. It has lanky black cormorants that fly arrow-like paths upstream while you paddle down, as though they don't want to watch what you're getting into. It has ten-pound trout, and if you handle your boat as ineptly as I occasionally handle mine, you might spend some eternal moments among them.

It has a rapid called Terminator.

Three clustered volcanic spires loom over the Futaleufu near its confluence with a smaller and cooler stream, the Rio Azul. The spires are known as Tres Monjas, the three nuns. They don't look like sisters of mercy, but they do add a lofty, cold beauty. There at the confluence with the Azul, on a small spit of land, sits Campo Tres Monjas. It's a quiet little outpost for kayakers, run by the world-renowned river athlete Chris Spelius.

Spelius, tall and blond, with wide shoulders and a square jaw, is the same complicated fellow whose fortunes I followed through a whitewater rodeo world championship. Though the family name is Greek, he looks like a Nordic heavyweight who might have beaten up on Sylvester Stallone in one of the *Rocky* films. As a former Olympic team member in flatwater kayaking and a granddaddy personage (mid-forties, and still competitive) on the rodeo circuit, he's famous on rivers all over the world—famous for his brashness as well as his skills. But the brashness has always been just a public facade for a sensitive and intelligent private man, and in recent years he seems altogether mellower. Probably his life in southern Chile has been part of the reason.

Finished with the flatwater racing grind, he went to Chile on a winter getaway in the mid-1980s and paddled the Bio Bio, in those days still the most celebrated whitewater run in South America. There on the Bio Bio, Spelius heard talk of another river, far to the south, that might be even more worthy of celebration: the Futaleufu. Two other American paddlers, Phil DeRiemer and Lars Holbek, had recently made what was probably the first kayak descent, and their take on it, as Spelius remembers, was "Oh, man, it's in a different league."

Spelius decided to see for himself. He ran the Futaleufu solo, carrying little more than a sleeping bag and a toothbrush. Each evening he beached his kayak, walked up to a campesino's house, knocked on the door, and—in his helmet and life jacket, looking like a giant otherworldly visitor—asked sweetly in broken Spanish if he could sleep in the barn. By day he paddled his way through a succession of thunderously difficult rapids, which are now legendary in whitewater lore under names such as Zeta, Inferno Canyon, Throne Room. Just a few miles below the tumult of Throne Room, Spelius encountered a lovely stretch with a very different feel. An aquamarine tributary joined the main river there, with a white sandy beach along the bank and three volcanic spires looming above. The little beach marked an idyllic refuge, a sort of hurricane's eye, near the middle of what was clearly the most bodacious river he'd ever seen. "This is the place," he recalls thinking. "I've got to figure out a way to live here."

At that moment the prospect of seeing this idyllic refuge buried beneath a hydroelectric reservoir was hardly imaginable. In the mid-1980s, even the celebrated Bio Bio seemed to have a free-flowing future. The very idea of damming a world-renowned Chilean river—entombing its human culture and its natural wonders beneath impounded water—was just a distant dark cloud in the west, moved by a distant and invisible wind that some people call "progress."

After many more trips and a slow process of building friendships, Spelius became not just a landowner in the Futaleufu valley but a real neighbor. The white sandy beach, along with a few acres of wooded land behind it, is now the site of his Campo Tres Monjas. The camp is a simple facility—a mess hall with a fine Chilean cook, an outhouse, a wood-heated shower and sauna, space enough for a dozen scattered tents—because Spelius hasn't wanted to erect any superfluous buildings that would detract from the majesty of the river. In addition to that reason, there may be another—wanting not to give his kayaker clients a perilously false sense of ease. Downstream from Campo Tres Monjas, after all, lie more thunderously difficult rapids.

The most formidable of those lower rapids is a certain thousand yard gauntlet, a prolonged class-five travail compounded of crashing waves and lurking rocks and a blind drop over a six-foot-high ledge, roiling eddy lines, surprise currents pushing every which way, pour-overs where you don't want to get poured, roaring water here, roaring water there, and amid it all a few hideous holes, some large enough to bite hold of a kayak and swallow it the way a coyote swallows a mouse. An impetuous paddler who heads straight down the gullet of this rapid might cover the whole thousand-yard stretch in two minutes, or then again, might never show up at the bottom at all.

About ten years ago, roughly when Spelius himself was discovering the river, an experienced rafter with major expedition credentials, Steve Currey, tried to lead a group through here. It would have been a notable feat—first descent of the lower river by raft. But Currey and company aborted their trip at the thousand-yard gauntlet, after dropping a raft into one of the holes and watching it get tumbled unrelentingly there for half an hour. Since this was their point of termination, the rapid became known as Terminator.

All right, time to get wet. We climb into our kayaks and launch from the sandy beach, peeling away one by one like fighter jets rolling out of formation. The current is powerful and quick even here, where the water is nearly flat. It's even more powerful than usual, because a rainy period just preceding our arrival has made the river exceptionally high.

This will be our second day on the water, the first having passed without untoward drama. There are ten of us, with two guides, and from yesterday's experience I know that I'm traveling with a fast crowd. The strongest and steadiest paddlers — John from Florida, Skip from Maryland, Dr. Dan from North Carolina, and my pal Mike Garcia from Montana, among others — are very damn strong and steady indeed. Skip, a magazine photographer who's here on assignment with me, is even capable of taking one-handed shots with his waterproof camera as we bob through the ten-foot-high waves. "David, turn around and smile!" he hollers, while my face is bloodless with concentration. Our guides are Ken Kastorff and Mike Hipsher, two of the pre-eminent guardian angels in the world of whitewater. Kastorff, when he's not helping Spelius or guiding his own trips in Costa Rica, is one of the best kayak teachers in America; Hipsher is a former world champion in wildwater racing, which entails running serious rapids in a sleek, unstable boat at top speed. The other paying clients are vigorous souls, excellent kayakers, several of whom have decided that since judgement is the better part of river running, they prefer the footpath detour around Terminator to the option of paddling through it.

And me? I'm a middle-aged fool with a desk job, who now finds himself parked in a small surging eddy just past the no-turning-back point at the top of Terminator. Yesterday I blundered through here without grievous mishap. Having plunged over the big ledge drop and felt myself shoved suddenly rightward, into the maw of disorder, I flipped upside down, rolled upright again, and paddled breathlessly out the bottom. Today I hope to do better. I have a mild case of jitters. If I were smarter or more prescient, I would be terrified.

At first we pick our way cautiously downstream along a rock wall on the left, eddy to eddy, dodging into the current and out again, with Kastorff leading. This whitewater strategy is called a sneak. Halfway down, though, we gather up in an eddy beyond which there can be no further sneaking. Now comes the hard part, and from here each of us will go alone. Sitting relaxed in his boat, delivering stern counsel from behind his zitzy sunglasses, Kastorff reminds us what to expect and what to do—or what to try to do, anyway. See the horizon line thirty yards down? He says. That's the big ledge drop. Take it at a point about eight feet from the left bank, but be angled toward the right. As soon as you've landed, stroke like hell back to the center. Avoid the nasty hole on the left, brace through the exploding waves, don't go *too* far right for God's sake, and be alert for the large pour-over rock farther down. Everybody got it? Duh, yuh-yes, we say. All right, Kastorff says, now watch for my signal from below. Then he toodles off downriver, disappearing over the ledge like a memory of confidence and safety.

I wait my turn. I splash myself in the face, rinsing the fog off my glasses. I watch for Kastorff's signal. Then I go.

I launch my boat over the ledge on a nice rightward angle and, landing, make my move toward the center. But as I drop into the maw, a wave arches up and smacks my chest, high and hard like a blitzing linebacker, knocking me dippy. Now I am upside down in the unholy chaos at the heart of Terminator, holding my breath and waiting for a good opportunity to roll. What I haven't yet realized is that there won't be any good opportunities, not in this stretch of water, and that I ought to seize a bad opportunity before I use up my air.

Finally I try. One roll attempt, unsuccessful. Another attempt, unsuccessful. The water is alive with turbulence, swirling furiously all around my body, snatching at my glasses and my paddle, refusing to let me pop up. The river seems godawful belligerent. Was it something I said? A third roll attempt raises me upright, for an instant, until another breaking wave knocks me back under. I make one more try: a weak roll, a moment's precarious balance, now if I can just catch a little breath, and sit forward, and plant a decent stroke, I might extricate... — at which point I drop backwards over the large pour-over rock, landing upside down in a sucking eddy. I lose my grip on the paddle, and it's gone.

Gaa. I've got no air, no stick, no strength. No recourse but to abandon ship. So I do what all kayakers' loathe doing. I yank up the spray skirt that seals me into my cockpit, push myself out of the boat, and swim. This is a form of ignominy, but with the ignominy comes oxygen.

I grab instinctively for a small nylon strap—the grab loop, it's called—that hangs knotted through the nose of my kayak. I cling to the overturned hull while gasping for breath. And then, as the boat eases itself out of the sucking eddy, back into the current, I ride along. Not far below, Kastorff paddles over to make the rescue.

I've lost one river shoe, and the paddle, and a bit of face. The shoe and the paddle are replaceable; the face is not crucial for a doddering writer with no pretensions to whitewater mastery. All considered, then, I drag myself onto the bank feeling that it wasn't such a terrible experience.

But maybe I'm wrong. Late the next evening another

paddling pal from Montana, Kevin Kelleher, confides to me: "That was the scariest thing I've ever seen."

Surprised, I ask why. Because when you swam to the surface, Kevin says, the suck of the eddy pulled you up-stream at once. If you hadn't grabbed that loop as you swept past the nose of your boat, he says, you would have gone back up into the hole and, buddy, you would have stayed there. He felt desperately helpless as a spectator, Kevin tells me, during that moment when it looked like I might not come out alive.

Rivers can die too. Rivers are animate, in their way. They move. They breathe. Every river, except the most hopelessly throttled or poisoned, constitutes a dynamic matrix for an elaborate, organismic network of biological relationships.

To drown a river beneath its own impounded water, by damming, is to kill what it was and to settle for something else. When the damming happens without good reason — simply because electricity is a product and products can be sold — then it's a tragedy of diminishment for the whole planet, a loss of one more wild thing, leaving Earth just a lit-tle flatter and tamer and simpler and uglier than before. Already this had begun happening with the Bio Bio, the Futaleufu's sibling to the north. By early 1994, the struggle to protect the Bio Bio from being dammed was a famous international battle that had been famously lost.

The Futaleufu, on the other hand, was still safe and obscure. Or so it seemed, until a private utility company called ENDESA (the same powerful corporation damming the Bio Bio) quietly filed a claim for water rights to the

Futaleufu, with a proposal for multiple-dam development that would put most of the valley's agricultural land, most of its homesteads, most of its riverine ecosystem, most of its grace, most of its heart, and all of its great whitewater under a pair of reservoirs. The ENDESA scheme would even bury the road, severing the valley's tenuous connection with the rest of Chile.

The people of the Futaleufu, including Chris Spelius and his campesino neighbors, only caught wind of ENDESA's move in late March of 1994, with barely enough time to file a counterclaim. Immediately they held a meeting, formed a defense committee on behalf of the river and its ecosystem (under the acronym CODDERFU), passed the hat for expenses, and sent two representatives to Puerto Montt to meet with a lawyer. They had grabbed the loop of this issue just in time, escaped from the suck of political docility, and now they were swimming in big water.

The first CODDERFU meeting was followed by many more, as concern spread and resolve stiffened throughout the valley. The local spokesmen for CODDERFU declared that the Futaleufu and its tributaries "should be preserved for outdoor recreation, for agriculture, and for tourism, which is their true value, as a National Park." It was also suggested that a reasonable alternative to damming the Futaleufu could be found—possibly by placing a hydroelectric plant at the outflow of Lago Espolon, a natural lake with significant potential for electrical generation. Then the whole issue, having been raised and polarized, passed into the opaque innards of Chilean bureaucracy, to be decided who-knows-when, on who-knows-what economic or political grounds.

Meanwhile, Spelius had sat down at his laptop and typed out an E-mail message to his boating friends around the world. "To dam *this river* would be like blowing up the Sistine Chapel," he wrote. From a strictly economic angle, it made no sense, there being more to be gained from long-term tourism than from a short-term flow of construction money. Furthermore: "The local populace does not want this project." He could say that with assurance, having spent many hours hearing them out. "This news has changed the priorities of my life," he added. Spelius was now a respected adviser to CODDERFU, and a key fundraiser, though remaining careful that his own voice was only one among many. The international river cowboy, the otherworldly visitor, had become a conservationist and a community pillar.

There are many cogent reasons why the world needs the Futaleufu River more than the world needs another dam project, generating bargain-rate electricity to be sold and, largely, wasted. Whitewater thrills for globetrotting kayakers and rafters are (notwithstanding the tourist revenues they bring) certainly the least of those reasons. Others range from the aesthetic to the ecological to the economic....

My own preferred argument for preserving the

> Rivers are one of the few items that can produce miracles. It doesn't rid a desert region of its obvious dryness to have water course through, but it does offer hope and the prospect of a sort of unreal, illusionary, diversity.
> —S. H. Semken, *River Tips and Tree Trunks*

Futaleufu, based on the moments spent contemplating my mortality in its clutches, is this: Humanity badly needs things that are big and fearsome and homicidally wild. Counterintuitive as it may seem, we need to preserve those few remaining beasts, places, and forces of nature capable of murdering us with sublime indifference. We need the tiger, *Panthera tigris*, and the saltwater crocodile, *Crocodylus porosus*, and the grizzly bear, *Ursus arctos*, and the Komodo dragon, *Varanus komodoensis*, for exactly the same reason we need the Futaleufu River: to remind us that *Homo sapiens* isn't the unassailable zenith of all existence. We need these awesome entities because they give us perspective. They testify that God, in some sense or another, might not be dead after all....

What more can I tell you about the Futaleufu River? I suppose I could describe those stupendous upper rapids, Zeta and Throne Room, which on a later day I view and appreciate from the safety of shore. I could mention the carcass of a forty-pound trout that lies stored—a tourist attraction now, a voucher for the local fishing—in a freezer at a little *hostelería* down the valley. I could recount the day we spend running the Rio Azul, a frolicsome stream in contrast to the demanding intensity of the big river. And I could end with another episode of my adventures and misadventures in Terminator. I could describe my final run through that rapid, on my last afternoon of paddling the Futaleufu—sneaking again down the left, pausing again in the crucial eddy, staring again at the horizon line, then launching myself over the ledge. I could tell you about the

thrill of running Terminator right side up, about the rapture of threading down through its unholy chaos with the
requisite strokes and braces and leans, about the satisfac-
tion of reclaiming just a bit of my confidences and face.
But somehow, in the context of other matters, that doesn't
seem important.

———— ⌾⌾⌾ ————

David Quammen has been awarded the Lannan Literary Award for
Nonfiction and an Academy Award in Literature from the American
Academy of Arts and Letters for his novels, stories, and essays. His books
include *The Song of the Dodo* and *Wild Thoughts from Wild Places*, from which
this story was excerpted. He lives in Montana.

Yangtze Goddesses

SIMON WINCHESTER

*An old fisherman recalls the
vanishing river dolphin.*

ZHENJIANG IS—OR RATHER WAS, DURING ITS
more glorious days in the Sung dynasty, between
the tenth and the thirteenth centuries—one of the
great crossing points of the Eastern World, for this is
where the East's greatest river intersected with the world's
greatest canal. The Grand Canal, which still lays claim to
being the longest man-made waterway, was built during
the Sui and Tang dynasties, mostly during the seventh century. While the Yangtze wanders in these parts from east to
west, the Canal spears directly north and south. The two
waterways intersect at right angles. The Canal enters the
river from the south a few miles below Zhenjiang, and it
leaves for the north at a point on the far bank almost
directly opposite the city.

Five hundred years ago, the waters around Zhenjiang
(the name means "guarding the river," and there was once a
huge military garrison) would have been busier than almost

anywhere else on the Yangtze. Up- and downstream commercial traffic, dominated by the huge wooden trading
junks whose descendants are the great iron barges of today,
would have mingled with the smaller and lighter but nonetheless important junks and skiffs that were involved in the
supply and military business for which the canal had been
built. Marco Polo, in the thirteenth century, noted the frantic activity on the waterways: this was a place, he said, that
"lived for commerce."

Lily and I walked down what was called Small Jetty
Street, aiming for the precise spot on the dockside where
Polo was said to have stepped ashore. The street itself had
much of the charm of old China—it was cobbled, and there
were well-worn stone steps, and every few yards an old
stone archway. Behind one of these was a tall Buddhist
stupa, which the locals said was 800 years old. It didn't look
it: I suspected that, like so many relics in China, this one had
been far too exuberantly restored far too often, and it was in
fact almost modern.

We reached the river, an opaque gray and chocolate-
colored flood with oil rings in the eddies, and clumps of
refuse bobbing on the wavelets. When Lord Macartney
came here in November 1793—he was the first foreign
ambassador to try to pry open China's locked doors to trade,
and he failed, signally—this stretch of the river was called
the Blue River: his diarist noted, as well he might, that the
name was rather ill suited, since the water's color was in fact
quite similar to that of the ocher-and-umber sludge of the
Yellow River; which they had seen only a few days before.
"The waves rolled like the sea," he said of the crossing

(Macartney's expedition, which was traveling southward on the Grand Canal, had to cross the Yangtze with the rest of the southbound Imperial traffic), "and porpoises are said to be sometimes seen leaping amongst them."

There was a fisherman sitting in a rickety-looking boat by the quay. He was puffing gently on a bamboo pipe, a smoldering nut of tobacco in its tiny brass bowl. I reminded Lily about the porpoises and the lovely little white dolphins, the *baiji*, once so common in the Yangtze and now said to be almost extinct. What did this man know about them? She shouted a question down to him.

At first he said nothing, but then as if by way of answer he slowly got up, walked to a locked box near the prow of his boat, and pulled from it a huge and tangled mess of fishing line that jangled and clanked with its several pounds of rusty ironmongery. He shook it at me, almost angrily, inviting me to take a look. But I knew what it was, instantly: this was an example of the very device that had put the pathetic little Yangtze dolphin into such grave danger: it was called a rolling hook trawl, and it was every bit as vicious a device as it appeared. It didn't just catch fish: it snared them, hurt them and killed them.

The Chinese once revered the Yangtze dolphin—five-foot-long, silvery-colored, bottle-nosed creatures that, it is said, have resisted evolution for 20 million years. Poets of the time were amazed at how gentle the creatures were, how they smiled and whistled, how they stood up in the water, breast-fed their young, seemed anthropomorphically charming. Dolphins appealed mightily to the mythmaking mind of the ancient Chinese. They called them "Yangtze

Goddesses," and the Sung dynasty poets had a ready legend for their creation: it involved a slave maiden who was being ferried across the river by a sex-starved boatman. He tried to rape her, she jumped into the water to preserve her dignity. God took pity on her and turned her into a white dolphin-goddess, while the boatman was tossed into the river and turned into a black finless porpoise which, also still found in the river today, is known in Chinese as a "Yangtze Pig." But whether Goddess or Pig, these two cetaceans are both in dire danger today—the industrial filth of the river being one reason, the invention of the cruel rolling hook trawls another.

Up until the late 1950s fishermen regarded the animals as simply too godlike to catch. If one turned up in their nets, they let it free. That was the rule, obeyed by all. But in 1958 Mao Zedong inaugurated the Great Leap Forward and declared that there were no more Heavenly Emperors and Dragon Kings: nothing was too revered for inclusion in the great maw of China's great Communist engine work. Overnight, whatever protection with which history and myth had invested the Yangtze dolphin was peremptorily stripped away. As one Hong Kong journalist put it, almost overnight "the Goddess of the Yangtze became lunch."

Catching the animals turned out to be ridiculously easy, quite literally like shooting fish in a barrel. The rolling hook trawl was invented to make it easier still: on each line were scores of eight-inch iron hooks, set two or three inches apart. This line was trawled from behind a boat like the one that was now bobbing beside us. When a dolphin was snagged on one hook, it panicked, thrashed violently around and, instead of freeing itself (as might happen had there been only one hook), was promptly caught on a neighboring hook and then by more and more until it was raked with slashes and cuts and was eventually dragged from the river bleeding to death from a thousand cuts. *Baiji* meat became swiftly abundant, and was to be found in the riverside markets costing only a few cents a pound. Leather factories opened to make goods from what little unslashed *baiji* skin was salvaged. *Baiji* oil was found to have magical healing properties for people with skin problems. And as the new trade flourished, so the number of dolphins in the river dropped dramatically, a tragedy for Chinese wildlife that makes the sad saga of the giant panda seem a triumph by comparison.

Now there are said by biologists to be only 100 *baiji* left in the entire river, maybe 150. Did the fisherman feel responsible? I asked. He nodded, and he did indeed look contrite. I let him explain. "Back in the 1960s we needed to eat. I took a lot of the dolphins out, and I sold them, or took the meat for my family. It didn't matter that we had once called them goddesses. We didn't care.

"But then as the years went by they became more and more difficult to find. We all"—and here he gestured to the other fishermen, who had gathered their skiffs around his and were listening to him, nodding themselves—"we all slowly realized what was happening. We knew we were wiping them out. We were killing them off, and by doing so we were helping to kill the river. And soon our attitude changed. Every time a *baiji* came out, cut to pieces by the hooks, we felt we had lost a little more. So we stopped using these rolling hooks. We went back to nets. And if we ever find a *baiji*—and I haven't seen one for six or seven years now—we throw it back. It's the rule again.

"Yangtze fishermen have good hearts, you know. We love this river. We love the fish. We love the dolphin and we revere her. But back then—back then it was very different. It was very difficult. Mao did some terrible things. We had to eat. We thought we had no choice. It was the dolphins, or it was our children. Which would you choose?"

Lily and I walked silently back up the worn old stairway. I could tell she was cross with me. A few days before, in talking to her about the well-publicized lack of fish and wildlife in China's greatest river, I had made some remarks about how it all seemed due to greed and to China's utter and contemptuous disregard for her environment. Perhaps some of this was true. But what this old fisherman had said rang true as well. It seemed something of an explanation, and a very sad one at that. Lily looked balefully at me from time to time. I made a silent vow as we tramped on upward, something to the effect that judgments about China should not be lightly made. So I mumbled an apology, and Lily grinned.

Simon Winchester is the author of *The Sun Never Sets, Korea, Pacific Rising, The Emergence of a New World Order,* and *The River at the Center of the World: A Journey Up the Yangtze,* and *Back in Chinese Time,* from which this story was excerpted.

Rafters in the Mist

GERMAINE W. SHAMES

*River spirits and ancestors go along
for the ride on a challenging
South American river trip.*

I T WAS THE SACRED WATERFALLS THAT DREW ME
to Ecuador's Rio Upano, the notion that these thundering cascades—so high they seemed to pour forth
from the clouds—flowed not with mere water but with
ancestral spirits. The Shuar Indians, I had read, made pil-
grimages to these sacred places seeking visions, hoping that
by thrusting their hands into the current they might capture
their immortal souls.

I am a beggar on this river. Cast adrift by the dry, brittle
gods of the Arizona desert and hungering for visions of my
own, I contrive confrontations with indigenous deities
whose faces I conjure in foam and spray. The Upano, tributary of the mighty Amazon, steals her crown of turbulence
from the Andean Cordillera. A temperamental river, an
unforgiving river, she has claimed this tangle of rain forest
and canyon for her own, turning back would-be conquerors,

toppling bridges, tempting prospectors with her gold, only to drown them in the reflection of their own dreams.

To run the Upano is to plunge into a time warp, an uncharted limbo somewhere between the Stone Age and Doomsday, to become a curiosity in polypropylene, a whooping fool, defying hydraulics and history for the raw, giddy rush of adrenaline. Fewer than 200 people have taken the ride. When adventure entrepreneur Peter Grubb made an exploratory trip in 1992, there was no known history of the river, no named rapids, no map. Local residents—Andean colonists and indigenous Shuar Indians—who had never seen a rubber raft or a sunscreened nose, looked up at him from their fish traps and sluice boxes in mute, bug-eyed incomprehension.

However high-minded my motives, I bear the taint of all who have come before me: conquistadors, slave traders, missionaries, harlots, prospectors, loggers, and mercenaries. Opportunists deaf to the cries of the ancestors, blind to the beauty of the forest, indifferent to the plight of the indigenous people whose lands they pillaged and whose sacred places they desecrated. With good cause do the river spirits spit and slap and roar. Slogging through the mud behind a red rubber paddle raft, I feel vulnerable and conspicuous, and oddly alone in the company of my fellow rafters, for whom the river seems to pose no such philosophic logjams.

We put in outside of Macas, a playfully static little backwater an hour and a half flight from Quito, which is just a short haul by bus from the disputed border with Peru. The town, in the throes of carnival when we arrive, rouses from its customary languor to dance and parade. The unwary get their first drenching here, accosted by water-throwing children whose laughter follows us to the river's edge.

Our first sight of the Upano washes myriad shades of gray and drab green, broken only by the occasional flash of plumage, the iridescent flutter of butterfly wings. Mist everywhere. Although we are splashing distance from the equator, the water remains cool to the touch. The water level has dropped to a scant ten feet, exposing boulders and branches, increasing the risk of our getting swamped or wrapped.

"The Upano's a Latin river," our guide Drew muses. "Think salsa, hot, unpredictable." The remark fails to raise a ripple. We are the only traffic on the river. Crude balsa wood rafts lashed with vines lie beached along the shores. Stillness. Slowed pulses. Yawning, Lance, a veteran of twenty rivers, fidgets with the Velcro on his rain jacket. A heartbeat later, the low roar of white water.

Churning rapids rip into the raft, a frenzy of silt and froth pummeling our faces. Then, "Highside!" We've hit rock. Braided water swirls and knots around us.

"This is starting to get amusing," Lance says, spitting river foam out from between the words.

Our first glimpse of the legendary Shuar Indian: a slight, bronzed figure in polyester shorts poised behind a geyser of river water. The man, busy wrapping a short cylindrical object in crumpled newspaper, takes no notice of us. As our rafts drift past, however, a deafening blast rings out. The Indian is dynamiting fish, Drew explains, shrugging. One of the world's most visible vanishing peoples, the Shuar, once warriors known for their insolence in the face of

Spanish authority and missionary zeal, have gradually suc-
cumbed to acculturation, seduced not by gold or gospel but
technology. The Shuar like things that go bang: guns,
explosives, loud keyboards. When they can no longer blast
their way clear of scarcity, they often sell their land for a
pittance and move downstream to Santiago and Morona,
malaria-infested border towns under permanent siege by
the military of four nations and riddled with an estimated
10,000 land mines.

The guides have cultivated "friendships" with four mar-
ginalized Shuar families, with whom rafters visit and trade.

"We've tried to keep impact to a minimum," asserts
Drew. "No money changes hands. They give us a basket, we
give them clothes or school supplies for the kids."

An intention as noble as it is unrealistic.

For camera buffs, the visit presents an irresistible photo
op. Our hosts pose willingly, but without expression; according to their beliefs, we are stealing their souls with
every click of the shutter.

"The families are changing," Drew admits. "They don't
seem as happy to see us."

More clicking of shutters. A Shuar girl chases a scrawny
chicken into a smoldering wood fire. Another, dressed in a
gleaming white polyester confirmation dress, stands shyly
off to a side with her eyes averted. Lalo, boyishly tentative
in his gestures, attempts to barter a beaded necklace
adorned with the severed head of a toucan.

I listen for the thunder of the waterfalls, but can hear
nothing. Perhaps the ancestors have ceased to speak to these
scattered families, cut off from community and tradition,

frozen in the glare of our electronic flashes. Like shadows, they cling to the banks of the Upano, pinned between the forest and the river, with nowhere to go but downstream.

The river rises eight inches overnight. Within minutes of launching we hit white water, rapids with names like Charybdis—named for the Homeric gates of Hades—and Kirruba, the Shuar chief who led the revolt that laid ruin to Macas in 1599.

The Upano would drive any reasonably meticulous cartographer mad: with each torrential rain, each landslide, the river remakes herself. Even the towering canyon walls cannot contain her; the fury of her passage devours earth, rock, and bough.

We put in for the night at a hilly site surrounded by sandbars. Rain streams down our already dripping faces. Mildew spawns in our blue bags. Tired and tight-lipped, we erect our tents beneath an increasingly menacing sky. Then, abruptly, the rain stops and an eerie silence descends on the camp. The evening's first fireflies, as bright as novas, circle overhead. Moving so quickly he seems to blur, a Shuar man darts through the camp and down to the river to retrieve a fish trap. At the same instant, we hear the aqueous war cry of rushing water.

"Flash flood!" cries Drew, as a murky torrent carries off his tent and dry bag. Racing for the bank, he barely manages to save the expedition's only solar water purifier before it is swept down the river like so much flotsam.

As we paddle toward Santiago, gradually losing altitude, peeling off layers of high-tech underwear, the river quickens.

Sweaty, mosquito-ravaged, our bodies a battleground of fungus and intestinal bugs, we brace for what promises to be the most technical part of the trip.

"If anyone goes overboard," Drew says casually, "this is the day it'll happen." The last group to run the river flipped one raft and dump-trucked another on this very stretch.

We swap tales, watch for omens. Spiders the size of crabs walk on water and stow aboard. The air grows heavier. I get a toehold with the less bruised of my legs. Lance flexes his wrists. In the distance, Gargantua—the most bullying of the rapids—dares us on.

Drew, flashing the "eddy out" sign with a sunburnt hand, concedes, "We'd better scout it." We watch the guides leap ashore and climb an overgrown embankment. Watertight cans clank open. A winded rafter huffs his way onto a ledge, brandishing a Nikon in each hand. We wait. We sweat. Sunblock dribbles into our mouths. Finally, the guides return and take their place at the oars.

"We're going for it," Drew says.

A brief float, as soundless as held breath, then Gargantua pounces on the raft like an angry river god settling a score.

"Punch it!"

Digging in, we paddle furiously. The water, foaming and full of holes, slaps at us from all directions. The raft plunges up, down, then without warning, veers. A wayward wave catches Kristin, a quietly intrepid paddler, off guard. With a grunt, she hurtles headlong over the rim. For what seems eons she thrashes in the surf beside the raft, her face pale and contorted. Lost in spray, Lance lunges across the raft and makes a grab for her life vest.

"I've got her," he cries, tumbling backward into the bow. In the scramble, a stray paddle whacks me in the nose.

The ancestors, having vented their rage, retreat to the outlying waterfalls. On this frothy, sun-spangled stretch of the Upano, the eye is drawn upward, above the treetops, beyond the swoop and flitter of wings, as high as the neck will crane and the imagination reach. The cascades hide their source in mist and wisps of cloud, then fall like an endless drink of water poured by a celestial hand.

Separating from the body of rafters, I wade through a rocky creek into a secluded pool whipped foamy by a towering waterfall the color of opals. Though the sun beats down hellish on my head, the water makes my pores prickle with gooseflesh. The river's flux drives me closer and closer to the cascade. I have no will to resist. Extending my hands toward the torrent in supplication, like the beggar I've become, I enter the whirlpool.

Voices. A low, hypnotic *"Tau, tau, tau…"* cry of the pilgrims who once flocked here to pay homage to the ancestors. As my hands make contact with the cool rush of water, I lose myself in the rapture of the moment, of the ages, hearing, feeling, tasting the aqueous soul of this dark equatorial heaven. The river flows. I flow.

The smell of brewed coffee and insect repellent hangs over camp. Fresh as week-old laundry, we heft our gear onto the rafts one last time and continue downstream. Gold panners line the shores. Waterfalls hurtle down the cliffs, wailing laments. The river ripples, undulates, but the brunt of her frenzy has passed. We coast the few remaining rapids, float the final leg, accosted by glimpses of rusted bulldozers, barracks, and khaki-colored uniforms.

Ecuador's border dispute with its neighbor, five-and-a-half-decades-stale, muddies this end of the river. What sort of reception we might receive, there is no telling. With every change in command, every political snafu, the shifting tide grows murkier.

This day, the border lies inert as a scab. As we take out on a buggy, black-sand beach just beyond an Ecuadorian army base, four soldiers armed with automatic rifles putter up in a camouflaged *panga*, amble ashore, and weave with darting glances among the beached life preservers, day packs, water bottles, duffels, gear boxes, and pit toilets.

"What took you so long?" Drew says with strained jocularity, laying aside his oars. "We could have made it to Lima by now."

A river trip, like a river, has no beginning and no end. Long after I fling my blue bag ashore and head for terra firma, the Upano stays with me. Haughty and unrepentant. Mighty and doomed. Her waterfalls crazed with the voices of forsaken deities. Her gold dust, her dead fish, her hydro-maniacal fits of pique…more than a memory, a dream.

Germaine W. Shames has written from six continents on topics ranging from the plight of street children to the struggle to save the Amazon. Author of *Transcultural Odysseys: The Evolving Global Consciousness*, she is the recent winner of a Literary Fellowship from her home state of Arizona. She was last spotted turning cartwheels atop the ramparts of a walled Moorish city in Andalucia.

Swiss Squeeze

PAMELA MICHAEL

Risk management on an Alpine river.

YEARS AGO, AFTER WATCHING A TERRIFIED tourist dangling from a speedboat-towed parasail slam into the facade of a beachfront hotel in Puerta Vallarta, I decided that were I ever to take up a dangerous sport, Mexico would not be the place to do it. The same wisdom prompted me to turn down free scuba diving lessons in Egypt. Risking one's life for *sport*—no matter how exotic or beautiful the locale—has always seemed insane to me. And yet I think of myself as a fairly brave person and something of a fearless traveler. But then, chancing ambush to see Angkor Wat is quite a different proposition than hang gliding or bungee jumping just for "fun."

Not long ago, however, when I was invited to join an "outdoor adventure" tour to Switzerland that promised paragliding, river rafting, and canyoning (sliding down waterfalls and belaying down cliffs, wearing a harness), so reassured was I by the Swiss reputation for precision and proficiency that I scarcely gave safety a moment's thought. A country that could produce more patent holders and Nobel Prize winners per capita than any nation on earth certainly could be counted on to muster guides I could entrust with my life.

My first few days in Switzerland only reinforced my admiration for Swiss competence, most visibly demonstrated by a remarkable transportation system of trains, ferries, funiculars, postal buses, and mountain railways that rendered one of the most dramatic and daunting landscapes in the world — 60 percent mountains and 25 percent forest — as accessible as a city park. What's more, I could check my luggage from one hotel to another, so that when I arrived at my next destination my suitcase would already be in my room. This was the kind of "adventure travel" even an out-of-shape, middle-aged woman could learn to love. Switzerland, as eighteenth-century tourist Johann Goethe noted, is the perfect combination of the colossal and the well-ordered. And nowhere is this lovely Heidiland fusion of pine forests, alpine meadows, hillside villages, and snow-covered peaks more sublimely realized than in the Engadine, the high valley of the En River, near the Italian border.

The Engadine is part of Switzerland's largest and most conservative canton, Graubünden, where women were given the right to vote only in 1971, where villages are connected by footpaths that date back 2,000 years to the Roman occupation. Indeed, the Bündner, as the residents of Graubünden are called, were the last people in the developed world to allow cars on their roads; they were banned until 1925. But even these stolid mountain people couldn't dam the eventual giddy flow of traffic to St. Moritz, the region's most famous resort town. Winter tourism to the Alps was virtually invented there by a hotelier in 1864 when he told his English summer guests that he'd pay their way home if they couldn't sit outside in their shirt sleeves in December.

The mild climate that delighted the visitors of that long-ago December was even more appealing in the June of my visit. Wildflowers dazzled the eyes and nose. Flocks of fuchsia finches eschered with yellow butterflies in the sparkling mountain sky. Cows, like four-legged vacationers, were arriving by train to summer in the high Alpine pastures. In September, I was told, they'd be brought down again, cowbells clanging, their horns and necks bedecked with flower chains, to join a day of music and merrymaking in the villages.

Mountains are great shapers of character, it is said. And great stimuli for engineers, too—the challenge of living in such difficult terrain has goaded the Swiss to tackle almost every peak with a cog railway, tramway, or tunnel. But it was the valleys and canyons that piqued my interest: the narrow gorges and wild cataracts of the Danube's scenic tributary, the En.

Our outfitters were something of an institution, it seemed. You'd see their colorful vans shuttling rafters along river roads, or gaggles of bicyclists with matching bikes and logoed helmets pedaling in slow motion up mountain passes. They had offices all over the country, many located in train stations. So practical, so convenient, so...Swiss.

Piling into the outfitters' van on the morning of our planned fourteen-mile rafting trip down the En, I had few misgivings despite the several Class V rapids we would face. "Without danger, the game grows cold," one of my traveling companions cracked as he threw himself into the back seat, rubbing his hands together in anticipation. I dismissed his comment as testosterone talk, the kind of bravado you might hear on ski slopes, rock faces, or race tracks. I'd never quite understood the appeal of sports that could, and did, with regularity, kill or maim their participants. Whatever it takes to jam your poles into the snow and push off from the top of a ski jump, or to consign yourself to gravity and leap out of an airplane with what amounts to a floppy silk umbrella strapped to your back, I knew I didn't have.

Moderate risk, like river rafting—that I understood; a little fear heightened the experience and afforded a great sense of accomplishment at the end of the day. But really hazardous sports, of which the otherwise sensible Swiss seemed to enjoy quite of few, were a mystery to me.

While there are several systems for ranking rapids according to their degree of difficulty, the most commonly accepted categories are:

Class I—Easy

Class II—Moderate

Class III—Moderately difficult

Class IV—Difficult

Class V—Extremely difficult

Class VI—Extraordinarily difficult.

—PM

Still, it was hard to feel in harm's way anywhere in Switzerland—everything worked so well. All the possibilities and contingencies of any situation seemed to have been taken into account. This assuredness that I was in good hands had settled into something approaching smugness on my part. I guess that's why I was taken so unawares by a rather unthinkable oversight on the part of the outfitters: they didn't have a wet suit large enough to fit me.

Now—it must be said—I am a big woman, at least the top half of me, which has become, in middle age, well… hefty. Though by some (almost cruel) twist of fate, I've retained the kind of strong, long Barbarella legs that thirteen years of ballet (and forty years of rock and roll) can forge. Consequently, I look rather as if I'd been together from the body parts of two different people. *But I'm not so large that there shouldn't be a wet suit large enough to fit me.* There are lots of men much larger than I, and quite a few women.

There I stood in the river rafting equivalent of the tack room, in front of my traveling companions and a few strangers, surveying hanging racks of blue neoprene wet suits, all with two-foot high numbers scrawled on the back—sizes one to five. Ah yes, I'd be a five, by the looks of it, I thought. Oh great. Just like the bowling alley humiliations of my childhood where the size—a big nine in my case—was printed right there on the back of your ugly shoe. Now I'm going to be crammed into a raft with a five on my back, surrounded by threes and fours and twos and maybe even a one.

"I'm not sure we have a wet suit to fit you," said the man handing out the gear, somewhat flustered.

"Do you have men's sizes?" I asked quietly, swallowing all pride.

"These are men's sizes."

"Oh." Tiny shiver.

"Why don't you try the five?" suggested our tour guide, ever optimistic.

I slunk off to the women's dressing room, a dank corner of the stone hut that housed the outfitters' extensive — but not extensive enough, as it turned out — gear. Other women were wiggling into their twos and threes, zipping them up the front with the tiniest of tugs, then skipping off like sprites while I struggled to squeeze my considerable belly into the clammy, sweat-soaked, foul-smelling suit so I could at least attempt to zip it up. Judging from the stench, there were no rest stops along the river — once this thing went on it stayed on until the end of the trip, no matter how long that happened to be. But mine wasn't going on in the first place. There was just too much of me bulging from the unzipped "V" in the front. No matter how elastic the suit, there was no way to zip all of me in.

My struggle was humiliating, so humiliating that I felt almost shrouded in a cloud of shame and frustration, cut off from the other women who were, no doubt, embarrassed to be watching me wrestle with my own body. The kindest of them broke through the cloud: "Want some help?"

Soon there were eight hands pressing, stuffing, cramming, and tugging at flesh and zipper and blue neoprene. Four voices laughed and shrieked and giggled, and one of them was mine. The mass of me was jollied up, up, up until it almost hit my chin. We got the zipper to about mid-

SWISS SQUEEZE   131

sternum and had no choice but to let my now enormous bosom, enlarged by folds of belly with no place else to go, balloon out the top like some cartoon decolletage.

"I feel like I'm wearing a full-body Wonder Bra," I joked. Humor to the rescue.

A bright red life jacket added even more bulk but, blessedly, hid the mortifying number five. I could only hope that it would also hide the bulk of me the wet suit couldn't cover. I looked like a multicolored Michelin Tire Woman in Ray-Bans. I could barely turn sideways. Would I even be able to paddle in this get-up? And how could I possibly bear the amused smiles of my fit, young, limber companions as I waddled down to the water's edge? But there was a river to run, and this was the only body I had at my disposal to run it with; I swallowed my pride, took a deep breath (as deep as my neoprene-constrained lungs would allow), and lumbered out the door.

Risk comes in many forms—physical, emotional, and even financial—but courage is a singular summoning of a part of ourselves and the universe that is as elusive as it is powerful. I was flush with newfound courage and determination as I joined the others on the rocky shore. The water was a milky blue-gray, from ground-up rock known as glacial flour. Six of us—five "adventurers" and one real adventurer, our river guide, a blond dreadlocked Aussie nicknamed "Home Boy"—set off in a fourteen-foot raft and were quickly swirling through rapids with names like Meat Cleaver, Happy Snapper, Nipple Rock, Prussian Sling Shot, and the aptly named *Kotzmühle*, the Vomit Mill.

Good river guides possess a necessary combination of

river skills—strength, caution, the ability to "read" the water—and people skills, the leadership qualities needed to make greenhorn rafters *Paddle Forward! High Side!* and *Hold On!* at just the right times. Home Boy was a Crocodile Dundee/Lord Byron hybrid; he had the perfect blend of daring and sensitivity and we adventurers were soon throwing ourselves from one side of the raft to the other without hesitation on his command. The Michelin Woman was a little slow to resume her paddling position on the rim at times, but she scrambled gamely and with only half a thought of how she looked hoisting herself out of the bottom of the raft. During the lulls, she even found herself relaxing enough to take in the beauty of the En Valley.

In the quieter stretches of water, Home Boy pointed out some of the many streams that fed into the river from tantalizing, lushly-forested side canyons. Several of the gushing tributaries had heavy loads of iron that stained the rocks around the confluences a shocking red. We saw abandoned old *trinkhalles* along the shore, remnants of spas from another age. The region, in fact, has been a popular healing resort since the sixteenth century and still has several operating spas, including a palatial new one at Bad Scuol, located in a romantic village in the lower Engadine that calls its mineral water "the champagne of the Alps."

We floated past the edge of the Swiss National Park, the oldest in Europe, established in 1914. In this oasis of wildness in the midst of a tamed and somewhat manicured country, it is possible to catch glimpses of marmots, red deer, ibex, lynx, and chamois. Sadly, the protection of the park did not come in time for the last bear in Switzerland: it was shot within sight of the river in 1904.

Halfway through our run we came upon a raft from another outfit, "wrapped" around a large boulder in the middle of the river. The paying rafters sat shivering, despite their wet suits, on the rock-strewn banks while their guide struggled valiantly to free the raft, now swamped with water and barely above the surface. Home Boy parked us in an eddy along the shore and leapfrogged from boulder to boulder to reach the stricken craft. The two guides tried ropes, wedges, all kinds of ingenious — and previously employed, it was clear — techniques, some of them quite dangerous, for at least an hour, in vain. The current had captured the raft and wasn't letting go. Disturbingly, we were in a particularly rugged and steep section of the gorge; it was clear there was no way to hike out from this spot on the river.

But this was Switzerland, the Disneyland of nations, by Gott, where

Many a time have I merely closed my eyes at the end of yet another troublesome day and soaked my bruised psyche in wild water, rivers remembered and rivers imagined. Rivers course through my dreams, rivers cold and fast, rivers well-known and rivers nameless, rivers that seem like ribbons of blue water twisting through wide valleys, narrow rivers folded in layers of darkening shadows, rivers that have eroded down deep into a mountain's belly, sculpted the land, peeled back the planet's history exposing the texture of time itself.
— Harry Middleton,
Rivers of Memory

everything was under control, so Home Boy fished out his cell phone and called in a rescue team. We squeezed a couple of the colder refugees into our raft and pushed off, leaving the rest of the stranded rafters to await the rescue boat. Just down river we rounded a tight bend and—*flash!*—saw an eagle take wing in a spray of sunlit droplets of river water, a squirming fish grasped in its talons. An icy dribble splattered my upturned face as the eagle flew over our heads. It felt like a benediction.

I had become, for a moment, just another element in a shimmering landscape of river, sky, tree, mountain, fish, bird. I let out an exultant whoop and fell back into the raft laughing, washed by waves of exhilaration, awe, and gratitude. I had triumphed over my fears and been rewarded with this yodeling, soaring Alpine high. And I hadn't risked my life, really, just my pride. Small stakes, when you think about it.

<hr>

Pamela Michael is the director and co-founder, with Robert Hass, of River of Words, an international children's poetry and art contest on the theme of watersheds. Her travel stories have appeared in the *San Francisco Examiner*, *Shape*, *Odyssey*, *Maiden Voyages*, and other publications. She hosts a travel radio show in the San Francisco Bay Area and is the author of *ROWing Partners: 101 Ways to Build Community Partnerships*, as well as the editor (with Marybeth Bond) of two books: *A Woman's Passion for Travel* and *A Mother's World: Journeys of the Heart*.

River and Road

KIM STAFFORD

*A river carves its history
in memory and lore.*

AN EARLY OREGON LAW NAMED EACH navigable river an official state highway. Among these was the Siuslaw, running west from the coast range into the sea. Where the river curved and shouldered against bluffs, a road was impossible in the early days, and traffic went by water—up from Florence at the coast, to Mapleton near the head of tidewater, fifteen miles inland. There was a kind of road threading along the ridge above the north bank, but locals called it The Goat Trail, and it was a shocker compared to the easy glide of flat water. The river was there; a real road might someday be made. Houses faced the water.

The river made a lot of sense, and a pioneer could make sense, too, by figuring out the river. Salmon came up the river, logs came down. The best farmland was right against the water. Every morning, the milk boat came by, then the fish boat, then the school boat, then the mail boat, and now

and again, the schooner from San Francisco. Before wildcat
logging clogged the channel with silt, two-masted schooners
could float all fifteen miles inland to Mapleton. If you
weren't on the river with a dock in good repair, you just
weren't part of modern life.

Rain, a glory of rain, made the river the natural ribbon
that bound everything up like a purse-seine slung across the
hills. The river was everywhere—not a place, but a way of
happening. Charlie Camp told me how the two happy
tourist ladies from California stopped to talk. They got on
the subject of rain.

"How much rain do you get here, Mr. Camp?"

"Oh," he said, "we get about eight foot a year. That's
common, but I've seen more."

"Now, sir, just because we come from California, we don't
need to believe that." They liked their old Oregon man.

"Ladies, you see that elderberry bush down there by the
barn? That's eight foot tall. If we took our year's fall of rain
in a day, that bush would be under the flood."

Was he right? He was. Mapleton, Oregon, right up
against the west jump of the coast range, combs off ninety-
six inches of rain in a common year. That's nothing compared to the twenty feet of rain that falls on the west slick of
the Olympic Peninsula, but it's wet. Charlie told me you
know you're in Oregon when you can stand on the porch
and grab a salmon fighting its way up through the thick
tumble of the rain. That turned into a song as I drove home:

> *Step to the porch, a salmon flies by—*
> *Hook him in out of the rain.*

You're pretty far gone, pretty far gone:
You're clear out here in Oregon.

When a baby is born, as everyone knows,
There's moss in its fingers, webs in its toes.
It's pretty far gone, pretty far gone—
It's clear out in Oregon.

There is the chill glory of baptism by rain every day of winter when you step outside. So why not use that water for a road?

One well-schooled pioneer played a little dance with the river out of sheer practicality. He staked his homestead claim on the good farmland up North Fork, but when he came to look for timber up to his high standard, he found nothing close by. Seeking the tree, he cruised four miles down North Fork to the Siuslaw channel, then a good twelve miles upriver to Mapleton, then another mile south up Knowles Creek. There he stood, a good fifteen miles from home as the crow flies, but the tree he found was too straight and the water too handy to do it any other way. He felled the tree parallel to the creek, and bucked out one good forty-foot log, five-foot through at the little end. He rolled that log to the bank of Knowles Creek with the help of a logging jack, a tool that stood about knee-high and asked for patience. Then he carved his brand on the butt end of the log, left instructions at the sawmill downstream, and went home to his tent.

When high water came in the spring, Knowles Creek rose, picked up his log sweet as you please, and carried it a mile down to the main channel of the Siuslaw at Mapleton.

From there, the log made its own way downstream to the mill above Point Terrace, where it was identified, barked, slabbed off, and run through the saws. The mill filled the order matched to the brand, took its own percentage of lumber out for the trouble, and stacked what was left on the riverbank.

When the moon was right and the tide deep, the man drifted down North Fork of a morning, rode the flood tide up the Siuslaw to the mill by skiff, dressed his lumber into a raft at slack tide, then herded it downriver on the ebb. The next turn of the tide put him off the mouth of North Fork, and he spent slack water turning his raft into the North Fork channel. When the next flood tide swung in, he rode his raft by dark up North Fork until he came to his claim. A nice two-story house came out of that one log, with siding left over for the barn, and the man passed on easy ways to his children.

He took the time, he knew the ways. The river did the rest.

The early drift-netters on the Siuslaw suffered under two delusions that sweetened their lives considerably. I talked with Trygve Nordhal, who remembered both. First, it seemed obvious that any motor on the boat would scare off the fish. Second, salmon can see, right? By day, they would surely stay out of any net you laid down. So the word went. So drift boats went by spruce oars only, and by night. You

The United States has 3 1/2 million miles of rivers and streams. Less than 2 percent are free-flowing, impeded by over 5,500 large dams and almost 80,000 small ones.

—PM

had to know every tree on the dim night sky horizon, sight them against the starlit clouds to turn and turn, to stay in the channel clear.

Every stretch of good drift water on the river had a name. There was the Barney Drift, where old Indian Barney once fished. There was the Squaw Drift, and to the side of it, little Papoose Drift, then the Town Drift, Woodpile, Stickpatch, Sandpile, Spruce Point, the Homestead, and Deep Hole Drift where the salmon crowded the deep channel against the north bank. At the Barney Drift, the best of them all as Trygve told it, "We'd go out about twenty oarstrokes, and then we'd lay net, and drift down to what we called The Gap, and pick up the net. Then we'd lay out again, and drift down to what we called The Three Shorts. And that was the end of the ebb-tide drift."

Talking of fish and the river, Trygve's voice spoke with the rush and ebb of water. There was the turbulent haste of his knowing words, then a milling around a slack, then a drift back down for ebb: "Early in the season, we'd go whenever the tides were right. If it was a minus tide in the evening, we'd fish below the bridge—if it was high tide in the evening, just about dark, why the fish would make it across the bar, clear up to North Fork before you caught them, and you couldn't catch a fish below the bridge. They never stopped. They came on the tide as far as they could. If it was low water in the evening, for some reason they came in on the morning tide, they flew around, and went back down for a minus tide—low water in the evening, first dark. But if it was high water in the evening, you could not catch a fish below Florence on high water slack. They'd all be up to Barney Drift. They'd catch a hundred fish to the boat up here. You wouldn't catch one below the bridge. They move in cycles like that. And you catch more fish if it wasn't raining. If it was raining, they'd move right up the river. Seemed like they don't go up the river until they have some fresh water."

The nets were twenty-five meshes deep for the lower river, thirty meshes deep for the upper channel. Meshes ran eight inches for Chinook salmon, six and three-quarters for silverside, six and a quarter for fall steelhead. Fishermen who didn't know the river spent their days mending net they'd trailed into snags. Not only the drift sites had names, but the hidden snags as well. Trygve: "Right off the Town Drift, downstream side, you had to pick up fast. A big spruce tree had fallen in the river there years ago, and it had The Eagle's Nest, they called it. Would just about take your whole net, if you got caught in that."

In one night with a set net, a farmer on the river could catch enough of the big Chinook to last all winter. One Chinook would fill several gallon jars for salt-fish, and a net could pick forty fish from the river in one night. No one recorded the Siuslaw Indian names for these fishing sites, but with a river so rich, they may have been similar to what Franz Boas recorded for the Kwakiutl candlefish stations way north: "Full in Mouth," "Fat," "Eating Straight Down," "Eating All," "Eagle Bowl," "Owning Many," "Place of Succumbing." When a Kwakiutl mother bore twins, she knew they were salmon; if they came near water, they might take off their human masks and swim away.

On the Siuslaw, when fall rain failed to fill the river deep, the grocery schooner from San Francisco couldn't make it in across the bar. Then people ate salmon and potatoes three times a day, every day, all winter long. Like the Siuslaw people before them, those pioneers ate the river.

Salmon came up, logs came down. There is one house on Cox Island with no road but the river—the Sanborne house, now windowless and sagging. Mrs. Sanborne told me how she stood by the top window at dusk, and saw her husband float past in a raw December storm, hopping from log to log on a big billowing raft that had broken loose. He glanced once at her lamplit shape, then turned furious to his work and drifted darker downstream west. That time, he lived.

Fred Buss told me how the river took a life. The tug was coming in to dock, and the crowd on shore was as turbulent as the water. People simply jostled Miss Sherman loose from balance, and down she went from the pier. A young man shucked his hat and went in after her, swam under the keel, but came up alone.

Miss Sherman had just become engaged, Fred said, and that softened his way with the story some, but he told it stroke by stroke as an oarsman would who lived by killing the river's fish and knowing its way.

"We watched for her three nights, thinking she'd come to our nets as others had, and every time we pulled in heavy, reached for some silver arm of fish by the lamp-box, it might be her. Fish drown, too, in the net, you know. They come in stiff, cold. And sometimes salmon come to the lamp, up out of the channel, and drop away again. But Miss Sherman stayed down three days.

"Then we were mending net on the dock in the morning.

My partner says, 'We'll see Miss Sherman soon. She ought to be floating by now.' And by God, there she comes, slow past our dock on the ebb, face down, white bump on the water. I was for putting a net out, but these damn fools had to turn her over with an oar. Of course her face was gone. Crabs had eaten that, breasts and all. I said to let her be, but they would not. Jesus, it made me mad. As she rolled up, her left fist came out of the water. There's her gold ring then, hanging by the fingerbone."

Kim Stafford was born in 1949 in Portland, Oregon, where he lives with his wife and daughter. He holds a degree in medieval literature from the University of Oregon, and currently directs the Oregon Writing Project at Lewis & Clark College. His publications include *A Gypsy's History of the World*, *Braided Apart*, *The Granary*, and *Rendezvous: Stories, Songs & Opinions of the Idaho County*. This story was excerpted from his book, *Having Everything Right: Essays of Place.*

The Song of the Bio Bio

MICHAEL SHAPIRO

Frankly my dear, I don't give a dam.

T O THE CASUAL OBSERVER, IT MAY HAVE appeared to be just another day on the river. A couple of guides were casually re-rigging their boats, some guests were nursing cold beers, and a raging game of kayak polo created waves in a big eddy near camp. It's a scene that's become commonplace on so many of the world's white-water rivers—the post-exhilaration rituals that boaters enjoy after a thrilling day of running the rapids. Yet this wasn't any old river: it was Chile's Bio Bio, one of the world's finest river trips, and the guests were enjoying the evening at View Camp, named for its stunning panorama of a nearby volcano. The fortunate few on this 1997 trip may well be among the last river runners to experience the stunning and diverse pleasures of the Bio Bio.

A trip on the Bio Bio is much more than a rollicking river ride. It's an opportunity to see a relatively unspoiled natural wonder, a living ecosystem of wildflowers, willows,

and red-backed buzzards; a chance to visit with the indigenous Mapuche (People of the Land), and see spectacular
waterfalls, some plunging 100 feet or more into the river.
Cascading over Class V rapids, the Bio Bio caresses the base
of the 10,300-foot Volcan Callaqui, its snow-capped pinna-
cle still steaming. Callaqui's fumerol could be seen as an
omen being ignored by government and business leaders
preparing to sign the Bio Bio's death sentence.

Though our trip's primary leaders deeply loved the Bio
Bio and the chance to share its joys with newcomers, they
said they'd give up running the river if that would preserve
it for the Mapuche. "We know it's not our river," says John
French (whom everyone calls Frenchy). His statement
reflects the deep respect he has for the local people, yet it's
not completely accurate. In a sense, through almost two
decades of running the Bio Bio, it has become, in a small but
significant way, their river. Just as the local people who live
along the river call themselves the Pahuenche (the people of
the pine nut trees, one of many Mapuche tribes), Frenchy
and his co-leader Butch Carber have become people of the
river, too.

The Bio Bio, with charms as subtle as the song of the
Chilean Elaenia (a bird that sings "bioooo-bioooo," the
source of the river's name), has worked its way deep into the
hearts of these men. "We're on the downside of our careers,"
Butch said, "but it's a shame that future generations won't
get to run this river." Though Butch has led about thirty
expeditions down the Bio Bio during the past twelve years,
he's still inspired by it. "Every trip I see something new. I
can't say I know it as well as I want to know it."

And he probably never will. In 1992, ENDESA, Chile's national power company, nailed the first spike into the river's coffin when it began construction of the Pangue Dam near the end of the prime white-water run. Pangue shut its gates in 1996, inundating about seventeen kilometers of river, drowning the Canyon of a Hundred Waterfalls and wiping out the roller-coaster rapids of the Royal Flush. "Those rapids were great—you couldn't have designed them better," Frenchy said. Added Butch: "That was the last waltz. It was big and technical and exciting. You had to be right on—it was a great way to end the trip."

Today the ten-day journey ends with a short float over the lake created by the dam. During the bus ride back, Butch sits on the right side of the bus so he doesn't have to see the devastation the dam has wrought. Though Butch has seen the dam before, our trip is the first time he witnesses the lake that has drowned the river he loves like a member of his family. As the bus bumps over a rutted dirt road, Butch sits silently, appearing stunned by what has been lost.

This crushing feeling of loss is not new for Butch. A few years back, his wife, the first woman to row a boat down several of the world's most challenging rivers, died after a protracted battle with cancer. Within two years he also lost his father; and when the Pangue Dam went in, he found the pain almost unbearable. "You can never bring it back—at least not in our lifetimes," Butch said. Some guides chose to work other rivers after the dam went in, unable to enjoy the Bio Bio after the river had been so brutally scarred. But for those who aren't accustomed to its past glory, the Bio Bio

still offers a tremendous river trip, and Butch is deeply committed to sharing his love for this place until it's no longer
possible. "Hopefully guests will take away an appreciation
of what is lost when you dam a river," he said.

Pangue is the first of six dams slated to be built along the
Bio Bio. The second, smack in the middle of the white-water
stretch near a rapid called Jugbuster, would effectively end
rafting on the Bio Bio. Some boaters may still be able to
navigate short stretches of the river, but the ten-day journey
we enjoyed would be a thing of the past. In mid-1997,
Chilean newspapers reported growing popular support for
the anti-dam movement, but the odds of stopping the second
dam, called Ralco, appeared slim.

So what about the argument that North Americans have
no right to come into a country like Chile and say it's a mistake to dam rivers for hydropower. "I think that's bullshit,"
Butch says. "We can learn from our own mistakes. That's
the only way we can change things."

From View Camp we start to hike through resplendent
fields of lupine into the foothills, getting a rare opportunity
to talk to local Pahuenche people. On the slopes of Callaqui,
an elderly indigenous woman named Maria, with a deeply
lined face, dark leathery skin, and sparkling eyes comes out
to greet us. She patiently poses for photos with some members of the group, as everyone struggles to communicate in
Spanish, the second language for all involved. Making the
conversation more difficult is Maria's unconscious tendency
to throw in a Pahuenche word when she doesn't know the
Spanish translation. And sometimes it's hard to hear her, as
pigs in the yard loudly crunch every cherry pit they can find

on the hard-packed, dirt floor. After some good-natured joking, the subject of the dam comes up.

"We have lived here for generations," Maria says. "My parents lived here, my grandparents, and my great-grand-parents before them. We are the people of the pine nut trees—our survival depends on these trees." Maria goes into the house and returns with a wicker basket of pine nuts and eggs. The brown-shelled nuts are about an inch and a half long, and are ground up to form a staple of the Pahuenche's diet. "If they move us away from our homes, we won't have these nuts," she says, extending a quavering handful. "We need these."

After visiting with Maria and the smiling kids that rattled through the yard, we continue hiking up Callaqui. After a challenging stretch called the Highway of

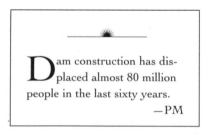

Dam construction has displaced almost 80 million people in the last sixty years.
—PM

Ball Bearings, we settle in a clearing about halfway up the mountain and make camp for the night. We rise before dawn and, as the sun rises, reach the level of the araucaria trees, deep green, spiky pines, that thrive at the cool climates of the higher elevations. The day breaks sharp and clear at the horizon, as clouds hug Callaqui's peak.

Those who make it to the summit don't return to camp until just before sunset and don't have much time to recover. We get up early the next day to prepare for the several Class V rapids that have given the Bio Bio an international reputation. Butch and Frenchy started the day by recapping the safety talk, emphasizing the need for quick high sides. (A high side is when one side of the boat starts to rise and boaters quickly jump to that side of the boat, using their weight to keep the boat from flipping.)

Though focused on the challenges ahead, it was hard not to be overwhelmed by the surrounding beauty. This stretch of river has been formed and sculpted by the dual actions of volcano eruptions and river erosion. The still-smoldering Callaqui's lava once flowed down to the Bio and blocked the river, and over time the Bio Bio has carved a detour around the massive toe of this lava flow. The result: steep, sharp drops and plenty of thrilling white water. Thundering waterfalls, such as the majestic Maya, shoot into the Bio Bio, creating an almost surreal, Hollywood-set-like beauty.

After successfully navigating some intermediate rapids (M&M, Snickers, and Milky Way, where Maya Falls plunges into the river), we approach Lost Yak. This rapid is named for a kayaker who flipped his boat and bailed out, then lost his 'yak in the tumultuous, frothy rapids here. The run here is to start center, move left, and navigate around a boulder that can flip a boat without a second thought. A couple of us join Butch in his boat to support his rowing with some paddling up front and to add some weight to the right spot if need be. Butch enters center, moves left and hits his target. But a hidden wave kicks the boat toward the rock and the front, left tube starts to rise. Butch screams "High side" and we fling ourselves at the tube, using our weight to slam it back toward the river. After a couple of interminable seconds of wondering whether the river would consume or spit out its prey, the front of the boat eases back down toward the river, we nudge our way around the boulder, and clear the rapid. A couple of the boats that follow have some scary moments, but everyone makes it through pretty clean.

Next: Lava South, famed for its fear-inspiring Whale's Tail, a must-miss "hole" or wave that curls in on itself. Rising several feet out of the water, the Whale's Tail seems to simultaneously beckon and threaten rafters. Lava South is a technical rapid, and a clean run at the top sets you up to bypass the Tail on the bottom. But one wrong move up high and you can easily get flung towards the tail and some serious consequences. A few years back, Butch ended up doing battle with the Tail, and he felt like his arm had been ripped out of its socket. A veteran boatman, he iced it with a cold beer and rowed the rest of the trip without complaining. A few weeks later, when he couldn't raise his arm above his shoulder, he finally saw a doctor and had X-rays. The diagnosis: a broken arm and badly torn shoulder muscle.

The scary thing about running Lava South is that a good boater will point the boat at the left bank, straight at the Tail. If run well, the curving wave above the Tail will lead the boat just to the right of the huge wave. We drop in and start accelerating toward the Tail. Usually, this is where slow-motion kicks in but this is over in a heartbeat. The curving wave swings us around, sets the nose of the boat just where we want it, and in a second we bypass the danger.

After a series of clean runs, we hit a few more exciting rapids, but nothing as heart-stopping as Lost Yak and Lava South. After tying up the boats the festivities began, as the guides mix up a concoction called Pisco Punch, which looks more frightening than the rapids. Pisco is one of Chile's national beverages, a potent grape brandy often mixed with fruit juice to create a drink that doesn't taste like alcohol but can knock you flat. One drink would have been plenty, so we all had two or three and settled down to a feast of lamb (freshly slaughtered for us and cooked on a spit at our campsite), *ensalada chilena*, and chocolate cake. After cooking dessert in a Dutch oven (a big cast iron pot with a lid), we walk about five minutes down the road to a natural hot springs, and sit alongside the river as an almost full moon rises.

As we soak, Frenchy starts talking about what makes the Bio Bio so special. Sure the rapids are exhilarating, but it's the local Chileans like Rosalva, an elderly woman who runs the house where the guides stay, that make it so rewarding. "One year on her birthday, a couple of us guides took her out for lunch, and the rest of the guides painted her house. We bring her the arthritis medicine she needs." Then there's Rolando and his wife, who drive the vans to the put-in. "Not only will we miss the Bio Bio but these people will miss

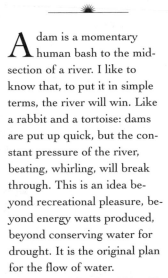

A dam is a momentary human bash to the midsection of a river. I like to know that, to put it in simple terms, the river will win. Like a rabbit and a tortoise: dams are put up quick, but the constant pressure of the river, beating, whirling, will break through. This is an idea beyond recreational pleasure, beyond energy watts produced, beyond conserving water for drought. It is the original plan for the flow of water.

—S. H. Semken, *River Tips and Tree Trunks*

us. The dam doesn't benefit these people. The farms they've worked for hundreds of years will be flooded—generations of labor and knowledge will be lost."

As I reflect in the deliciously warm water, it becomes clear that my lasting memories will be of the people as well. Of Butch and Frenchy; of Maria showing me her pine nuts in Callaqui's shadow; of Rolando who, when asked to be in a picture, joked that he'd do it for some change; of the other rafters, who come from Hawaii, Colorado, and London.

My final view of the river wasn't pretty: a dry canyon below the dam. But then I thought about the last time the river was blocked: after Callaqui's last major eruption. As the centuries passed, the Bio Bio worked its way around this obstacle, creating one of the most magnificent stretches of river on Earth. And though it probably won't happen in my lifetime, I know that someday the Bio Bio will again flow free, and the Chilean Elaenia will sing in the treetops above it.

Michael Shapiro has turned over boats on California's Kern, wrapped boats around rocks on Oregon's Rogue, perched in the middle of Idaho's Main Salmon, and forgotten how to call commands in Spanish on the Rio Cahabon in Guatemala. He now volunteers as a guide with a group that leads disabled people on white-water trips and sea kayak voyages. He is the author of *Michael Shapiro's Internet Travel Planner*, and he also writes for magazines and newspapers, including *Arthur Frommer's Budget Travel, Yahoo Internet Life, Trips, San Francisco Examiner*, and *Dallas Morning News*. He lives in Sonoma County, California with his girlfriend and big-boned Maine coon cat.

What My Father Told Me

MICHAEL DELP

*A tale of a life lived in communion
with water.*

WHAT MY FATHER TOLD ME, HE MOSTLY
told me when we were fishing. It didn't matter
that we had skipped church for the hundredth
time, or whether he had walked into my school and gotten
me out of class. He wanted to tell me things, he said, and the
best place, he felt, was on the river. He said the river was as
close to time as you were going to get. No sense, he said,
watching a clock to learn about time. It wouldn't even do
you any good to study rock stratification or fossils, like some
scientists believed.

What seemed to arrest my father's attention the most was
the fact that rivers were always full of water. He would often
stand on the banks of our cabin on the North Branch and
ask over and over where all that water was coming from. Of
course, he knew. And one summer when it was over ninety
for almost two weeks in a row we sweated our way north of
Lovells and found the source: a small fingerlet seeping out

from under a hummock in a swamp. Another time we stopped along the mainstream and my father showed me what he called a sacred spot. There was an iron ring in the ground, and looking into it was like peering into the eye of a river god, my father whispered.

My father taught me about perfection too. Often I heard him say "perfect, everything is perfect" and when I asked what he meant, he'd always say, "Just look around." But I remember him telling me a story about perfection, just to illustrate that perfection wasn't always an absolute quality in his life. Once in Montana he had been fishing a section of the Madison when he stopped in mid-cast to admire what he considered to be absolute perfection: a clear, evening sky, five-pound rainbows rising to midges, alone and miles from any house. Suddenly he heard the sound of tires squealing, then the crush of metal against the guard-rail a hundred feet above him and a Ford Pinto flew over the exact spot where he was fishing, landed in the river and sank in front of him. The driver swam toward him, my father half cursing his bad luck, but marveling at his one chance to see a car fly.

He taught me about glaciers and about how glaciers literally carved out the bellies of rivers. Move this water out of here he'd say and all you got is a meandering single track through the woods barely deep enough to spit in, but add water and you've got a living vein. My father never talked much about God or religion except to say that whatever made rivers had to be wild.

My father loved wildness. He loved the fact that you

could stand only so long in the current of a river until your feet started to drop out from under you. And he often said, over his shoulder when we were fishing together, that you could take something out of your imagination you didn't like, just like you would out of your pocket and let it go into the river and it would never come back.

He told me that whenever he felt any sense of failure, he would go to the river and just let whatever was bothering him loose in the water. He said he felt wild when he drank from the river, or caught brook trout and ate them on the same day. Trout particles he called them and he was sure they had lodged in his bloodstream over the years until, he said proudly, he was more brook trout than man.

When I was twelve he took me to the Upper Peninsula for a fishing trip on the Big Two-Hearted. He was careful to point out that the river wasn't the real river Hemingway was writing about, that was the Black, further east of the Two-Hearted. This was before the Mackinaw Bridge, when you had to take a ferry across the Straits. We holed up in the station wagon, listening to Ernie Harwell call a late Tigers game. I could smell the odor of wet canvas. Tents and fishing bags. Fishing tackle.

On our way into the river my father told me that of all the places he'd been, all the rivers he'd fished, this place we were going meant the most. In the '40s he and Fred Lewis had fished this water for weeks at a time. Years later, when Fred went blind, his wife dropped him off and he fished by himself for two weeks.

I still have pictures of Fred Lewis in my albums at home. In one, he's wearing a red-plaid wool shirt. My dad says those were the best shirts you could wear to fish in. He told me to always have a fishing shirt handy. Never wear it for anything else, he said. And never, never wash it. If you can, he said, the first time you wear it, you need to anoint it with the blood of a few night crawlers and brook trout.

That's what my father fished for most. Brook trout. He could sneak into the smallest, brushiest streams where you'd swear there wouldn't hardly be any water. He'd dangle a short rod over the bank and slip the worm in without making a ripple. Then he'd mutter a prayer to the fish gods, to keep them close, he'd say, and then he'd lift the tip of his rod so slowly you couldn't see. I remember brook trout coming out of the clear water, how they looked like miniature paintings, vibrant and loose with color.

My father told me sitting on the banks of the Two-Hearted that the best way to cook brook trout was in the coals. Pack them in river clay, he said and put it in the fire. When the clay cracked, the fish was done.

We ate fish like that for a week. My father drinking small glasses of wine. Sometimes he'd let me sip some and we'd lean back against the trees, our faces hot from the flames. Coming through the fire, his voice sounded like the voice of a god. It sounded hollow and large, like it was coming from somewhere under the earth.

My father told me that rivers weren't really natural phenomena at all. Rivers, he said came directly out of the veins of the gods themselves. To prove it, he said, try to follow one. When you tromp through a swamp for a day or two, following something that's getting smaller and smaller and then finally vanishes under a hummock in some swamp

somewhere, he said, you'd need to go down under the earth
to find the source.

The source was in wildness, he said. A wild god making
a river come up out of the ground by opening up one of his
veins and letting his divine blood sift upward toward blue
sky. When I think about my father now, I think about gods
under the earth and about blood, about how he baptized
himself there on the Two-Hearted that summer.

I'd already been baptized twice. Once in church when I
was a baby, he said. But he'd had second thoughts about
what went on, about who was sanctifying what. And another time by my grandfather with a handful of lake water.
Now, he told me, I needed to drink from the same river that
he drank from.

We were standing knee deep just about the mouth.
Lake Superior was crashing below us. He lifted a cupped
hand to my mouth and I drank and then he drank. Blood,
he whispered. Keep this wild blood in you for the rest of
your life.

When my father wasn't working or fishing, his other great
joy was quoting short lines of poetry while we fished.
When he wasn't talking about the connection between
rivers and the spiritual territory he tended so seriously
inside me, he was talking about the wildness he loved in
poets he'd read. I always thought it odd that a man brought
up around huge tool and die presses would come to something so seemingly fragile as poetry. He particularly loved an
ancient Irish poem, "The Wild Man Comes to the
Monastery." Some nights when he was a bend or two

below me I could hear him calling back, "though you like the fat and meat which are eaten in the drinking halls, I like better to eat a head of clean watercress in a place without sorrow." At twelve, those lines meant little, but over the years, something seeped in and built up, an accumulation of images, he liked to say to me, would get me through the hard times when my life would go dark. To keep away the loneliness, he'd say, and then whisper another line from Machado, or Neruda. Keep these poets close to your heart, he would admonish me and so I fished for years listening to the great Spanish surrealists drifting upriver to me in the dark.

Weeks later we were drifting on Turk Lake trolling for pike. It was almost dark and my father was looking back over the transom, watching his line. One word came out of his mouth, storm. I looked into the western sky and saw huge clouds boiling in, black and inky, the curl of them like a huge wave. Keep fishing, he said. Keep casting from the bow. The pike will feed just before it hits, keep casting, cast your heart out, he said.

From where I stood I could see a white belly slashing up toward my lure. I could see my father etched by lightning, his rod low, then him striking, both of us fighting fish under the darkening sky.

We lost both fish. The sky seemed to literally fall on us. My father told me later in the cabin, that we'd been lucky, foolish, but lucky, he said. He told me that luck was when skill met necessity and that his lightning theory was worth proving. Besides, he said, we had fished in the wildness of a storm, and what better way to end a day than to be wring-

ing the wildness out of your wet clothes, sucking the wild
rain out of your cuff, thirsty for more.

What went into a boy, stayed inside. I hid it away, kept my
father's voice inside me, packed in close to my heart. Whatever my father told me I always regarded as the absolute
truth. I believed in the river gods. Believed that river water
came from their veins; that if there was one god, He must be
made entirely of water. That was years ago. For years I kept
lists and journals of what I remembered my father telling
me. It was all good.

Take the river inside as you would a text he would tell
me more than once. He knew that once inside you could
memorize every pool and run, every rock in a stream and
unless there was a winter of bad anchor ice, you could
come back in the spring for opening day and look for every
mark you'd imagined in the winter. Even better, he told
me, was the ability to enter the river inside whenever you
felt the need to. "I got to light out for the territory" he was
fond of saying, a good part of him given over to the wildest
parts of Huck Finn's personality. And always there was
that dark, brooding sense of the surreal, the river looming
up inside both of us as if it were alive and breathing
through our skins.

But, what I remember most clearly now is the way his
voice sounded on the day he died. He was barely coherent,
wandering through the double stupor of morphine and the
cancer in his head. He was almost dead, but you could tell
his mind was still reeling with images. On this last day he
was talking rivers, and trips he'd taken, I showed him a new

reel and he launched himself into a beautiful story about
fishing the Two-Hearted again. Then, he said he had been
overtaken the night before by a dream that he had turned
into something purely wild. He didn't know what it was, he
said, but he knew he had moved with grace, and that he had
moved under the earth with great force. He said that when
he woke up, he felt a part of him was missing and that he
had some sense in the dream that he had been deposited
somewhere. Surely, he said, he must have dreamed himself
into a river. He knew, and I remember him telling me, that
there were Sioux Indians who could turn themselves into
rivers. He said he had seen one such man when he was a
boy traveling through Nebraska with his father. The Sioux
had simply lain down, begun singing in low tones, stretching himself out further and further until he literally flowed
past his feet.

My father's last dream
had taken him back to
that day, back to that
wondrous opportunity to
see flesh transcend itself.
Now my father, weak
from disease, lay still in
his bed, only his mouth

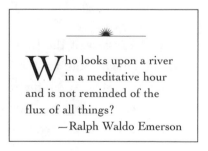

Who looks upon a river
in a meditative hour
and is not reminded of the
flux of all things?
— Ralph Waldo Emerson

moving. What he told me on that last day was to honor my
promise to take him away, to take him back to the river.

I remember my father telling me he had scouted years
for the spot. He was never one for fanfare, nor ceremony,
and the measure of a good day was calculated by hard
work. A good spot had requirements he had said: shade

most of the day, a gravel bottom and a mixture of currents, a mixing place. We visited only once. That afternoon he sat with me and talked mostly of dams. It was either a wing dam, he thought, or more probably a coffer dam.

In the sunlight that filtered through the trees he drew diagrams in the dirt. Head the river off gently, he said, or it would surge over everything. With leaves he made the wash of the river, traced it exactly over the spot where he wanted the grave. Mud he said, the trunks of trees jammed by the current against steel rods driven into the bed of the river to hold back the water. He was firm about this desire, and his firmness carried itself into the waking dreams I had of the dam, the daily visions I had of myself felling trees, driving the steel rods, packing mud like a beaver.

After he died I simply carried him off from the funeral parlor, out the back door and into the truck. His friends buried the coffin in the cemetery on the hill and I drove his body to the river.

I worked most of the first day cutting. The trees came down on the bank and I moved over their limbs as if the saw were a scythe. He lay up higher on the bank, his head on a rock like he was sleeping. I drove the stakes in two feet of water, then rolled the trees in, guiding their huge trunks against the stakes.

That night I worked against the river, my hands digging up river stones, mud, clay from the banks. I looked often at him lying up above me, his face barely visible in the cast of light from the lantern. I had made the cuts like he had instructed. Like putting a log cabin together he had motioned in the dirt that day, one log grooved, the other mortised. The seam of the logs joining together was barely a scar against my hands.

I slept off and on, working, sleeping. Packing mud and clay, repacking small spots where the water wanted to get in. When I finished I was standing in something that looked like a wooden arm growing out of the bank and angling back against the glow of the river. At the lip of the dam I held my hand against the water then turned back to look at the moist bottom of the river below me open to daylight.

I dug down below grade, through rocks and smaller rocks, into the clay that cradled the river, the water seeping into the grave.

No mumbo-jumbo he had said, no remorse, just let me go back. I laid him face up at first, then rolled him to his side so one ear might be toward the river, the other toward the sky. I packed him in, tight he had said, wedged into the bottom of the river and then I covered him, first with clay and heavy stones, then with lighter rocks and pebbles.

I waited until early evening, lit the lantern and then began dismantling the dam, only enough to let the water in, letting two logs drift away in the darkening current. The water sluiced over the dam, now inches under water, over the stones, and sifted down, I am sure into my father's lips. I wanted to speak something to him in the dark but couldn't. He had wanted silences; wanted the sound of the river all around us.

Now, in summer I drift over his spot. The remnants of the dam still hold. I imagine my father has gone back completely by now, and only his bones are held in the belly of the river. I think of him often, how he carried me far beyond the years he could. How his life merged and moved with mine and then swept in another direction. I think of him alive and casting, examining and selecting flies like a surgeon, his love of poems and wildness fused together and fueled by his desire to take in all of the world in front of him. I think of how his life comes back to me each time I fish, each time I step into the current. Mostly, I think of how both of us are carried by rivers, how his memory sifts through me like the current where only his bones are left to tell the story.

Michael Delp is the director of creative writing at the Interlochen Art Academy. He is the author of *Under the Influence of Water*, *On the Graves of Horses*, and *The Coast of Nowhere: Meditations on Rivers, Lakes and Streams*, from which this story was excerpted. His poetry and prose have appeared in numerous anthologies and publications as well as in a handful of chapbooks.

PART THREE

STREAMS OF CONSCIOUSNESS

Waiting Out the Platte

CARA BLESSLEY

*Sandhill cranes and geese ply
the Midwest flyway.*

F ROM THE ONE-ROOM SCHOOLHOUSE I CAN
hear the cranes singing their hypnotic *kerr-loo, kerr-loo* before first light. They are silent most of the night and like a haunting they begin, one after another, until the chorus of bird voices on the river grows and sings with a voice of its own. With a sudden movement, the cranes break from the shoulder-to-shoulder contact they've maintained throughout the night and explode into the dawn, the mass trumpeting signaling they've made it through another night. The *whish-whish* of the river fades into a din behind the pounding of wingbeat and water rushing from the birds' legs. The river, wrestling with entire trees, driftwood, whatever finds its way to the throat of its current, is silenced.

I trek down to the Platte at dawn, following the cranes' call. Cold spring morning, frost outlining the bare silhouettes of cottonwood trees; their branches have not yet come to bud. Overhead, the cranes are on the move. The river at

my feet seems confined and rushes by fast, furious in places.
The surface undulates and winds around the level sandbar
islands and keeps on going. There are no calm pools, no
place where the water is gathering, eddying against a fallen
tree or boulder thrust out from the shore. The current is too
strong and carries these intrusions away without hesitation.
I watch the water come down fast around the island, nearly
reaching the blind. Water rushes in and in spite of all the
damming with sandbags and rip-rap, it doesn't look like the
blind is going to make it.
With every hour, the river
rises. The island is disappearing day by day.

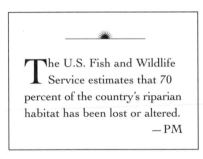

The U.S. Fish and Wildlife
Service estimates that 70
percent of the country's riparian
habitat has been lost or altered.
— PM

Harold Mangelsen settled
on the Platte in the 1930s.
On a hunting trip east of
Grand Island, he met an
old sheepherder who owned land that Harold needed to
cross in order to access the river. The two men, sharing a
common love for Nebraska, became friends. By the time he
passed away, the sheepherder had sold his 240-acre farm to
the Schneider family, with the stipulation that Harold could
continue to use the property. In the spring of 1952, Harold
located an abandoned schoolhouse outside Prosser,
Nebraska. The original structure had been destroyed in the
mid-1940s by a tornado that ripped through the prairie
lands of central Nebraska. Even though it was only five
years old and in perfect condition, the recently built schoolhouse was left empty and hardly used when the students

were moved to a different school. The schoolhouse was auctioned off, along with its accompanying outhouse. Harold bought the outhouse first and when he began to bid on the schoolhouse, the auctioneer could plainly see what he was up to and kept the auction going. Eventually, they settled on the price of $1,500.

With his new purchase, Harold gathered some friends and his two oldest boys and together they jacked the schoolhouse up off its foundation and moved the entire structure on a flatbed trailer, intact, to the rim of Schneider's farm. It was situated under the shade of a cottonwood and painted bright red, just 100 yards from the Platte River.

I first came to the Platte in the fall, right in the middle of goose-hunting season. During that time of year, geese are everywhere, vying for a secure place on neighborhood ponds, vacated sandpits filled with water, or golf courses deserted after the first freeze of the year. The geese are constantly alert. Instinct tells them where their boundaries of safety lie and they adhere to what seems to be a universal code among geese during hunting season: stick together and stay near water.

Flying over the blind on the Platte, the geese see lifelike decoys, figures that flap plastic kite-wings in the wind. They hear the nasal *waack-waack-waack* of their clan members and call out to them to fly along. The decoys insist that here, on this sandy island that parts the river, feeding is good. This place is safe. It is a good time to rest your wings and get your strength back for the long flight south. This dialogue continues until the geese fly on or decide to check out the island, come in for a closer look. But they are still hesitant. They don't dive bomb in an excited rush to land but descend cautiously, letting out the occasional vocalization to make sure their varied but convincing friends below will still respond.

The energy in the blind builds and while some members of the group continue to wheeze away into their goose-callers, others reach behind them for their guns, undo the safety latch, and hold very still. The elders allow the younger kids to aim first. One has never gotten a goose; others have been unlucky so far this season. With the first crack from the barrel, the geese, already gliding in on cupped wings, turn and bank sharply to the left, to the right. They flap and flap, harder than they flapped coming in or soaring overhead. In a mad rush to get as far away from that island as they can they break their landing pattern for a few seconds and their sole aim is to get back up into the wind as fast as they can. Other shots fire, the river rushes by outside. The decoys stand dumbfounded and quiver on their sticks.

The moment passes. The quiet tension dissipates into soft laughter and comments about the near-miss, the one that was headed straight for the island, why so-and-so didn't shoot. Everyone reassumes their favorite seat in the blind. The collapsible camp chair, one on top of the cooler, another stretched out on the fold-away cot. We are hungry. The sun has been up for two hours and it's time to fix breakfast, put another pot of coffee on the stove.

Later in the day when the hunt is over, we gear up in our waders and head back across the Platte. The pull of the river around my legs is strong. My thighs yield to the pressure of the current and I drag each leg with my entire body, leaning

into each step. I hold my arms above my head when the
water gets deep and the small waves lapping against my
chest threaten to fill the waders and float me downstream
like a raft. Yeller, the yellow Labrador retriever, swims
alongside me. The river is cold; slush ice is beginning to
form. I pull my body to shore.

The Platte wanders like a tangled vein through the heart of
the Midwest. It originates in the Rockies of Colorado and
Wyoming, born from the snowpack of high mountain alti-
tudes. What begins as a trickle of a stream grows, gaining
momentum and bulk as it moves east, descending in altitude. In its wake, the river carves out canyons and creates
new life zones as it shifts and extends its path.

This is the most crucial stopover point for migratory
waterfowl on the central flyway. In spring, tens of thousands of Canadian and snow geese and sandhill cranes pass
through the area between the towns of North Platte and
Grand Island, Nebraska. They rely on the abundant food
sources from the surrounding farmlands; islands on the
Platte serve as a safety zone from predators at night.

After the cranes leave the river at daybreak they make
their way to nearby fields. There they feed on leftovers from
last autumn's corn harvest, wandering away from each
other, grazing and browsing for food all day long. In the
evenings, the cranes return to their sanctuary on the sandbars of the Platte.

Harold's grandkids spent the better half of yesterday
trying to save the blind. They dragged iron fence posts to
the island to make a dam, filled in the dissolving banks with

willow branches and brush. The ice broke up two weeks ago and is trapped in a jam down river. The ice travels until it reaches a point where it can go no further. It begins to pile up, the pressure from more ice coming in causing a massive damming of the water flow. All the way to Grand Island and beyond the river is flooding. The river has nowhere to go.

It used to be, when Harold's boys were growing up on the Platte, that the river would disappear come July. It would completely vanish, leaving only a wide sandy gap in the middle of so many cottonwoods and cornfields. Seventy percent of the water rights were doled out to farmers for irrigating crops during the summer months and to electric companies to generate power. With all the pressure and overuse of the river's resources, it would dry up on an annual basis.

Harold took advantage of this freakish phenomenon to prune back overgrowth on the islands. Islands suitable for blinds were referred to as "toeheads," flat islands covered with willows and shrubs. First Harold would hook up a grass mower to the back of an old Willys jeep and drive it across the dry river bed to the toeheads he wanted to build blinds on for the fall hunting season. He would mow down the brush and grass and then he'd bring out a tractor and level off the island with a disk. This served two purposes: it made room for the blind and kept back the encroaching growth of willows and scrub thickets to foster crane habitat.

By mid-September, and sometimes as late as October, word would travel from town that the river was coming. As a family, Harold and his boys would run out to the middle of the dry Platte River bed and wait. Soon enough they would see it; a long, thin trickle, leaving a dark streak in its path. The river did not come in a rush, but crawled down the parched, desolate bed. Its pace was so slow that no one could believe the Platte would eventually be running full, let alone engulfing the islands that once stood at the highest point the entire length of the river.

Twenty years ago you could see the river from the front stoop of the schoolhouse. The cottonwoods have grown to a point where the river is no longer visible but you can still hear it. A hint of it is there hiding behind the trees. Down on the bank, the sand is spongy and dampness is in the air, the ground, on my skin—the river is everywhere. Inside the blind hangs a leather bag filled with ammunition Harold put inside years ago, ready for the next outing on the Platte.

Cara Blessley is a natural history writer and photographer based in Moose, Wyoming. An avid lover of the outdoors and wild places, she has traveled to India, East Africa, the Canadian Arctic, and South America, observing and documenting the natural world. She is the editor of *Polar Dance: Born of the North Wind*, which was awarded Best of Small Press at the 1997 Book Expo America, and the author of *Spirit of the Rockies: The Mountain Lions of Jackson Hole*. She divides her time between the northern Rockies and the mountains of southeastern Arizona.

The Magic of the River Soča

DR. FRANJO ZDRAVIČ

*A peaceful mountain river nurtures
a man and his family.*

I T WAS LATE AUTUMN 1947 WHEN I STRUGGLED
with my old bike up a steep dirt road in northwestern
Slovenia through the Vršič mountain pass and down
into the valley of the Soča River. At that time, shortly after
World War II, a bicycle was the only available means of
transportation; few people had automobiles and trains or
buses were infrequent. The brakes of the bike were not too
reliable, so I had cut a small pine tree and tied it to the frame
in such a way that its branches increased the braking power
and made the descent safer.

My first glimpse of the Soča came unexpectedly, after I
had crossed a small bridge. The river was not as spectacular
as I had expected from the stories I had heard. But only a
little farther down the road I came to a second bridge and
stopped, for now a long stretch of the river was before me.
It was very clear, of a particular blue-green color. Its sound
had an unusual quality, a weaving of many water melodies

and the sound of rocks tumbling in the riverbed. It was fast but there was nothing aggressive about it; its movement was quick and vivid, like a ballerina's. As I stood looking and listening, I was pervaded with a sense of peace and gratitude that Mother Nature had created such beauty.

At this time I was a young doctor on assignment in Bosnia, looking after a great number of young people who were involved in the construction of a railway from Šamac to Sarajevo. I took care of everything from vaccinations to minor and major injuries to diseases that ranged from common colds to typhoid fever. Doctors were scarce, and each of us had many patients, so we worked long hours and had to be available day and night. As the months wore on I had become progressively more tired. I had begun to dream of water, of a clear, cool river somewhere in the mountains. It was the desire to rest beside such a river that drove me to go on an autumn bicycle journey. I had but five days to spend.

From the bridge I continued slowly down the riverside road for about two kilometers, then stopped at a mountain inn called Zlatorog, at the entrance to a village called Trenta. It was a simple but very friendly place, where you immediately knew that you were welcome. There were few tourists, mostly local people, and some hunters. These hunters, all excellent mountain climbers, also take care of the game, mostly chamois, high up in the Julian Alps. They are, in effect, national park rangers in the service of the local government. In the years to come, I would become good friends with most of them.

The sound of water pervaded everything in the valley— the river, its tributaries, the waterfalls on the opposite bank of the river worked like a sleeping pill and a tranquilizer combined. I slept well that night. The next morning I continued my journey down the valley, passing the village of Soča, the small towns of Bovec, Kobarid, and many other pleasant villages as far as Gorica, about 80 kilometers from Bovec. Here the Soča crosses the border into Italy for the last stretch of her journey; at this point she is just a slow-running large river, tired after her long journey, flowing into the Adriatic Sea.

Of course, you cannot understand a river on your first visit, as you cannot understand a human being after only one meeting. To truly know her you must visit her often. I returned to the Soča Valley whenever I could, and was soon joined by my family, friends, and colleagues with their families. In time we acquired an old abandoned farmhouse on the riverbank and spent many hours repairing and renovating it in our spare time. It became our true home, even if we lived most of the time in Ljubljana. Visitors came both from home and from abroad over the years. We even had small medical meetings there, and scientific workshops with prominent scientists from many countries. These meetings were combined with leisure and long walks in the surrounding countryside. The sense of peace and contentment that pervaded the Soča Valley immensely improved our lives and was, in addition, a continual source of energy for coping with hard work and the problems of existence in the post-war period in Slovenia.

Water is deep in our genetic memory, and it has a healing power. We are all instinctively attracted to it, so that when we go on holiday we want a room that looks out on the sea, a lake, or a river. On the Soča, our children, especially, were always eager to go down to the riverbank. They found stones of many shapes and colors there, and piles of firewood brought down by the frequent floods. Sometimes they would go for a quick swim in the ice-cold river (at most 8 degrees centi-

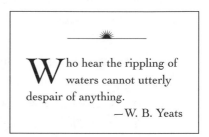

Who hear the rippling of waters cannot utterly despair of anything.

—W. B. Yeats

grade), then run back to warm themselves by the fire we kept going most of the time in a big outdoor fireplace.

I came to think of our exceptional river as a reflection of the many phases of human life. She starts in the depths of snow-covered high mountains and seems to be projected by some hidden force down the steep riverbed through narrow passages, deep canyons, over precipices. When squeezed too much, she reacts by loud sounds of distress, like a human being. When her path becomes easier, her sound changes to a pleasant murmur, which diminishes as she moves through the flatland in the last stretch of her journey. Then merging with the Adriatic Sea, and through it, with all the oceans of the world, the Soča River gets her deserved rest.

We learned to know the Soča in all her changes through the seasons, but not until my son grew up and became a filmmaker and sound artist did our river's underwater life become visible to us, through his work. He recorded the river's journey, using special underwater equipment, creating a film-poem of great beauty. This is a particular comfort for me, for this river may not be the same in the future, unless humanity ceases its course of self-destruction.

The Soča should remain a river for thinking and dreaming and enjoying the company of friends, and also for promoting constructive work and good decisions. Her banks are the right place to make a bonfire for special celebrations and pay respect to the gods. Or to light a candle and weep for those beloved persons who are no more.

I had a dream the other night. When my journey here comes to the end it would be nice to find on the other side, as I did in my dream, a river like the Soča. And maybe even a nice little white dog like the one who was my companion for many years in our wanderings along the Soča.

---∞∞∞---

Dr. Franjo Zdravič was a surgeon and professor of reconstructive surgery and burns. He was head of the Department of Plastic Surgery and Burns at the Medical Center in Ljubljana, Slovenia, for many years. During his career, he shared his medical expertise with many developing countries, including Algeria, Laos, and Kuwait. He died in December, 1999.

Headwaters

REBECCA LAWTON

*Following in the footsteps of Meriwether Lewis,
the author struggles to adjust to life "off the river."*

REVISITING MY FIRST TRIP TO THE MISSOURI
Breaks country means going back twenty years to
Indian Summer in northern Utah. Three friends
and I had just finished warehousing our rafting gear after a
season of white-water guiding. The cottonwoods shivered
amber in cool drafts off the Uintas, and Andy, Debbie,
Miles, and I knew we had to move fast if we wanted to head
north. We stuffed our river bags into Miles's dark-green
Pinto station wagon to drive to Montana. We'd heard of a
stretch of the Missouri River that runs more than 150 miles
between the town of Fort Benton and the Fort Peck reservoir. We knew little of the river, except that part of it winds
through the Breaks, a high-plains badlands near the Canadian
border. And we knew that Meriwether Lewis and William
Clark had traveled *up* the river, which is not much for
rapids—but who needed white water anyway? We'd been
running big rapids all summer for many seasons. Anyway,

we had maps and the name of a canoe rental outfit. These were enough. We made Fort Benton our destination.

We drove straight through for a day and a night, stopping to sleep for only a few hours near a high pass in the Yellowstone. On the second day, we reached the town of Three Forks, Montana, where we detoured to the Missouri Headwaters State Park. We pulled in on a dirt entrance road that led to a day-use parking lot near a river. Although I expected to see your classic headwaters, a tiny spring issuing from the earth amid mossy boulders and maidenhair fern, we found instead a quiet confluence in an open, sunny plain with grasses long since turned brown by summer heat. There the Jefferson, Gallatin, and Madison Rivers flow together to form the Missouri. The interpretive signs said that Lewis and Clark, with their band of discoverers, arrived at Three Forks in July 1805. They'd already traveled up the Missouri nearly 3,000 miles from St. Louis, wintering over along the way in present-day North Dakota. When they came to the Three Forks confluence, they recognized it as the river's headwaters: all forks measured nearly 90 yards wide, so to call any one the Missouri would have

Lewis and Clark were sent by Thomas Jefferson to find the fabled "Northwest Passage," the link between the Great Lakes and the Pacific, sought since the time of Columbus. In earlier times river exploration was eagerly followed by the public in periodicals and lecture series, with much the same enthusiasm that later glued people to their television sets to watch moon landings and space walks.

—PM

been to give it "a preference wich its size dose not warrant as it is not larger than the other." After naming the streams and scrambling for a few days to figure out which stream to pursue farther west, the party continued up the Jefferson toward the Continental Divide.

We piled back into the Pinto and proceeded on toward Fort Benton, where we would provision our trip, rent two canoes, arrange a shuttle, and launch the next morning after breakfast. Before all this, though, we stopped at the Great Falls. We'd scoffed at reports that called it unrunnable. Of course Lewis and Clark had to portage around it—they were headed upstream. And of course the portage lasted for weeks—they were pulling their boats and supplies overland. But that was nearly two centuries before. In 1979, when boatmen could navigate just about anything in neoprene rafts, we wondered how great Great Falls could be.

Imagine our surprise to see a formidable set of cascades at Great Falls, not Niagara maybe, but fully spanning the river.

"You couldn't run this in a million years," I said.

The fall's rock ledges rose like giant stair-steps in the riverbed. Muddy water frothed and crashed over them.

"Jeez," said Miles. "Maybe Lewis and Clark were badderass guys than we thought."

To run the falls looked hopeless, but to portage them heroic. We stood in silence, humbled in the shadows of giants. We remembered what we had forgotten: that immense spirits precede us—always—when we travel on rivers.

I have an affinity for Meriwether Lewis. Perhaps not because he was handsome, accomplished, and competent, which history says he was, but because of his mental illness. Not many of our national heroes have taken their own lives, but Lewis did. He was believed to have been prone to depression that in the end overwhelmed him. So I empathize greatly—I too fight the demon depression, although it's a beast that seems smaller than Lewis's.

His biographer Stephen Ambrose has said that Lewis "pretty clearly was" manic-depressive, meaning that he dealt with surges of euphoria and invincibility alternating with waves of nausea and utter helplessness. We have it on Thomas Jefferson's own authority than Lewis fell into "sensible depressions of the mind" that Jefferson believed had genetic roots: "Knowing their constitutional source, I estimated their course by what I had seen in the family." While Lewis made his westward journey, though, he seemed fine—in fact, Ambrose has pointed out that neither Clark nor the enlisted men made note in their journals of any strange behaviors on the part of Lewis. Lewis neglected his own very important journal writing from September 1805 to January 1806, speculatively because of depression, but he never failed the expedition. Instead he conducted himself nearly flawlessly for the entire 8,000-mile journey by river, on horseback, and on foot. In his musings after Lewis's death, Jefferson wrote that the strenuous daily activity and decision-making of the expedition must have put off Lewis's usually troubled mind.

I'm no expert on manic-depressive disorders, but I have studied depression in general. In short, it's caused by brain chemistry out of balance. Low levels of the neurotransmitters serotonin, dopamine, and norepinephrine bring on feel-

ings of worthlessness, low energy, and fatigue. We'll probably never know what Lewis's specific brain chemistry was,
but I often wonder if it could have been managed by proper treatment. A modern course of drug therapy, psychother-
apy, and diet monitoring, had it been available, might have
eased his agony. I don't know, but I do know what depression feels like, and when I meditate on Lewis, his suffering
feels familiar. I'm with him as he reflects in a funk on his
failures at age thirty-one, writing that he had "as yet done
but little, very little indeed" in his life (although he had just
successfully reached the Continental Divide, discovered the
Missouri headwaters, met peacefully with the Shoshones,
and traded for all the
horses he needed to con-
tinue west). I shiver with
empathy as he writes des-
perately of his failed
attempts to marry. I ago-
nize over his struggle the
night he took his life—his
pacing restlessness as he
prayed that Clark would
come, his shouting argu-
ments with himself, his emotional end. His final hour, which
must have felt so private, has become shared posthumously.
With me, with thousands of others.

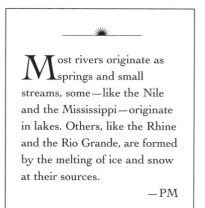

Most rivers originate as
springs and small
streams, some—like the Nile
and the Mississippi—originate
in lakes. Others, like the Rhine
and the Rio Grande, are formed
by the melting of ice and snow
at their sources.

—PM

News of our Missouri expedition preceded us down the
river. During the day farmers and ranchers wandered to the
shore to say hello. In the evenings they politely left us alone.
River residents treated us well, like honored guests, offer-

ing fresh drinking water and vegetables pulled up from late
summer gardens.

It's big country, and we were moving fast. We discovered
that we could rig sails by stringing ponchos between paddle
shafts held vertically on each canoe. Because the river flows
east in a country of prevailing west winds, we sailed 15, 20,
and 25 miles a day downstream on the same winds that
would have blown us upstream on our home rivers across
the Divide. We weren't in a hurry, but with the going so
easy we couldn't help sailing as far as the winds would take
us.

Such stark landscape. As Andy put it, "It looks like we're
on the moon." Not so much the White Cliffs area, with its rock
walls and spires that resemble the canyons of our home rivers,
but the Missouri Breaks, the downstream part of the run. The
badlands country has soft and sloping hills with little runs of
juniper stringing up gullies. But the folds of the gullies lie
mostly hidden to the boater looking downstream. As we sailed
through the Breaks, we gazed out at mile after mile of sere
grassland. And the bald, lunar-like surface seemed to curve
away from sight with the arching surface of the earth. At night
I pondered Andy's words as a slip of crescent moon sank
between two cottonwoods, the only large trees for miles.

But after dark, black moods gripped me. I grappled with
an internal dialogue I'd grown so used to during bouts of
depression. What do I do in the winter? Who will I be once
I'm off the river? Some evenings the melancholy came on
right after dinner, and I slipped into silences.

Debbie asked me about it. I replied, "I'm feeling an end-
of-season gloom."

"Yeah," she said. "The back-to-the-real-world blues."

"You too?"

"I've had it before. Always in September."

By morning each day, though, any storms in my mind had cleared. They seemed to be gone by the time we packed up the canoes in the morning. And they stayed away all day. They didn't plague me as I walked by the river, or rigged our poncho sails, or cleaned up camp in the crisp twilight before bedtime.

In the months leading to his suicide, Lewis abused himself badly with drink and drugs and couldn't focus on his responsibilities. His depression seemed to be made worse by his depraved lifestyle and inactivity. Had he been engaged in the "constant exertion" that Jefferson knew calmed him, could Lewis have staved off his "hypochondria"? Could he have functioned well again, married happily, written and published his account of the journey to riches and acclaim? Jefferson blames the "sedentary occupations" set before Lewis after the expedition for the return of his troubles. I don't dispute Jefferson's diagnosis, but I believe that Lewis needed the river itself as much as he needed the challenge of his explorations. Boating on a gentle river has been shown to boost serotonin levels in the brain. Rafting white water supposedly elevates dopamine and norepinephrine. Whether moving up the Missouri or down, or wandering on foot in search of new discoveries, Lewis was never far from moving water, an experience that I believe helped keep him in chemical balance for as long as it lasted.

None of us who traveled on the Missouri likes to sleep in tents, so each night we lay out in sleeping bags under the stars. By morning a blanket of dew covered our bags. The dew invaded camp as a silent intruder, waiting until the deep hours to steal over us. Normally we rested snug in our bags, immune to any chill. But being the restless one in the group, often visited by nagging spirits after midnight, I awakened one night toward the end of the trip during the dewy hours and felt the cold.

My strategy at such times is to sit up and meditate. I pull my waterproof river bag close for a backrest and wrap up in my sleeping bag. The practice settles my mind, transforming sad feelings to a blank weariness that eases me back to sleep. As I sat in the dark of that night on the Missouri, my mind relaxing, I felt the calm that hung in the air. The coyotes had long since stopped howling for the night—in fact, the air sounded so still I could have believed they never had wailed. Andy, Debbie, and Miles slept on, unmoving lumps visible under a waxing moon. Moonset was still a short time off, and I decided to walk the river. I dressed in several layers while still in my bag and slipped out into the night.

Once up, I followed the riverbank. The moon illuminated the ground well enough to light my way along the water, which shone with a muted glow. The incised gullies of the Breaks rose and fell across the river, casting shadows. I moved upstream, following a sweet, familiar scent I'd picked up on the wind. The breeze smelled of ripening rose hips. I stopped, transfixed by this symbol of the high country where the wild roses grow with other untamed things. If the rose hips really were there, ripening on uplands, perhaps a group of explorers laboring slowly upstream after months on the hot plains in 1805 had also caught their scent. If so, along with the river growing clearer nearer to its source and the feel of fall hanging in the air, the rose hips would have conveyed great promise and the nearness of mountains.

The breeze blew colder and I shivered. I decided to run back to camp. The moon was sinking fast and would leave me in utter darkness in big country.

Packing up the canoes in the morning helped my mental state, as did focusing on general camp activities such as cooking and washing. While doing chores, my internal chatter ceased. My thoughts turned to the Missouri, and my mind filled with the simple tasks to be accomplished to proceed down the river. The days teemed with places and their names: Lundy Ranch. Virgelle Ferry. Coal Banks Landing. Marias River. Judith River. Clark named the Judith for his cousin Julia Hancock, whom he later married. Lewis named the Marias for his cousin Maria Wood and the "pure celestial virtues and amiable qualifications of that lovely fair one." Perhaps he wished to wed his cousin, too, but Lewis was not to marry in his short life.

While he was on the Missouri, Lewis did not fail. Although he didn't find an all-water route to the Pacific, it was only because it did not exist. If such a route had been anywhere within 3,000 miles, Lewis would have found it. He did explore the river's headwaters, of course, the great source of the river. Not only the confluence of young streams at Three Forks, but the place in the mountains where the waters begin. The journey to the source absorbed him completely, keeping him functionally healthy for two and a half years. It brought him together with a corps of discoverers who trusted him thoroughly, and it joined his name for all time with Clark's. In the great-hearted middle of his journey, Lewis pledged himself "to live for *mankind*, as I have heretofore lived for *myself*." He couldn't have appreciated at the time just how many lives he would affect, but anyone who knows rivers and the American West knows Lewis. Through his strenuous explorations, he found a point of origin, the place where we inner-are.

The rivers are our brothers. They quench our thirst. The rivers carry our canoes, feed our children. If we sell you our land, you must remember, and teach your children, that the rivers are our brothers, and yours, and you must henceforth give the rivers the kindness you would give any brother.

— Suquamish Chief Seattle (1854)

For all the wild country we were accustomed to in our occupations as river guides, the Missouri Breaks counted among some of the most remote. The northern prairies stretched in all directions, rolling up to vast Canada less than 100 miles north. The coyotes we heard sang in packs that sounded big and diverse. Beavers worked at night, tail-slapping the water as we drifted off to sleep. Over everything arched a bowl of stars wider than we'd ever seen. Orion stood among the constellations, one obvious sign that we'd shifted seasons and moved under a winter sky. Sometimes I lay awake pondering the same sky Lewis measured with his sextant in 1805.

In my fits of wakefulness, I contemplated reaching the end of our time on the Missouri and the prospect of returning to the real world. On the trip's last night, I tossed and turned again, sat up to meditate once more, and focused on the darkness inside my eyelids. Time passed and I felt calmer. Soon I zipped out of my bag and rose to find drinking water.

A light shone in camp. Andy and Debbie had cleared the kitchen table. They sat on ammo boxes on either side of it, playing cards in the glow of Andy's candle lantern. I gravitated toward the light like a lured insect.

"Join the club," said Andy. "No doubt Miles will be arriving soon, too."

Barely twenty yards away, Miles rolled over and propped up on an elbow. "What're you playing?" he asked.

"Hearts," said Debbie. "The cure for restlessness."

"Deal me in," said Miles.

"Me, too," I said, pulling up my ammo box.

We played for hours, not talking about the coming winter. We'd left the river before, we could do it again. How hard could it be, anyway, to return to civilization?

Rebecca Lawton was among the first female river guides in California, Utah, Idaho, and Arizona, spending ten of her fourteen seasons in Grand Canyon. She has published short stories and essays about river life in numerous anthologies and small journals. "Headwaters" is part of a nonfiction collection-in-progress titled *How to Read a River*.

River of Hope

LORI UDALL

Thousands of Indian villagers vow to drown themselves in the rising waters of a sacred river.

T HE FIRST TIME I TRAVELED TO MANIBELI village, it was the dry season. The Narmada River was quite low, and I stood on top of the hill where the village began and looked down across the brown, dry landscape to some wooden boats near the river's edge. I sat in front of one of the mud and bamboo huts nestled in the hillside and watched the young women in their bright pink and yellow saris walking down the barren hill with copper jugs on their heads to get water from the river. It was just a sleepy tribal village then. At night, you could see the bright lights from the construction site of the Sardar Sarovar dam, the project that would eventually result in the partial submergence of the village. The massive lights in the distant skies were a foreboding invasion into such a tranquil existence, a village where electricity was unknown.

On this trip, I had come to Manibeli to meet and travel with Medha Patkar, a grassroots activist who was opposed

to the dam and was working with the villagers who were
going to be forcibly resettled. It was a long morning trip in
a taxi from Baroda in Gujarat state, past the gigantic dam
site, across the Narmada River in a long wooden tribal
canoe, and then a short hike up the hill to Manibeli. It was
late June of 1993, and the beginning of the monsoon season. As I hiked up the hill I noticed three brown tents on a
bluff opposite the village. Men in light brown uniforms
were milling about or sitting at a table. Some of them had
guns and long nightsticks hanging from their belts.

"What are they doing here?" I asked Sanjay, an activist
who had come to meet me at the river.

"The police have stationed here temporarily for the monsoon. The officials are afraid people will drown when the
river swells and they say they are here to save us from ourselves," he explained, with a trace of irony in his voice. "It's
brought a lot of tension to village life. They're afraid there
will be a police invasion like last year."

In 1991, Manibeli became the center of the grassroots
struggle against the dam, and since then had become a
symbol of the resistance to the project. Villagers from the
surrounding area and Manibeli residents had taken a vow
to drown rather than move. In the Gandhian tradition of
nonviolent noncooperation, they had staged a protest they
called a *satyagraha*. During the monsoon, while the waters
rose from the partly constructed dam, the local villagers
would stay in Manibeli watching the water rise higher and
closer to their huts. Activists and supporters from as far
away Bombay and Delhi had also come to join the *satyagraha*. In the Spring of 1992, police and government offi-

cials had invaded Manibeli to "help" dismantle the homes of some villagers who had agreed under pressure to move to Gujarat. But it was clearly an act of intimidation. During the invasion, there were clashes between the police and the tribals who were refusing to go. A camp of over 100 police had been set up in the village during that monsoon season.

As we climbed the last hill to Manibeli we walked under a metal sign that formed an arch over the trail. The message was in Hindi. "It says 'only educators and social workers may enter,'" explained Sanjay, letting out a laugh. "It's a signal Manibeli won't cooperate with the officials or police who want to make them move. The resettlement officials are not welcome here anymore."

We reached Manibeli and Sanjay led me to a large thatched hut where Medha was holding a meeting. There was a large crowd of women standing outside. Medha barely acknowledged me as I entered and went on speaking to a room filled with tribal men. Medha was almost in the center of the hut, with men completely surrounding her. Medha is a petite Indian women with a round, pretty face and piercing brown eyes. She wore her black hair in a long braid down her back; her burgundy sari tucked under her legs. A social worker, originally from Bombay, Medha had been living and working in the villages for years. It seemed the tribals had accepted her as one of their own.

There were no other women in the room. The tribal men, Sanjay told me, were from many neighboring villages, some were village chiefs. Some were dressed in traditional clothes with a *lunghi* and turban. Some had bows and arrows. Others wore a combination of traditional and modern attire such as western pants and shirts with a turban. I looked around the room and could see the women outside were peering through the slats of the bamboo wall, listening intently to the discussion inside. I sat near the door with Sanjay so he could translate for me. Medha was speaking in Marathi, the language of Maharashtra State, which most of the tribals knew, in addition to their own languages. Sanjay explained they were talking about immunizations that were available to the tribals and which clinics they should go to.

Medha is known for holding long, long meetings and this one was no exception. By late afternoon, the meeting was still in full swing, with breaks for singing. When they started talking about the dam project and the upcoming monsoon *Satyagraha*, the tone of meeting changed, and there were dramatic charged statements from a few elder men waving their arms angrily, who stood up in the center of the hut. Then one man started a chant:

Koi nahi hatega, bandh nahi banega.
No one will move, the dam will not be built.

After several hours, I slipped out the door and walked along the hill looking down at the river. The river was quite high, even for the early monsoon. Narmada is a river that means many things to the people along her banks. It is one of the holiest rivers in India. It is said that all sins are washed away by bathing once in the Ganges, three times in the Saraswati, but that a mere look at the Narmada absolves one's sin completely. Many a pilgrim in search of enlightenment had passed this place on a 1,600-mile spiritual journey called a *parikrama*. The *parikrama* course starts at the sea and follows the river to its source and returns on the opposite side. The journey is said to take a total of three years, three months and three days. The pilgrims visit 142 sacred spots, some which are ancient temples or ruins. The pilgrims are a familiar site to villagers here, who often offer them a meal or shelter for the night.

In many parts of the world rivers are referred to as "mothers": Narmadai, "Mother Narmada"; the Volga is Mat' Rodnaya, "Mother of the Land." The Thai word for river, *mae nan*, translates literally as "mother water." Rivers have often been linked with divinities, especially female ones. In ancient Egypt, the floods of the Nile were considered the tears of the goddess Isis. Ireland's River Boyne, which is overlooked by the island's most impressive prehistoric burial sites, was worshipped as a goddess by Celtic tribes.

—Patrick McCully,
Silenced Rivers

Like all of the villages on the banks of the Narmada, in Manibeli, there is an intrinsic connection with the river. The river is a vital part of the tribal's life and culture. The river provides irrigation for rice paddies, fish, drinking water, water for bathing and washing clothes, and transportation. It is also the source of many myths and legends, some which have been buried with the past or died with tribes that had only an oral culture. Narmada means "giver of merriment." Researchers have uncovered over thirty other names for the Narmada, including Karabha (one who radiates happiness),

Vipapa (without sin), and Maharnava (survivor of world destruction). The Bhils and Bhilalas, the tribal groups in the submergence regions of the dam, hold the Narmada in deep reverence, often referring to the "Goddess Narmada" or simply "Ma" which means mother. As they share the river, they also share other resources: the agricultural land, the forest from which they gather fruits, herbs, roots and medicinal plants; and the common grazing land for their cattle.

I walked into the Shoolpaneswar Temple, which I had passed earlier while coming in to the village. The temple is one in a series of ancient structures along the river that serve as pilgrim sites, worship places, or just a spot for a peaceful night's rest. Once when I had been in Manibeli before, I met a priest who had been living there. As I wandered in this time, it seemed deserted. There was no longer a ceiling, (or maybe there never been one), but most of the four crumbling walls and various icons suggested a once-majestic place. I walked around to the front of the temple where an arched stone doorway looked out toward the river. Framed in the doorway were the earthy brown hills, feeding into the blue-brown of the river, the hills on the river's other side, and then the greying sky. I sat on the steps under the arch, and looked at the river. It wasn't raining but the valley before me was becoming misty. A deep stillness settled over the valley, as the timelessness of the place enveloped me.

As it grew darker, I walked back to the bamboo hut. People were milling around outside, and it seemed that the meeting was breaking up. Medha came out the door, and greeted me. "So, welcome to India and Manibeli. You've been away too long." I thought we would get some time to talk and plan our itinerary through the villages along the river, but she told me she had a hold a meeting with the women. I followed her out to a stone wall in the back of the village and sat with her among ten other women. Ostensibly, the meeting had been set up to discuss some personal problems of some of the women, but the conversation gravitated to resettlement. I sat next to Medha who translated for me. "The women have much better ideas than the men." she whispered, as she leaned over closer to me.

"Why can't you just let them come in to the main meeting?" I asked.

"I imagine eventually they will be allowed. But I can't disrupt their cultural norms. I have suggested it lightly, but there was no response. Women actually do most of the work, but the men are the decision makers. Traditionally, when decisions are made for the community, it's the men who do it. It's only been recently that the women have participated in some of the marches, so I see that as encouraging," she explained. The women were involved in an intense discussion. I watched their faces, as the shadows from the evening light darkened their images and brilliant saris.

Moving is the worst thing you can do to a people, next to killing them, I had read once in a report of a renowned anthropologist who had worked on many involuntary resettlement schemes caused by large-scale development. As I listened to the women speak with such emotion, I realized the tribals knew that instinctively, even if they hadn't already heard back from the villagers that had been forced to move to unliveable resettlement shacks in the neighboring state of

Gujarat. Their tie to the river and the land was too deep and inextricable to forfeit and there was no moving now...even if it meant death or drowning.

After the women's meeting broke up, several of the men came up to Medha excitedly, and circled her, all talking at the same time. I saw Medha let out a big smile and nod her head in agreement. "They want to go confront the police in their tents," she said as tears welled up in her eyes. "They're becoming so courageous. Many of them were beaten up last year by police."

Medha and I followed the group of tribals down the trail leading to the river until we reached the metal arch. Under the arch, the men gathered in a close knit circle, as though to protect themselves. Then they started singing, and later chanting. The more chants they did the louder and more boisterous they became, as though they drew strength from the sound of each other. I watched them, yelling with glee at the police tent across the gulch, so proud and defiant. Their fists were in the air, and they were jumping up and down. Medha was laughing and joining the chants:

> *Doobenge par hatenge nabin.*
> *Hamare gaon mein hamara raj.*
> We will drown, but not move.
> Our villages, our rule.

Some project promoters call the Narmada "the river of hope" because of the claimed irrigation and drinking water benefits to wealthy farmers and villagers in the command area. As a witness to that night, the words "river of hope" held a much different meaning for me. The Narmada had become a symbol and source of hope for the many lives of men and women who came together to save the river and themselves from someone else's idea of "development." And here they stood, a tribal group on the fringes of Indian society, whose impending displacement and fate was being repeated over and over again in tribal communities throughout India as a result of large-scale development projects. Hundreds of thousands like these people standing before me had already been displaced in other projects, and left with nothing, migrating to the slums in Bombay or Delhi. But this group, tonight, on the banks of the Narmada was responding and saying: *No. You cannot do this to us. We won't go.*

As they shouted the chants over and over, I was slowly mesmerized by the sound of their voices. The chants echoed across the gulch, as a misty rain started coming down. There was only silence from the police tent, the sight of it lost in the blackness of the night. But the words of the tribals floated past the tent, on down the hill to the river, mixed with the Narmada's song and danced out farther into the night.

<hr>

Lori Udall has worked on international environmental and human rights issues for fifteen years. She writes poetry and literary essays, and her work has appeared in *Sidewalks, Artisan, Phoebe, The Ecologist,* and *Multinational Monitor.*

Drought

BARRY LOPEZ

*When a river sings its swan song,
sometimes dancing is the only
thing to do.*

[handwritten: meaning?]

[handwritten: some one died → people inquiring]

I AWOKE ONE NIGHT AND THOUGHT I HEARD
rain — it was the dry needles of fir trees falling on the
roof. Men with an intolerable air of condolence have
appeared, as though drawn by the smell of death, dressed
comfortably, speaking a manipulated tongue, terminally
evil. They have inquired into the purchase of our homes.
And reporters come and go, outraged over the absence of
brown trout, which have never been here. The river like
some great whale lies dying in the forest.

In the years we have been here I have trained myself to
listen to the river, not in the belief that I could understand
what it said, but only from one day to the next know its fate.
The river's language arose principally from two facts: the
slightest change in its depth brought it into contact with a
different portion of the stones along its edges and the rocks
and boulders midstream that lay in its way, and so changed
its tone; and although its movement around one object may

[handwritten: "read the river"]

changing river

seem uniform at any one time it is in fact changeable. Added
to these major variations are the landings of innumerable
insects on its surface, the breaking of its waters by fish, the
falling into it of leaves and twigs, the slooshing of raccoons,
the footfalls of deer; ultimately these are only commentary
on the river's endless reading of the surface of the earth over
which it flows.

It was in this way that I learned before anyone else of the
coming drought. Day after day as the river fell by impercepti-
ble increments its song changed, notes came that were
unknown to me. I mentioned this to no one, but each morning
when I awoke I went immediately to the river's edge and listened. It was as though I could hear the sound rain begins to
make in a country where it is not going to come for a long time.

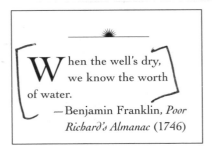

W hen the well's dry,
we know the worth
of water.
   —Benjamin Franklin, *Poor
Richard's Almanac* (1746)

As the water fell, how-
ever, nothing unexpected
was uncovered, although
the effect of standing in
areas once buried beneath
the roar of the river's current was unsettling. I
found only one made
object, a wheel, the kind
you find on the back of a child's tricycle. But I didn't look as
closely as the others. The wailing of the river over its last
stones was difficult to bear, yet it was this that drew me back
each day, as one visits those dying hopelessly in a hospital
room. During those few hours each morning I would catch
stranded fish barehanded in shallow pools and release them
where the river still flowed. The bleaching of algae once

waving green underwater to white; river stones once cool
now hot to the touch and dry; spider webs stretched where
there had been salmon eggs; snakes where there had been
trout—it was as though the river had been abandoned.

During those summer days, absorbed with the death of
the river and irritated at the irreverent humor of weather
forecasters in distant cities, I retreated into a state of isola-
tion. I fasted and abstained as much as I felt appropriate
from water. These were only gestures, of course, but even
as a boy I knew a gesture might mean life or death and I
believed the universe was similarly triggered.

From this point on, the song that came out of the river
did not bother me as much. I sat out of the way of the
pounding sun, in dark rocks shaded by the overhanging
branches of alders along the bank. Their dry leaves, stirred
by the breeze, fell brittle and pale around me. I slept on the
bank regularly now. I would say very simple prayers in the
evening, only an expression of camaraderie, stretching my
fingers gently into the darkness toward the inchoate source
of the river's strangulation. I did not beg. There was a
power to dying, and it should be done with grace. I was
only making a gesture on the shore, a speck in the steep,
brutal dryness of the valley by a dying river.

In moments of great depression, of an unfathomable
compassion in myself, I would make the agonized and tentative movements of a dance, like a long-legged bird. I
would exhort the river.

What death we saw. Garter snake stiff as a twig in the
rocks. Trees (young ones, too young) crying out in the
night, shuddering, dropping all their leaves. Farther from

the river, birds falling dead in thickets, animals dead on the
paths, their hands stiffened in gestures of bewilderment and
beseeching; the color gone out of the eyes of any creature
you met, for whom, out of respect, you would step off the
path to allow to pass.

Where a trickle of water still flowed there was an atmos-
phere of truce, more dangerous than one might imagine. As
deer and coyote sipped from the same tiny pool they abro-
gated their agreement, and the deer contemplated the loss of
the coyote as he would the loss of a friend; for the enemy,
like the friend, made you strong. I was alert for such moments, for they were augury, but I was as wary of them as
of any lesson learned in death.

One moonlit evening I dreamed of a certain fish. The
fish was gray-green against light-colored stones at the bottom of a deep pool, breathing a slow, unperturbed breathing, the largest fish I had ever imagined living in the river.
The sparkling of the water around him and the sound of it
cascading over the creek bed made me weak and I awoke
suddenly, convulsed. I knew the fish. I knew the place. I set
out immediately.

The dry riverbed was only a clatter of teetering stones
now, ricocheting off my feet as I passed, bone weary, feeling disarmed by hunger, by the dimness of the night and by
the irrefutable wisdom and utter foolishness of what I was
doing. As I drew near the mouth of the creek the fish began
to loom larger and larger and I could feel—as though my
hands were extended to a piece of cloth flapping in the
darkness—both the hope and the futility of such acts.

I found the spot where the creek came in and went up it.

I had seen the fish once in a deep pool below a rapids where
he had fed himself too well and grown too large to escape.
There was a flow of night air coming down the creek bed,
rattling dry leaves. In the faint moonlight a thousand harle-
quin beetles suddenly settled on my clothing and I knew
how close I was to a loss of conviction, to rage, to hurling
what beliefs I had like a handful of pebbles into the bushes.

The beetles clung to the cloth, moved through my hair,
came into the cups of my hands as I walked, and as suddenly were gone, and the area I stood in was familiar, the
fish before me. The rapids were gone. The pool had become
a pit. In its lowest depression the huge fish lay motionless,
but for the faint lifting of a gill cover. I climbed down to him
and wrapped him in my shirt, soaked in the pool. I had
expected, I think, a fight, to be punched in that pit by the
fish who lay in my arms now like a cold lung.

Climbing out of there, stopping wherever I could to put
his head under in some miserable pool, hurrying, I came to
the river and the last trickle of water, where I released him
without ceremony.

I knew, as I had known in the dream, the danger I was
in but I knew, too, that without such an act of self-assertion
no act of humility had meaning.

By now the river was only a whisper. I stood at the indis-
tinct edge and exhorted what lay beyond the river, which
now seemed more real than the river itself. With no more
strength than there is in a bundle of sticks I tried to dance,
to dance the dance of the long-legged birds who lived in the
shallows. I danced it because I could not think of anything
more beautiful.

why capitalized?

animals speaking...?

The turning came during the first days of winter. Lynx came down from the north to what was left of the river. Deer were with him. And from some other direction Raccoon and Porcupine. And from downriver Weasel and White-footed Mouse, and from above Blue Heron and Goshawk. Badger came up out of the ground with Mole. They stood near me in staring silence and I was afraid to move. Finally Blue Heron spoke: "We were the first people here. We gave away all the ways of living. Now no one remembers how to live anymore, so the river is drying up. Before we could ask for rain there had to be someone to do something completely selfless, with no hope of success. You went after that fish, and then at the end you were trying to dance. A person cannot be afraid of being foolish. For everything, every gesture, is sacred.

"Now, stand up and learn this dance. It is going to rain."

We danced together on the bank. And the songs we danced to were the river songs I remembered from long ago. We danced until I could not understand the words but only the sounds, and the sounds were unmistakably the sound rain makes when it is getting ready to come into a country.

rain dance

I awoke in harsh light one morning, moved back into the trees and fell asleep again. I awoke later to what I thought were fir needles falling on my cheeks but these were drops of rain. *ref first sentence*

It rained for weeks. Not hard, but steadily. The river came back easily. There were no floods. People said it was a blessing. They offered explanations enough. Backs were clapped, reputations lost and made, the seeds of future argument and betrayal sown, wounds suffered and allowed, pride displayed. It was no different from any other birth but for a lack of joy and, for that, stranger than anything you can imagine, inhuman and presumptuous. But people go their way, and with reason; and the hardness for some is all but unfathomable, and so begs forgiveness. Everyone has to learn how to die, that song, that dance, alone and in time.

The river has come back to fit between its banks. To stick your hands into the river is to feel the cords that bind the earth together in one piece. The sound of it at a distance is like wild horses in a canyon, going sure-footed away from the smell of a cougar come to them faintly on the wind.

Barry Lopez is a contributing editor to *Harper's* and *North American Review*, and has received an Award in Literature from the American Academy and Institute of Arts and Letters, the American Book Award, and the John Burroughs Medal, among other honors. He is the author of *Arctic Dreams*, *Of Wolves and Men*, *Crossing Open Ground* and *Desert Notes: Reflections in the Eye of a Raven; River Notes: The Dance of Herons*, from which this story was excerpted. He lives in rural Oregon.

River Towns

WILLIAM LEAST HEAT-MOON

Riverscapes from a 5,000-mile watery journey from sea to shining sea.

THE MISSISSIPPI AT STE. GENEVIEVE WAS 10 feet above flood stage and still rising, and we'd heard that the Missouri, only 75 miles away, would crest about the time we reached it, a concern because the Corps of Engineers might "shut down the river"—not its flow but navigation on it. I'd become confident *Nikawa* could handle the flood, but would the necessity of catching the spring rise in the Far West allow us to accommodate regulations 2,000 miles east?

As I oiled the engines and refueled, I talked with a man who had arrived a couple of days earlier from Florida, on his way to Chicago in a 50-foot motor yacht, a boat bigger than its length alone suggests. He had used 450 gallons of diesel to run the 122 miles from Cairo to Ste. Genevieve, at a cost of 700 dollars. He said, "That damn current ate my lunch." I told him we'd come almost 2,000 miles from the Atlantic Ocean on only a third more than that. "Sure," he said, "but you're in a toy." The eye of the beholder: I'd considered boats like his the toys. The weather was about to turn again, and already the wind was reaching 20 miles an hour, but it was generally blowing upriver to give us a push against the current. Every few miles we had to stop and raise the motors to clear the props of drift while *Nikawa*, indeed, bounced like a toy. We took one hard hit that knocked off a piece of propeller first damaged in Lake Chautauqua, but it wasn't enough to stop us. When people asked, as they often did, "Is it fun?" I remembered the perpetual threats, a sure depressant of that so American thing called fun. I thought, Toys are fun—cross-country river trips are something the hell else.

Above the Ste. Genevieve ferry, rocky bluffs come down to the river along the Missouri shore, and where quarries have not destroyed them, the cliffs are lovely, seated in maples and cottonwoods, topped with cedars and hickories. On the Illinois side a long line of levees protected a bottom cropland of grains and legumes. For more than a thousand miles, the Mississippi from above St. Louis to below New Orleans runs as an engineered conduit with either levees or bluffs penning the river, a circumstance that makes the roll of a flood faster, deeper, meaner. Like the Missouri, the Mississippi can no longer significantly spread high water full of slit into lowlands to diffuse the flow and enrich the soil. Of the hundreds of uses of this river, the Army Corps of Engineers for years tried to operate it for only one—barge navigation. The old steamboats, of course, hauled freight and people when the Mississippi was still nearly a wild river, but then those boats and cargoes were smaller; today, shipping companies speak only about economies of scale, and well they can, since on the broad Mississippi a full fifteen-barge tow can carry as much as 870 semi trucks.

The river has been not just caged, it has also undergone considerable straightening—channelizing—another element adding to the severity of a modern flood. And sometimes the Father of Waters takes things into his own hands. Mark Twain wrote in *Life on the Mississippi*:

> In the space of one hundred and seventy-six years the Lower Mississippi has shortened itself two hundred and forty-two miles. That is an average of a trifle over one mile and a third per year. Therefore, any calm person, who is not blind or idiotic, can see that in the Old Oolitic Silurian Period, just a million years ago next November, the Lower Mississippi River was upwards of one million three hundred thousand miles long, and stuck out over the Gulf of Mexico like a fishing rod. And by the same token any person can see that seven hundred and forty-two years from now the Lower Mississippi will be only a mile and three quarters long, and Cairo and New Orleans will have joined their streets together, and be plodding comfortably along under a single mayor and a mutual board of aldermen.

Villages and towns along this portion of the river, unlike on the Ohio or the Allegheny, do not commonly sit right on the edge of the banks; rather, they're behind a levee or a natural

rise, frequently some distance away, so for hours the traveler
may have little relief from the miles of willows and maples,
shrub and brush, with no main drags—often named Water
or Front Street—to offer a pause to body or a boost to
imagination. If you want
to know you're passing,
say, old glass-making
Crystal City, population
4,000, you have to look at
a map. Despite these
drawbacks to the jour-
neyer, the Mississippi, of
all our waterways, has

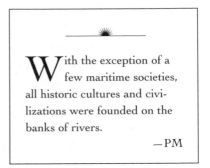

With the exception of a
few maritime societies,
all historic cultures and civilizations were founded on the
banks of rivers.

—PM

spawned a greater number of river narratives than any
other, a happenstance brought about more by the spell of
Twain than any magic in the lower Mississippi itself. I had
a couple of years earlier traveled it from New Orleans to St.
Paul, and below St. Louis the river isn't by any means one
of my favorites, so I moved along that day with a near
eagerness to get off it and take on the longest river in
America, of which an old pilot once said, "We used to separate the men from the boys at the mouth of the Missouri.
The boys went up the Mississippi and the men up the
Missouri."

The day became progressively darker as we banged on
north, and by the time we passed the mouth of the Meramec
River, the sky had turned oppressive and the industry of St.
Louis started showing itself. A fourteen-year-old boy,
Auguste Chouteau, began the construction of the city
named to honor Louis IX of France and, indirectly, pay

regard to the boy's current king, Louis XV, that self-indul-
gent, lecherous profligate who inherited the mightiest
monarchy in Europe and proceeded to give up much of it
while he pursued, among others, Madame Pompadour, a
woman whose counsel almost made him into a good king. It
was this Louis who purportedly said, "After me, the flood,"
words that often have an ironic ring to them in St. Louis. In
fact, the day we arrived there, the Mississippi was inching
its way up to the foot of the great Gateway Arch, the tallest
national monument in America.

Three miles below the heart of the old waterfront where
the teen-aged Chouteau first put saw to timbers, hammer to
pegs, we searched out a moorage [First Mate] Pilotis had
recently arranged with the Corps of Engineers on the inside
of its big dredge *Potter* and two service barges. Tethered off
the bank, the boats formed a narrow chute free of the roiling water on the channel, a safehold further quieted by a
driftwood dam beavers
had built between the
Potter and the shore. We
were only 20 feet from the
open Mississippi, but the
chute was gentle enough
to shelter a dozen black-
crowned night herons giv-
ing out their guttural

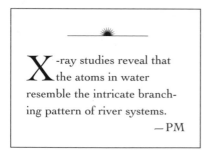

X-ray studies reveal that
the atoms in water
resemble the intricate branch-
ing pattern of river systems.
—PM

quok! quok! quok! at our arrival. I once heard the birds called
river ravens, and assuredly the evening fit their dark plumes
and mournful quothings.

We phoned a friend to ask for a lift from under the actual shadow of the second-largest brewery in the world to a small pub serving its own cask-conditioned ales and a potently spiced white-bean chili. I called on our musician to play. As he blew his bag full, the windy night began to rattle the windows of the St. Louis Brewery, lightning flashed, and rain got dumped everywhere, but he merely glanced into the blackness and piped away, and women rose to dance to "Garry Owen," lifting their smooth knees high, hands clapping above their heads, and inspiration flowed like the sky.

When we returned to *Nikawa*, she was low in the stern from rain in the welldeck, and a young man from the Corps lent me an electric bilge-pump to empty her. Off and on the rain came down through the thunder-and-fire-rent night, a storm to extinguish the flames of Hell, and I had no doubt that the great Missouri, which would hold our lives for at least the next six weeks, was announcing itself, already testing our mettle.

William Least Heat-Moon, of English-Irish-Osage ancestry, is the author of *Blue Highways, PrairyErth,* and *River Horse: The Logbook of a Boat Across America,* from which this story was excerpted. He lives in Missouri, the state where he was born.

PART FOUR

STILL WATER

Baptism

LORIAN HEMINGWAY

The power of water to heal and purify
illuminates a childhood summer.

OUTSIDE THE PAPER MILL TOWN OF PINE
Bluff, the Arkansas River spreads out broad like
a plain, meeting up with young boys gone for a
summer swim, and swallows them whole without ever asking their names. It is the river from my childhood, clouded
by red clay, steady and deep, its current forceful as an
avalanche. In spring when the floods came I would watch
the river from the safety of the high, sandbagged levee, its
dark water clogged with mangled car parts, whole trunks of
trees uprooted by tornadoes, and tangled fists of rusted
barbed wire. It was a seasonal ritual in Pine Bluff, watching
the gruesome bounty of the floods, and I was as shameless
as any in my curiosity.

I saw the body of a young girl once, flying in that water,
her thin blond hair matted with twigs and reddish foam that
churned in the wake of the surge as she slid down the chute
of the river, far from where she'd started out, far from the

calm of that spring morning before the storms came. Her eyes were wide-open like two cat's-eyes marbles, and the skin around her mouth was as blue and transparent as oiled paper. I remember understanding in that instant of seeing her—a girl my own age, dead—the unchecked power of the water that bore her up. And I understood then that a river could murder, randomly, with no thought to the lives it pulled into its fury.

I used to think a lot about that girl, imagine where she'd lived, what she'd been like, why she'd ended up a broken, dirty doll flying past my high perch on the levee. I told myself she had wanted to swim in the waist-high flood that spring, be carried, weightless, by the current into some new place she'd yet to see. Every kid wanted to ride the floods but few were allowed. She was the one who'd dared to do it, ignoring her mother's warnings. She'd swum into a whirlpool and couldn't get out. A tree branch or an old car part had clobbered her. She'd been knocked unconscious, then drowned. I dreamt about her for a while, and in my dreams, she'd always come to life just as she bobbed past, raise her head up out of the blood-colored water and call to me, "It's O.K. Come on in," and I'd turn my head quickly in the dream, remembering the glassed-over eyes of the real girl, afraid that if I stared too long she'd seize my hand and pull me into the spinning water.

For a long time I feared death by water, yet summer after summer I still made treks to the clay banks below the levee, usually with my Aunt Freda. We'd spend our afternoons pushing worm-rigged cane poles into the muddy water of the Arkansas, sunbathing in the humid mornings before the mosquitoes settled in, thick as fog. I ate great handfuls of the river mud on particularly idle days, tempted by the potent scent of minerals in the red clay, and smeared what I didn't eat on my body, watching it dry orange in the sun, so tight on my skin it cracked and fell off in chunks as I ran into the water.

Freda was often my only companion during those summers that could last from March until October, a half-Cherokee woman raised in a Catholic orphanage who later became a Carmelite nun, and later still gave up the order and the church entirely for full-time exploration into the theories of Carl Jung. She was Pine Bluff's token eccentric—many called her crazy—whose physical beauty was matched only by her complete disregard for conventional thought. I was her student in summer, a refugee from Mississippi, beguiled by her beauty, completely willing to sit at her feet on the sun-baked clay, listening.

Freda told me that the Arkansas, as red sometimes as leaves in Indian summer, was very like the blood of Christ itself, capable of healing and life—sustaining grace, a benefactor, in a way, to those who availed themselves of its power. This notion went contrary to the cold-blooded slaughter I had witnessed in these waters just a few summers before, and I suspected that Freda was, perhaps, as crazy as people said. I'd sit quietly, staring up at her as she talked, my eyes wide, as she agreeably allowed me to stuff my cheeks with mud, thinking, I imagine now, that I was merely indulging a sacrament.

We took a picnic basket to a grove of cottonwoods along the riverbank one Sunday morning, Freda and I, in the summer of my fifteenth year. It was clear and hot already, and I could smell the clay damp along the banks from dew that had settled. It smelled like the ravine behind my mother's house in Mississippi, wet earth and minerals so potent my mouth watered when I breathed deep.

As she started out across the river, Freda was drinking ice water from a fruit jar. I was spread out on the blanket we had brought, eating a meatball sandwich, one of Freda's specialties. She wasted nothing. When the sauce was gone, out of the pot came the meatballs. She'd crumble them up on eggs or mix them with the fried okra; this morning they'd been sliced dry onto two pieces of Sunbeam bread, the kind you can mash into a ball, throw at the ceiling, and have it stick.

Freda turned around to look at me, smoothing out the blanket, something her mother had given her, all orange and green and purple in a crazy pattern.

"You hear that?" Freda asked me, turning away quickly.

"Hear what?" I asked.

"Listen."

I listened, thinking maybe it was the river noises.

"I don't hear anything," I said. "What am I supposed to be hearing?"

"That," she said impatiently, moving her arms out in a direction upriver from us.

There was no wind and sounds came up on you suddenly. I could hear something now, the way you do when a radio knob is turned up slowly, the music coming closer and then filling my head. I thought I could feel the ground start to vibrate under me.

"What is it?" I asked excitedly.

"Sssh. Quiet." Freda said.

I had heard the sound before, rising up on a Saturday night from the tiny church that fronted the alley behind Freda's house. It was a gospel song—not a hymn, slow and reverent—and the voices yelled at full timbre and harmonized. Glory! Glories! It grew stronger and stronger, moving through the cottonwoods with such force I saw birds scatter from the trees. When I listened to that chorus of voices from my bed at Freda's, I'd be covered in goose flesh, the hair on the back of my neck pricking up, throbbing with the pulse of the music.

"Here they come," Freda said, pointing in the same direction, "right through the trees."

I looked down at my arms and watched the skin rise up. I saw them then, a whole congregation of black people, maybe 200, coming down the bank through the cottonwoods, their long robes trailing across the red clay until they looked as if they'd been dipped in blood, their mouths open so wide as they sang I could see the soft pink of tongues and the flashing of gold teeth in the sun.

"Lord Jesus meet us by the river," I heard them sing in full-bellowed voices, not one timid note among them.

"Wash us in the blood,
in the blood
oh the blood, dear Jesus
of the lamb."

Several called out "Hallelujah!" and fell to their knees on the shore.

I looked at Freda and she put a finger to her lips.

"If we're quiet," she whispered, "they won't go away."

The head of the congregation, a big man the color of jet, held his arms up high and spread them wide.

He looked as if he were ready to ascend, his robe blowing back from a wind that had quickly risen. He called out to his people in a deep, full voice. "Brothers and sisters, walk with me now. Let these waters re-*leve'e* the sins of this earth. Be saved, in the name of sweet Jesus, by the miracle of the water. By the miracle, children. Let the Lord hear you, children, shout Hallelujah, brothers and sisters."

He took a breath, his arms still raised high, and I could see his chest swell beneath the robe, full as a ten-year oak.

"Into the waters, sisters, into the water now, brothers. Cleanse your souls shiny white as these robes, white as the light of Jesus.

"Sing Hallelujah, children."

"Hallelujah!" they shouted back, so long and loud I could see the ice in Freda's water jar rattle.

Verily, verily, I say unto thee; except a man be born of water and of the spirit, he cannot enter into the Kingdom of God.
— John 3:5

My head was light with the sound of them, Hallelujahs rising in my own throat, choked back and then free again. I wanted to sing with them, thrash on the bank and roll limp into the river. The feeling was so strong I coughed and sputtered until Freda slapped me hard on the back.

They started into the river then, dozens of them, beckoned by the preacher who called out as they passed, "Bless you, sister, bless you brother, sweet Jesus, bless you all. Taste the Glory, children. Submerge your souls in the light. Praise Jesus. Hallelujah!"

And the gospel blues pulled them straight toward the water as if they had been born of it.

I watched as their robes billowed up around them, pockets of air caught in the fabric carrying them high over their heads, and then they went down, swaying with the current, one by one, the preacher laying his broad hand atop each head, crying out, "In the name of the everlasting blood of the lamb, I baptize you."

As they went under, their robes caught in the water like dying swans and went down with them. Some held their arms up as they went under, and I thought I could hear a "Praise Jesus" bubble to the surface.

For an instant I moved to stand up, the call in me so strong I had to fight it. We watched them struggle up out of the water, singing as they came to the bank, their robes heavy now and flattened against their bodies. I noticed some of the women had huge breasts, round as melons beneath the wet fabric, and that the men looked like boys, shy, surrounded by all this womanhood. They sang louder when they were clear of the water, clapping wet hands together and moving like a black and white snake, single file through the trees. In their retreat I could see the women shake their hips in rhythm to the music, and I felt a sweet pain low in my belly. If they had seen us, they had not let on.

I looked down at my arms, at the goose flesh risen up in dark points on this hot summer morning, and wished I had followed them in. I turned to Freda sitting there on the

old Indian blanket, her bright, beautiful face lifted high, a
peculiar smile on it that made me happy.

"I'm going in," I told her. She nodded as if she already knew.

I didn't sing as I moved down the bank toward the water,
looking across to the other side where two young boys
fished with cane poles. I didn't know anything to sing except
"Honeycomb." But I could still hear them far down the river
and imagined I was part of their congregation, about to be
made pure and simple, washed free of something whose
name I did not yet know. I'd seen their faces when they'd
come out, lost in something that brought amazement to their
eyes. They were free. Oh yes. I could see it. A miracle had
taken place in that water. I swore to myself it was so. I'd
seen that same look they'd had, once, in an airport, on the
face of a tall black woman. She wore a two-inch-high rhine-
stone pin on her jacket that read JESUS. I remember
reaching out to touch her as I walked past—wanting to
touch her—and how she turned around quickly and smiled
at me, her eyes patient and understanding, filled with a
notion of heaven.

The water felt warm at first, then cooler farther out
where the bottom started to slip away. I felt a slow panic
begin to move in me, starting at my knees, then filling my
chest, as I remembered the girl, her arms limp in the river
swell. I looked back toward the bank and saw Freda watching me.

"I'll hold my breath," I called out, asking for reassurance.

"I think you should," she called back.

I went down slowly, the thin cotton of my t-shirt turning
wet against my breasts.

I stayed down as long as I could, my cheeks puffed out like a guppy's, feeling the current pushing between my out-spread legs, my toes gripping the firm river bottom. I felt like a reed in some underwater wind, not sure what I was doing. The water was cool and heavy with the current, and I imagined it was as deep as outer space. I spread my arms out the way the preacher had done, and a thought came into my head so loud and clear my eyes opened in the dark water.

"Help me," it said, over and over, first deep, then high, then meek as a child's plea. "Help me." My mouth opened in surprise and I tasted the rich blood of the water choking me; and the voice grew louder. I imagined the girl there with me, her hand outstretched in the current, fingertips gripping mine, her flesh as warm as the water in which we floated. I imagined, too, the firm hold of her hand as we burst together into the air, our lungs filling in a rush, greed-ily, our arms outstretched held high above our heads.

"You baptized yet?" Freda called from the cottonwoods as I walked slowly from the river, falling to the red clay bank, exhausted. I raised my arm and waved my hand once, a signal, yes, and saw for a brief moment the girl there beside me, her hair bright in the warm August sun.

———— ⌘ ————

Like her grandfather Ernest, Lorian Hemingway is a writer and fishing enthusiast. Her award-winning books include *Walk on Water* and *Walking Into the River*. She directed the prestigious annual Lorian Hemingway Short Story Competition, based in Key West, Florida, for more than a decade.

Sacred River

ROGER HOUSDEN

*A river fuels the hopes and dreams
of an entire culture.*

THE DOOR OF OUR ROOM WAS OPEN, SO WE
could hear the rush of the river outside. As we
were sitting there, watching the day, the cleaner
crept in with his brown reed brush. He was stooped, older
than his years, a sad little man. I was prompted to ask if he
had a family. "Yes," he said, and then after a pause, "but wife
sick, and children, too. No money for medicines, very difficult." He spoke without a trace of guile, with no hint of a
suggestion that we should give him money. He was just stat-
ing the facts of his life. He made to start his work, and then,
as if remembering something, he turned and pointed
through the door to the river. "But Ma Ganga will take care
of us." Without another word, he began sweeping the floor.

That exchange took place some years ago in the tourist
bungalow at Haridwar. "Ma Ganga will take care of us"—I
had never heard anyone speak of a river in that way before.
For this man, the Ganges was a living presence, a protector,

a healer of ills. I came to realize during that stay in India that the sweeper was not alone. The Ganges is as alive as it ever was with the hopes and dreams of an entire culture. Even Nehru, that arch-modernist, asked that his ashes be cast into the Ganga at Allahabad. For him, too, the river was India, more than any political party or ideal could ever hope to be. The whole Hindu world still comes to its banks to sing, to pray, to wash, to ask favours and blessings, to urinate, to barter, to die. For the rest of our journey, that great river kept insinuating itself into my thoughts.

It is great, not because of its size (it is 2,500 miles long, but there are many longer and wider rivers) but because, more than any other river on earth, it is a living symbol of an ancient culture's way of life and of the sacred dimension of nature itself. Of all the Hindu goddesses, Ma Ganga is the only one without a shadow. She is the unequivocal fountain of mercy and compassion, here in this world only to comfort her children. Her waters are the milk, the nectar of immortality, source of all life and abundance. She is often shown carrying a plate of food, and an overflowing pot. In Bihar, farmers put a pot of Ganga water in the fields before sowing to ensure a good harvest, while newly-married women unfold their sari to Gangaji and pray for children. It is her physical presence that offers such consolation. The river itself, rather than her image as a goddess, is the one who attracts devotion and worship. Countless flowers are strewn across her body daily; millions of lights set sail every evening upon her waters. While stories of gods and goddesses come and go with the ages, while one myth replaces or rivals another, the organic presence of Ganga continues as ever, absorbing her devotees' offerings and ashes in the same way she has done since time immemorial.

My first contact with Ganga the living Goddess, via the sweeper, and subsequent hours spent by the riverside at Haridwar, fired my imagination sufficiently to impel me to return to India three years later in order to follow its course. I decided to go on foot, by boat, and by bus from its headwater in the Himalayas to Banaras—half the length of the river.

A cave, Gaumukh—the cow's mouth—is the source of the river. Hindus carry it with them whenever they go to the Ganga: the spout of the brass pot they use to scoop up holy water for their personal rituals is often in the shape of a cow. Out of the cow's mouth pours the Ganges, by a glacier some 15,000 feet up in the mountains. A sadhu lives there all the year round without a stitch of clothing. It was October when I reached him, and the pilgrim traffic was quiet. I had walked the narrow path from Gangotri, the nearest village, aided at times by the wooden rail that follows the cliff above the stream. The terrain is stark and rocky, with snow-covered peaks looming above on either side. I was cold, hungry, and my head was spinning with altitude sickness. I smiled wanly. He looked at me as if he had seen it all before a thousand times. His matted hair fell below his shoulders. A tiny rag was thrown across his thighs. "Which country?" he said. "England." He nodded. I sat there a few moments longer, trying to feel the sanctity of this source of all mercy and compassion. God knows I needed it; but it was not forthcoming in a way that my senses could register. I sat there an hour with the sadhu, aware through a haze of the

austere grandeur not only of the mountains but also of him;
aware also that some hours of stiff walking still lay between
me and Gangotri if I was to return there by nightfall. Many
pilgrims camp at Gaumukh, and still higher up at a spot
called Tapovan; but altitude affects me more than most, and
the walk down to Gangotri held out more relief at the end
than a night with the sadhu....

In the morning I headed off downstream, feeling lighter
by the minute as the way fell in altitude. I was following
paths that wound through forests of cedar and pine from
one tiny hill settlement to the next. The walking, as always,
threw me into a rhythm that my body and mind were thank-
ful for. It aligned me with the motion of animals; with the
occasional mule or goat that passed me at times on the way.
It allowed for conversation in sign language with strangers,
for a shared pot of tea with some herders. I could dawdle
and watch the birds with tails a foot long, iridescent blue,
flutter clumsily on wings too small for their bodies back
and forth across the river. And always, I could hear the per-
sistent rush of wild water through the mountain gorges; see
its turbulent white tufts, its fierce eddies and whirlpools.

The second morning, I awoke on a ledge of turf by the
water to see, here and there at the water's edge, a rock
turned on its end and crowned with flowers. A man stood
facing the rising sun, still dripping ice-cold water after his
immersion in the stream, eyes closed and palms together in
traditional greeting. He murmured some prayers under his
breath, then turned in a circle on the spot, bowing to the
four directions and letting a trickle of water fall back into
the river from a brass pot he held out before him. He placed

two marigold heads on an upright stone, lit a cone of incense
between them, and with a final bow to the flowers and the
river, he went on his way. To his tailor's shop, perhaps, or to
his field. So simple: no fuss; not even the slightest self-con-
sciousness at the presence of some open-mouthed foreigner.
This was his way of starting the day, every day of his life, as
it is for millions of Hindus who live near a river, a lake, even
a pond.

Some days later, I was camped on a white spur of sand
just upstream from Rishikesh, the gateway to the vastness
of the Indian plain, the first town the river reaches on leaving the mountains. The stream that had tumbled through
canyons and ravines up in the mountains was now a fully-
fledged river. Ma Ganga is wider, slower, here; half-tamed
already, with the features of a civilization shaping her
banks. The straw huts of orange-robed renunciates line the
river edge; large ashrams and temples dominate the town.
This is where the Beatles came all those years ago to sit
with the Maharishi, whose ashram is still one of the largest
in the vicinity. People are bathing, doing their laundry,
praying, casting flowers on the water, selling pots. Bright
swathes of colour fill my eye; fine turbans, yards of cloth,
blue and yellow, trailing from a woman's shoulder; eternal
gestures, the languid folding of saris, the passing of money,
the feeding of children, begging, always the begging, and
the placing of the sacred mark on the brow; the grace,
wholly unselfconscious, of a woman stooping to place an
offering, a leaf-boat of flowers, into the water. Everything,
just as it has always been.

Walking along the bank one day, I passed a group of *san-*

nyasins in their orange robes chanting over an armchair in which an old woman was sitting. Someone was beating a drum, and a boat was tying up alongside. As I drew closer I realized the old woman was dead. She was tied to the chair, still in her renunciate robes. Next to her was a large box. Chanting continuously, several *sannyasis* lifted the chair into the box, and began placing stones around the old woman's feet. When they had added enough ballast, they nailed the lid down, and with some heaving and shoving, managed to haul the box onto the waiting boat. The boatmen rowed out into midstream, and unceremoniously tipped their cargo over the side. *Sannyasis* have no need of cremation, since their impurities are consumed while still alive with the fire of their spiritual practice. Small children forego the fire as well, since they are deemed too young to have accumulated bad karma.

Haridwar, half an hour downstream from Rishikesh, is one of the seven sacred cities of India. Two million people visit the town every year, to bathe in the bend of the river known as the Brahmakund, Brahma's basin. This is the place where Brahma greeted the celestial Ganga on her descent to earth; it is also where Vishnu (Hari) left his footprint, so another name for the same place is Hariki-Pairi, Hari's Foot. The footprint is venerated in the Gangadwara (Gate of the Ganga) temple on the right bank. Haridwar's waters are doubly sanctified, then, and it is known as the city of salvation. Criminals come here to disappear into the multitude of renunciates; runaways from ill-fated marriages and family problems, bonded laborers on the run from tyrannical landlords, respectable families from

Delhi, businessmen from the Punjab, villagers from Rajasthan, the whole world of northern India throngs in a mass along the river banks, all of them equal at the Gate of the Lord, Haridwar.

At dusk the river at Hariki-Pairi twinkles with a thousand lights. Leaf-boats bob in the water with their cargo of flowers and a camphor flame, sent on their way by pilgrims anxious to secure with their offering the good favours of Ma Ganga. Bells chime across the town, priests are chanting down by the river bank, waving brass candelabra, ablaze with light, in the shape of the sacred sound *Aum*. Pilgrims throng the Hariki-Pairi ghat, the most auspicious bathing place in the town; the entire river, as befits a goddess, is garlanded with roses and chrysanthemums, and a carpet of petals undulates on the waters.

From Haridwar I took the train to Allahabad, the ancient Prayaga. Another of the seven sacred cities, it in its turn, is doubly holy due to its position at the confluence of the Yamuna and the Ganga. Geographical peculiarities add to the power of the land, and a river confluence is especially holy, suggesting to the Hindu mind the image of the *yoni*, the vagina, the gate of all life. Prayag is blessed not only with the confluence of two rivers, but three: the Sarasvati, an invisible underground stream, is held to flow into the Ganges at the same point as the Yamuna.

I had met up with a couple of friends in Allahabad, and we intended floating downstream to Banaras, fifty miles on down the road, and three days away by boat. We had an agent arrange the boat for us, and early one morning he ushered us onto one of the small craft that lie in the shadow of the great fort. The skiff we stepped into had nowhere to place the legs, nothing but bare boards to sit on, and scant cover from the sun. In the prow sat a shifty-looking, one-eyed character whose legs were thinner than my wrists. He rowed a few languid strokes, and then gave us to understand that we had to wait for his son. We were still waiting half an hour later. All the boats alongside us seemed sturdier than ours, they all had cushioned seats, and all the other boatmen seemed to be in the prime of their life instead of the eclipse under which our own man seemed to be waning. When I made to leave for another boat, One-Eye immediately discovered a hidden vigour and lurched us into midstream with the assurance that it was unnecessary to wait for his son after all.

His enthusiasm was short-lived. Other boats, far more laden than ours, packed with fat pilgrims from Delhi or Bombay, sped past us towards the confluence, one of the most venerated spots along the whole length of the Ganga. At Allahabad, the Ganga begins to take on the proportions of an epic waterway. At the confluence, the river has the appearance of a huge lake, with dozens of pilgrim boats moored there, out in midstream. Our boatman seemed to be taking on this formidable waterway with an attitude more fitting for an afternoon excursion, rather than a trip that was to last three days. At this rate we would be rowing long into the night.

Despite ourselves, we began to settle down to One-Eye's pace, and soon all that could be heard was the creaking of oars (poles with bits of an orange box nailed to them) and the distant chants and calls from a huddle of boats at the confluence, a kilometre or two from the town. As we made towards the main river, the union of the Ganga and Yamuna, I noticed a figure walking in our direction across a curving sandbar on the farther bank. The boatman edged us in the direction of the shore, and the figure walked through the shallow water and out to our boat. It was the son. Everyone smiled; it was all preordained. It was only we who had been in the dark. In every small matter of life, and within the heart of all its chaos and confusion, India has her own inexorable logic that the visitor can only learn to fall into. It is useless, utterly useless, to resist, or to attempt to make things otherwise.

We were almost the only boat on the river. We saw one fishing boat, and just a few small dredgers laden with sand being hauled upstream by men on the towpath who were tied to the end of a long line attached to the mast. The sand had been scooped up from the central channel by buckets on the end of bamboo poles. There were no boats with engines. The one outboard motor I saw in the whole journey was on the ferry at Rishikesh. The only other craft we passed after Allahabad was a small, wide-bottomed boat piled high with reeds. Among them, a flat, high-cheekboned face draped in white cloth peered out from over the steerage.

As we left the city, we wound our way into a land that could barely have changed in a thousand years. In high contrast to the India that most people encounter, the river was silent except for the lap of the water against the boat and the cries of birds overhead. India has to be one of the noisiest lands on earth. Indians are entirely relational: they walk in groups, sit in bunches, travel in families. Their constant ban-

ter frequently reaches a decibel level far beyond that of con-
versational speech. They like to play loud music, of the
Indian film variety, to attract customers to their shops, to
celebrate a festival (there is always a festival to celebrate),
and to call devotees to the temples. The temple loudspeakers
begin at four a.m. and leave no corner of a neighbourhood
unscathed. On the roads, day and night, Indian truck and
bus drivers, who make up 90 percent of the traffic, keep
their fist permanently on the horn, the volume and pitch of
which is at the level of an air raid siren. The river, then, was
a sanctuary, an echo, perhaps, of what India might have
been like fifty years ago. We passed between high banks, a
dirt path spiralling up every now and then to some village
above. A woman with a pot on her head swayed up steps
that were etched in the mud, children played by the shore,
a grandmother washed her linen, buffalo bathed in the
river, vultures huddled on the sand.

In the late morning, a band of vultures gathered on the
left bank, taking turns at picking the remains from a
blanched skeleton which had run aground on the sand. A
little later, just before running aground too, One-Eye surprised us with two words of English: "Dead body!" he
exclaimed, pointing proudly into the water. The swollen
corpse of a man, bottom up, still clothed, brushed by our
starboard side.

Final dissolution in the Ganga purifies on the one hand,
yet to the contemporary eye, seems to pollute on the other.
Hindus are generally convinced that nothing can pollute
their sacred river, and many tests seem to show that Ganga
water does seem remarkably capable of retaining its purity.

Other tests prove the opposite, that Ganga is as susceptible as any other body of water to the pressures of modern society and a burgeoning population. The matter rests, for the present, in one's own belief system. "Yes, our water is perfectly good to drink," my hotel owner in Haridwar had assured me, with a smile. "It comes from Ganga." I decided to opt for the bottled water.

Hindus are obsessed with purity, and for them, Ganga is so pristine that the pollution accrued daily through contact with lower castes and other undesirable situations can be erased with a mere handful of river water over the head. To be brushed by a breeze that is carrying even a drop of Ganga water is sufficient, the Agni Purana says, to erase all sins. In temples of the Gupta period, statues of Ganga and Yamuna often grace the entrance, purifying all who pass through the door. The very land the Ganga flows through is purified by her presence, a view more acceptable to the contemporary mind. What defies logic — but then India does not live by Western logic — is that this most sacred of all sacred rivers is used as an open sewer. Cities pour their excrement into it, millions of individuals use it freely as a public toilet, and of course, industrial plants use it to dispose of their effluent. It seems a strange way to treat a goddess. In his first speech to the Indian Parliament, Rajeev Gandhi declared the Ganga a national heritage, and earmarked substantial central funds to deal with its pollution problems. As is the way in India, projects at the local level were hastily conceived and improperly executed; and as always, corruption made off with a large proportion of the allocated funds.

Western countries are more guilty than most for the

earth's pollution, a fact I had always attributed in part to the
Western dissociation between nature and God. If nature is
inert matter, you can treat it with impunity. If she is a goddess, a manifestation of the divine, I would expect her to be
treated with more care. Meanwhile, the devotee by the
Ganga continues to wash away his sins downstream from
the sewer.

As the sun drew near the horizon, the wind died, and
dolphins, dozens of dolphins, wheeled and dived alongside
us. The boatmen took an oar each. They seemed unable,
however, to row in rhythm, so that one soon fell behind,
until the other caught him
up again. For a few sec-
onds they would row as a
team, and then fall out of
rhythm again. An hour
after dark we saw the
flashing light of our
agent, who had already
set up camp on the bank.
Two days later, through
an early evening haze, we
glimpsed the outlines of
the palaces and temples,
all pink and brown, that
grace the riverfront of
Banaras. We were edging

> Just as Muslims strive to
> visit Mecca, so all Hindus
> dream of visiting Varanasi
> (Banaras) to bathe in the
> Ganges at least once in their
> lives to cleanse themselves of a
> lifetime of sins. It is considered
> particularly desirable to die in
> Varanasi—your soul is said
> to go straight to heaven—and
> the town, one of the oldest on
> Earth, is full of the aged and
> dying.
>
> —PM

our way round the only bend in its entire length where the
Ganga makes a turn back towards the north, the direction
of wisdom, and away from the south, the direction of death.

The bend is in the shape of a half moon, like the one on Shiva's brow. We were finally entering Shiva's city, then, where death is defeated—the one place along the whole length of the river where the great god's fire is cooled by the element of water. In Banaras, the fire and the water, life and death, are reconciled. From the source to The City of Light I had come. I cupped my hand in the water, lifted it to the dying sun, and let it trickle back into the stream. I remembered the sweeper in Haridwar, and knew the water to be on my own breath now.

———— ⬧⬧⬧ ————

Roger Housden has been a student of the spiritual traditions of India for over twenty years. His books include: *Fire in the Heart*, *Retreats* and *Travels through Sacred India*, from which this story was excerpted.

Anchors

TED LEESON

*A model of form and function, the elegant drift boat
is perhaps the best craft for savoring a river.*

T O LOCATE YOURSELF IN NEW TERRITORY
and lay some claim more consequential than a mail-
ing address, I believe you must seek out what could
be called its "sense of place," that particular weave of relationships among plants, animals, people, landscape, ideas,
and history that flourishes more or less uniquely under local
circumstance. I know of only one way to go about the
search—take up a single thread of the fabric, follow it, and
just let one thing lead to another. If you fish, you already
have the advantage of a starting point, so when I dropped
anchor in Oregon ten years ago, I bought a new fly rod, tied
up some local patterns, and went looking for steelhead.

Above all other fish, steelhead were to me the most
intriguing natives of the Northwest. They defined its
angling identity. Even though from northern California to
Alaska, there were thousands, perhaps tens of thousands of
miles of steelhead water, my imagination returned always

to a few rivers—the North Umpqua, the Deschutes, the
Rogue. Steelhead could be found elsewhere, but Oregon
was steelhead country. That first winter, I fished eagerly,
often, and in deep ignorance. When the run at last tailed off
in March, I had hooked exactly four steelhead and landed
two of them. There are advantages to being self-taught; the
quality of instruction is not one of them.

The summer steelhead, I'd heard, came more readily to
the fly. But when summer came, I found myself too
absorbed in trout fishing to bother, and the steelhead season
passed without a single trip. During the warm months I
nevertheless incubated little plans for the upcoming winter,
read up on the subject, tended pet theories, tied new flies.
The second winter went a bit better than the first, and the
next year a bit better yet. Eventually, I logged enough river
time and caught just enough steelhead to realize that I had
neither a taste nor an aptitude for it, though I never deter-
mined which of these was a cause, which an effect. The fishing cooled of its own accord, trips tapered off to four or five
a year, and I now find myself in the heart of steelhead country, lamely explaining why I fish them so seldom.

In fact, I raise the subject at all less for itself than for
what the fish unexpectedly led me to. The first steelhead
trip, and many thereafter, were undertaken with a partner,
also new to Oregon, in a borrowed McKenzie River driftboat—a shameful, wooden disaster of archaic design, dry-
rotted in a few vital areas, with oversized oars. It seemed to
float by accident. Neither of us knew much about running
it, though, and for many seasons it functioned better as a
boat than we did as boatmen. Its virtues on the water and its

fittedness to a landscape of rivers were instantly apparent to me. Driftboats belonged in the place, and to know them, I felt, would be to understand something of importance. If you approach it properly, fishing has no end points, only new points of departure. I had sought out wild steelhead as an embodiment of some native idea, some spirit that made the place itself. The pursuit led, eventually and obliquely, to the discovery of a second indigenous form. From that moment on, steelhead and driftboats have been inseparably linked in my imagination.

Their connection goes beyond the coincidence of private experience; the two share deeper affinities. Like steelhead, driftboats are anadromous, descended from the double-ended ocean dories that were launched through the breakers and rowed out to meet the incoming salmon. The lineage extends still further back, possibly through the river bateaux, to the banks dories of the North Atlantic cod fishery. In the Northwest, the design idea migrated up the McKenzie River and spawned. Becoming smaller and more maneuverable, the boats adapted to survive in the swift, churning currents and bouldered drops of white-water rivers. They evolved at last into a separate race altogether, like the steelhead that long ago ascended prehistoric rivers, lingering there to become strains of resident rainbows that never again looked seaward. In recent times, both the fish and the boats have been transplanted to other regions, but they remain authentically native forms, quick and stream-lined, thriving in rough water through slipperiness and cunning rather than raw strength. Down to the finest detail, they are perfectly suited to their regional habitat.

The evolutionary adaptations of the driftboat are ingenious. They are unusually beamy craft, with wide, flat
bottoms and high, flaring sides that produce a remarkable
stability. A driftboat will tolerate an angle of heel that would
capsize most small boats; you can stand on the gunnel without tipping one over. Built for buoyancy and shallow
draught, the hull draws less than six inches of water and will
slip over the shallowest flats. Stem and transom are sharply
angled. From stem to stern, the bottom is not flat but
severely rockered, curved fore and aft, and the combination
of broad beam and rocker puts the center of gravity almost
at the oarsman's feet. A well-made boat answers the oarsman's lightest touch; it will turn, stop, pivot, and deftly pick
its way through the obstacle course of a rocky rapids with
astonishingly little effort.

Like steelhead, a driftboat is the perfect union of form
and function, all beauty and business, and one of the most
honest things on the planet. Few other craft will perform the
same function, and none with such elegance. A white-water
raft will transport you downriver, but it is sluggish and
clumsy, handling precisely like what it is—an ungainly bag
of gas. But the hull of a driftboat is geometric grace, a cur-
vature in space defined by smooth, arced planes that intersect like the vault of a cathedral. It holds no hint of ugliness.
A driftboat has a simplicity, a clearness of vision, and a sense
of purpose so absolute that it might have sprung from the
uncluttered heart of a Shaker.

Were it possible to separate a river into the physical
components of water and current, to divide the liquid from
the flux it expresses, the water would settle into a formless

calm. But the current would be shaped like a fish, or the wing of a bird, or a driftboat—things not merely stream-lined but streamlike. They are formed to slip with a minimum of disturbance through worlds where the most compelling fact of existence is friction. This, I think, is one of the deep attractions of driftboats. They seem to be on the water rather than in it, propelled by the flow but somehow above it. The flat, stable bottom is as perfect an observation deck as it is a fishing platform, and I've never drifted with any-one who did not become completely absorbed in watching the landscape glide by. Moving but motionless, you come to feel invisible and weightless, slipping silently past deer, otter, herons, and fish, so that a driftboat now seems to me less a way of traveling a river than a way of inhabiting it.

There's one last thing, and perhaps the most important one. Most small boats are designed to hold a steady course, to oppose crosswinds and currents that would deflect them from the line of travel. To this end, they are built with keels that are aligned on the hull like a compass needle and use the resistance of the water itself to maintain a steady bear-ing. Keels are inertial, an argument for the way things are; they enforce constancy and direction, which is precisely their value. But the flat bottom of a driftboat is keelless, offering nothing to hinder transverse motion. It rides the uppermost sheet of water and shunts the current aside, slip-ping obliquely over the surface and outwitting the flux. A driftboat invites the sidelong and tangential, offering above all else an overwhelming sense of frictionlessness as the ordinary drift of things slides past.

Keellessness is a reversal that inspires a distinct kind of

navigation. Maneuvering a boat on moving water requires resistance; some force of push or pull is necessary to steer a course. Most craft achieve steerageway by traveling faster than the current, keeping always a step ahead of the river. This kind of boat-handling takes alertness, quick thinking, and instinctive reactions. But steerage velocity is relative, and you control a driftboat by going slower than the current instead of faster. You face downriver, but like a steelhead, your navigational orientation is upstream. Without a keel, the boat pivots and swivels in an instant, traverses the river from side to side, and holds against the flow, not by resisting it but by offering as little resistance as possible. You don't try to outrun the river; you gradually lower yourself down it, moving not with the speed of reflex but of reflection.

In the right water, a little trick can be worked that never fails to confound the first-timer. Where the river runs swiftly over shallow bedrock, a line of standing waves will develop. If they are spaced just right, you can trap the boat in a trough between two crests. Though the water rolls and swells on all sides, the waveform remains stationary, and the boat sits calmly amid the turbulence in apparent

---

The face of the water, in time, became a wonderful book—a book that was the dead language to the uneducated passenger, but which told its mind to me without reserve, delivering its most cherished secrets as clearly as if it uttered them with a voice. And it was not a book to be read once and thrown aside, for it had a new story to tell every day.

—Mark Twain, *Life on the Mississippi*

defiance of some law. You occupy a place within a place, holding in the flux, anchored by the water itself. And you see the river with new eyes.

To forgo a keel is not to forsake direction but to invite a kind of suspension, one that multiplies the dimensions and degrees of freedom in which you move. You can pursue a sense of place in the particulars of landscape, but you ground that sense, I think, in your own vision. I first sought out steelhead as an incarnation of native form, some key to the lay of the land. One thing led to another, and I dis-covered in driftboats a second indigenous idea, a way of exploring the first that in time became anchored to a way of seeing. Still later I would learn that you don't even need the boat, that the anchor alone is sufficient.

—————⬡⬡⬡—————

Ted Leeson is a contributing editor to *Fly Rod & Reel* magazine. His articles on fishing and fly tying appear regularly in *Field & Stream, Gray's Sporting Journal, Fly Fisherman*, and a variety of other outdoor publications. He lives in Corvallis, Oregon, and teaches English at Oregon State University. This story was excerpted from his book, *The Habit of Rivers: Reflections on Trout Streams and Fly Fishing*.

A Step in the River

CHRIS OFFUTT

On the banks of the Iowa River, a young man navigates his journey to fatherhood.

SUMMER FOR ME HAS ALWAYS BEEN A TIME OF hibernation, a hallucinatory season to be endured. This one is passing in a fury of photosynthesis and intimacy. Rita has kept her job for the insurance, while her belly grows. A small magazine has accepted a short story and sent me a check for fifty-four dollars. It's my third publication, the first that paid. Rita is happy. The check validates her decision to have a child with me, proves that my days as a bum are gone. I take her to town for dinner. The bill is low since Rita is eating five small meals a day instead of three large ones.

The rest of the money buys fabric to make curtains for the baby's room. After borrowing a sewing machine, I manage to produce two hemmed strips that will fit no window in the house. They hang at a slant. Sunlight borders the sides; the bottom is eight inches below the windowsill. I am prouder of them than of getting published.

Every morning I take coffee to the river and sit in the same chair where I ended the previous night with beer. I prop my feet on a sandbag left from the flood. Now, in late July, drought is killing the corn, and the river has dwindled to a creek. The morning stillness is broken only by the symphony of birds claiming turf, and my neighbor's boat as he checks his catfish lines. To him the river is a tool. He's trapped and fished it for two decades.

Twenty-five hundred years ago, a Greek named Heraclitus said, "You can't step into the same river twice." I climb down the bank and remove my shoes and socks. The river is warm on my skin, a continuous flow that is immediately gone, yet remains. The water surrounding one leg is not the same as around the other leg. Sediment drifts away and it occurs to me that you can't even step on the same bank twice. Each footstep alters the Earth.

Heraclitus is known as "the Obscure" because none of his writings survived. My neighbor has no use for his ideas. To him the river is always the same, moving past his house, providing food.

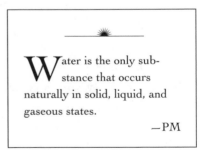

Water is the only substance that occurs naturally in solid, liquid, and gaseous states.

—PM

He steps into it every day. He gauges the spots to set his poles by the texture of mud beneath his feet. I spread my legs as far as I can. One foot is Heraclitus, the other is my neighbor. I am floating somewhere in between. Wind in the high boughs makes the leaves ripple like water, producing a distant whisper. Fish eggs cling to rocks along the shore.

Rita's eggs are thirty-four years old. She wanted amnio-
centesis to eliminate the worry of producing a baby less than
perfect. Her uncles, aunts, cousins, and grandparents all died
in World War II—some in combat, some in death camps.
Rita can never be sure what genetic oddities run in the family.
Her feet are flat and she has dyslexia. One of my eyes is far-
sighted, the other nearsighted. As a kid, I had big teeth
bucked so badly that four molars were yanked to make room.

Standing in the river, I imagine DNA as something large
and visible, extending from throat to navel, full of unruly
tangles that produce cowlicks, walleyes, and pinheads. I was
against the test, afraid that if our child turned out damaged,
it would mean that I was, too. Even worse, if the results
showed a Down's baby, I would want to keep it anyway.
The test is for throwing it back.

Rita prevailed, and two weeks ago we went to the hospital. She was told to drink sixteen ounces of juice. Half an
hour later a nurse strapped her to a table. Above Rita's head
sat a sonogram screen that would monitor the probing of her
gut. The nurse lifted Rita's shirt, pulled her pants down, and
swabbed her belly with a clear gel. She nodded to the doctor, another woman, who pressed an ultrasound transducer
to Rita's stomach. The sonogram screen filled with a murky,
mobile image that looked nothing like a child. The white
areas were tissue, the black was fluid. The spine looked like
a zipper. The doctor measured the skull and thigh. She
checked the heart, which was working fine. Flowing along
the top of the image were horizontal layers of uterine wall
and placenta, bringing to mind a summer sunset, changing
with the light of the heart.

The doctor manipulated the sonogram until two vertical images bisected the screen. She froze one, enlarged the other, and took photographs. "There's a hand," she said, indicating a pale blot. "We're looking at the baby as if it was sitting in a chair and we're underneath. It's mooning us. The legs are crossed, so we can't see the genitals. It's shy."

I watched the screen, trying to see as the doctor did, but found only a shifting landscape of black and white, a bubbling tar pit that caught light and held bones. "It looks good," she said. "Fifteen-point-nine weeks along."

She pressed several buttons and changed the image to a cone that represented a three-dimensional cross section inside Rita's belly. As the doctor moved the transducer, the image in the cone changed. She was hunting for a large space, far from the fetus, close to the amniotic wall. "There's one," she said. "Perfect."

The screen showed a dark gap surrounded by gray and white like an astronomical photograph. The nurse handed her a syringe. The needle was very long, a beak. She used both hands to insert it into a guiding tube that was pressed tight to Rita's belly. Rita closed her eyes. The doctor watched the monitor, moving her hands by rote, pushing the needle into darkness.

"Tenting," she said, and the nurse repeated the word. I asked what it meant.

The nurse explained that the amnion was tough enough to resist the needle; it was like pressing a stick against the wall of a tent. After several tries, the doctor breached the amnion. The syringe sucked pale liquid into its chamber, and I had a sudden impulse to drink it. My knees felt trem-

bly. A gray fog crowded my vision. The nurse took my arm
and led me to a chair, advising me to place my head between
my legs. She cleaned Rita's stomach. The final image on the
monitor showed a section of Rita's interior in the shape of a
cornucopia, the horn of life.

We drove home and Rita went to bed. For two hours I
watched her sleep. The baby was missing an ounce of life
already, a shot glass of amniotic fluid, and I was afraid
that it might notice. We had taken its water away, like
drought. I sat on the bed and apologized to Rita's belly for
our invasion.

The two-week wait went slowly. Today's mail should
contain the results of our amnio. I leave the river and climb
the bank to my chair. Maples crowd the opposite bank, their
leaves tinted yellow by lack of rain. The yard is brown and
I think of lush summers in the hills at home. The grass is
always greener where people die young. Our child is an
underground spring straining at the confluence of Rita and
me. The amnio will tell us if it's polluted.

The river is sinking like a lost continent, a misplacement
for which we all suffer. Yesterday I took the boat out, but a
light breeze halted me in a holding pattern between current
and wind. I had to wade home, pulling the boat with a rope,
wondering how much further the river can shallow itself.
Maps show it as a thin blue line the color of a vein until oxygen turns it the hue of mud. Should drought drink all the
water, the other side of the river would still be this side.
Herons would lose their safety, and bridges would have no
meaning. If the waterways lay empty to the sea, the ocean
would run backwards into the vacant riverbeds, rubbing salt

against the open wounds of earth. Drought and flood, that slow sabotage of the soul, would never matter again. The dam that holds nothing back becomes a tombstone for the river.

At two in the afternoon I fill a canteen with water and walk the half mile to my mailbox on the blacktop. The dirt road bisects a cornfield that is, as the farmers say, "standing dead." Each step raises a plume of dust beneath my foot. I stop three times to sip water in the oppressive heat of prairie summer. The handle of the mailbox burns my hand. Inside are two bills, a newspaper from Kentucky, and a rejected story. The amnio results are in a plain brown envelope, which I carry carefully, holding it away from my body like a snake. The mail is damp from sweat by the time I reach the house.

When Rita comes home from work, she makes me open the envelope. There is a four-by-four-inch photograph of the baby's chromosomes separated into pairs like matching flatworms. An accompanying letter says that the test has shown them to be structurally sound. The kid has a solid foundation. If it turns out to be a terrorist, the fault will be environmental, not genetic. Rita and I hug each other for what seems like hours. Her eyes are damp. I sense that I want to cry, but something deep inside forbids it, like a safety on a rifle, or a childproof cap. I cannot muster the courage of release.

I go to the room we've prepared for the baby. In the center stands a white bassinet, a lifeless picnic basket on legs, the same one I slept in as a newborn. My mother insisted on shipping it from the mountains to the prairie. She'd kept it, she said, against this very time. The bassinet is curved into an oval the shape of an egg. The light is dim. Everything has been placed with care. The whole room has an ethereal, expectant quality, like that of a cathedral in which miracles are rumored to occur.

I was my parents' first child and it occurs to me that my father must have regarded this same bassinet with similar trepidation. I suddenly realize that I've been misreading the myth of Oedipus all my life. Drinking mother's milk does not beget a thirst for father's blood. The tragedy belongs to Lairs, the father. Oedipus didn't fulfill his own destiny, he lived up to his father's terror.

I step outside to sit by the river in the streaming red light of summer dusk. Mosquitoes are working hard. I've hung old gourds on a frame to attract swifts because they feed on mosquitoes, but the birds care little for such accommodation. A great horned owl delivers a bellow that hushes the floodplain woods. A light rain blows downriver, a few sprinkles that pass rapidly as blown confetti.

The pregnancy is four months along, five to go. Rita dozes on the couch. The embryo has already set cells aside for its own offspring, like a farmer saving seed corn for next year's crop. Female mosquitoes land on my skin, needing fresh blood for their young.

<hr>

Chris Offutt was born in 1958 and grew up in the Appalachian region of eastern Kentucky. His stories have appeared in *Esquire* and other literary magazines, and his work has received an NEA grant and a James Michener grant. He is the author of the story collection, *Kentucky Straight*. He lives with his wife and two sons. This story was excerpted from his book, *The Same River Twice: A Memoir*.

Recommended Reading

Abbey, Edward. *Down the River*. New York: Plume/Penguin, 1991.

Altschuler, Stephen. *Sacred Paths and Muddy Places: Rediscovering Spirit in Nature*. Walpole, N.H.: Stillpoint Publishing, 1993.

Anderson, Lorraine. *Sisters of the Earth: Women's Prose and Poetry about Nature*. New York: Vintage Books, 1991.

Bachman, Ben. *Upstream: A Voyage on the Connecticut River*. Chester, Conn.: Globe Pequot Press, 1988.

Bangs, Richard. *The Lost River: A Memoir of Life, Death, and Transformation on Wild Water*. San Francisco: Sierra Club Books, 1999.

Bangs, Richard, and Christian Kallen. *Riding the Dragon's Back: The Race to Raft the Upper Yangtze*. New York: Dell Publishing, 1989.

Bennett, Charles E. *Twelve Along the River St. Johns*. Jacksonville: University of North Florida Press, 1989.

Bennett, Jeff, and Tonya Bennett. *A Guide to the Whitewater Rivers of Washington* (2nd Edition). Portland, Oreg.: Swiftwater Publishing, 1991.

Berger, Karen, and Daniel R. Smith. *Where the Waters Divide: A 3,000-Mile Trek Along America's Continental Divide*. Woodstock, Vt.: Countryman Press, 1997.

Bolling, David M. *How to Save a River*. Washington, D.C.: Island Press, 1994.

Boote, Paul, and Jeremy Wade. *Somewhere Down the Crazy River: Journeys in Search of Giant Fish*. London: Hodder and Stoughton Ltd., 1992.

Braddon, Russell, Christina Dodwell, Germaine Greer, Roger Laughton, William Shawcross, Brian Thompson, and Michael Wood. *River Journeys*. New York: Hippocrene Books, Inc., 1985.

Brown, Bruce. *Mountain in the Cloud*. New York: Simon and Schuster, 1982.

Burmeister, Walter F. *Appalachian Waters: The Hudson River and Its Tributaries*. Oakton, V.I.: Appalachian Books, 1974.

Burroughs, Franklin. *The River Home: A Return to the Carolina Low Country*. Boston: Houghton Mifflin, 1992.

Carrier, Jim, and Jim Richardson. *The Colorado: A River at Risk*. Englewood, Colo.: Westcliffe, 1992.

Cassady, Jim, Bill Cross, and Fryer Calhoun. *Western Whitewater*. Berkeley: North Fork Press, 1994.

Chamberlain, Lesley. *Volga, Volga: A Voyage Down the Great River*. London: Picador, 1995.

Chapple, Steve. *Kayaking the Full Moon: A Journey Down the Yellowstone River to the Soul of Montana*. New York: HarperCollins, 1993.

Clark, Robert. *Rivers of the West: Stories from the Columbia*. New York: HarperCollins, 1995.

Cody, Robin. *Voyage of a Summer Sun: Canoeing the Columbia River*. Seattle: Sasquatch Books, 1995.

Coffey, Maria. *A Boat in Our Baggage: Around the World with a Kayak*. London: Abacus, 1994.

Collins, Robert O., and Roderick Nash. *The Big Drops*. San Francisco: Sierra Club Books, 1978.

Cone, Joseph. *A Common Fate: Endangered Salmon and the People of the Pacific Northwest*. New York: Henry Holt, 1995.

Cooper, Bill, and Laurel Cooper. *Back Door to Byzantium: To the Black Sea by the Great Rivers of Europe.* Dobbs Ferry, N.Y.: Sheridan House, 1997.

Cowan, James G. *Letters from a Wild State: Rediscovering Our True Relationship to Nature.* New York: Bell Tower, 1991.

Cronin, John, and Robert F. Kennedy. *The Riverkeepers.* New York: Scribner, 1997.

Deitrich, William. *Northwest Passage: The Great Columbia River.* New York: Simon and Schuster, 1995.

Delp, Michael. *The Coast of Nowhere: Meditations on River, Lakes and Streams.* Detroit: Great Lakes Books, 1997.

Dennis, Jerry. *The Bird in the Waterfall: A Natural History of Oceans, Rivers and Lakes.* New York: HarperCollins, 1996.

Dietz, Lew. *The Allagash: The History of a Wilderness River in Maine.* Thorndike, Maine: Thorndike Press, 1968.

Duncan, David James. *River Teeth: Stories and Writings.* New York: Doubleday, 1995.

Duncan, David James. *The River Why.* New York: Bantam Books, 1988.

Ehrlich, Gretel. *Islands, The Universe, Home.* New York: Viking Penguin, 1991.

Eyden, Pamela, Molly McGuire, and Reggie McLeod, eds. *Big River Reader.* Winona, Minn.: Big River, 1996.

Fisher, Hank. *The Floater's Guide to Montana.* Helena, Mont.: Falcon Press, 1986.

Fletcher, Colin. *River: One Man's Journey Down the Colorado, Source to Sea.* New York: Vintage Books/Random House, 1998.

Fradkin, Philip L. *A River No More: The Colorado River and the West.* New York: Alfred A. Knopf, Inc., 1981.

Gertler, Ed. *Maryland and Delaware Canoe Trails.* Silver Spring, Md.: Seneca, 1989.

Gibbal, Jean-Marie. *Genii of the River Niger.* Chicago: University of Chicago Press, 1994.

Gidmark, David. *Birchbark Canoe: Living Among the Algonquin.* Buffalo, N.Y.: Firefly Books, 1997.

Gordon, I. Herbert. *The Complete Book of Canoeing.* Old Saybrook, Conn.: Globe Pequot Press, 1992.

Gullion, Laurie. *Canoeing.* Champaign, Ill.: Human Kinetics Publishing Inc., 1994.

Gutheim, Frederick. *The Potomac.* New York: Holt, Rinehart and Winston, 1974.

Hall, Oakley. *Separations.* Reno: University of Nevada Press, 1997.

Harden, Blaine. *A River Lost: The Life and Death of the Columbia.* New York: W. W. Norton and Co., 1996.

Harris, Eddy L. *Mississippi Solo: A River Quest.* New York: Harper & Row, 1988.

Harris, Thomas. *Down the Wild Rivers: A Guide to the Streams of California.* San Francisco: Chronicle Books, 1973.

Heat-Moon, William Least. *River-Horse: The Logbook of a Boat Across America.* New York: Houghton Mifflin Company, 1999.

Hiestand, Emily. *The Very Rich Hours: Travels in Orkney, Belize, the Everglades, and Greece.* Boston: Beacon Press, 1992.

Hildebrand, John. *Reading the River: A Voyage Down the Yukon.* New York: Houghton Mifflin Company, 1988.

Hoagland, Edward. *The Tugman's Passage.* New York: Lyons & Burford, 1982.

Housden, Roger. *Travels Through Sacred India.* London: Thorsons/HarperCollins, 1996.

Hundley, Norris, Jr. *The Great Thirst: Californians and Water, 1770s-1990s.* Berkeley: University of California Press, 1992.

Huser, Verne, ed. *River Reflections: A Collection of River Writings.* Chester, Conn.: Globe Pequot Press, 1988.

Jenkinson, Michael. *Wild Rivers of North America*. New York: E. P. Dutton, 1981.

Jerome, John. *Blue Rooms: Ripples, Rivers, Pools and Other Waters*. New York: Henry Holt, 1997.

Jettmar, Karen. *The Alaska River Guide*. Seattle: Alaska Northwest Books, 1993.

Johnston, Tracy. *Shooting the Boh: A Woman's Voyage Down the Wildest River in Borneo*. New York: Vintage, 1992.

Kane, Joe. *Running the Amazon*. New York: Knopf, 1989.

Kinseth, Lance. *River Eternal: The Wonder of Common and Ashen Days Alongside a Prairie River*. New York: Viking Penguin, 1989.

Kolankiewicz, Leon. *Where Salmon Come to Die*. Boulder, Colo.: Pruett Publishing, 1993.

Krakel, Dean II. *Downriver: A Yellowstone Journey*. San Francisco: Sierra Club Books, 1987.

Lee, Katie. *All My Rivers Are Gone: A Journey of Discovery Through Glen Canyon*. Boulder, Colo.: Johnson Books, 1998.

Leeson, Ted. *The Habit of Rivers: Reflections on Trout Streams and Fly Fishing*. New York: Lyons & Burford, 1994; Penguin Books, 1995.

Lembke, Janet. *Skinny Dipping and Other Immersions in Water, Myth and Being Human*. New York: Lyons & Burford, 1994.

Leopold, Luna. *Water, Rivers and Creeks*. Sausalito, Calif.: University Science Books, 1997.

Leopold, Luna. *The View of the River*. Cambridge, Mass.: Harvard University Press, 1994.

Lewis, Dan. *Paddle and Portage: The Floater's Guide to Wyoming Rivers*. Douglas: The Wyoming Naturalist, 1991.

Lopez, Barry. *Desert Notes: Reflections in the Eye of a Raven; River Notes: The Dance of Herons*. New York: Avon Books, 1976, 1990.

Lourie, Peter. *River of Mountains: A Canoe Journey Down the Hudson.* Syracuse, N.Y.: Syracuse University Press, 1995.

Macintyre, Ben. *Forgotten Fatherland: The Search for Elizabeth Nietzsche.* New York: Farrar, Straus & Giroux, 1992.

Maclean, Norman. *A River Runs Through It.* Chicago: University of Chicago Press, 1976.

Madson, John. *Up on the River: An Upper Mississippi Chronicle.* New York: Viking Penguin, 1985.

Mancall, Peter C., ed. *Land of Rivers: America in Word and Image.* Ithaca, N.Y.: Cornell University Press, 1996.

Martin, Marian. *The European Waterways: A Manual for First Time Users.* Dobbs Ferry, N.Y.: Sheridan House, 1997.

Madsen, Ken. *Tatshenshini Wilderness Quest and Other River Adventures.* Vancouver, Canada: Primrose Publishing, 1991.

Madson, John. *Up on the River: An Upper Mississippi Chronicle.* New York: Nick Lyons Books, Inc., 1985; Penguin Books, 1986.

Maxwell, Gavin. *People of the Reeds.* New York: Harper & Brothers, 1957.

McCully, Patrick. *Silenced Rivers: The Ecology and Politics of Large Dams.* London: Zed Books, 1996.

McGuffin, Gary, and Joanie McGuffin. *Where Rivers Run: A 6,000-Mile Exploration of Canada by Canoe.* Toronto, Canada: Stoddart Publishing, 1988.

McNamee, Gregory. *Gila: The Life and Death of an American River.* New York: Orion Books, 1994.

McNulty, Tim, and Pat O'Hara. *Washington's Wild Rivers: The Unfinished Work.* Seattle: The Mountaineers, 1990.

McPhee, John. *Coming Into the Country.* New York: Bantam Books/Farrar, Straus & Giroux, 1981.

McPhee, John. *The Control of Nature.* New York: Farrar, Straus & Giroux, 1989.

McPhee, John. *The Pine Barrens.* New York: Farrar, Straus & Giroux, 1978.

Meloy, Ellen. *Raven's Exile: A Season on the Green River.* New York: Henry Holt, 1994.

Middleton, Harry. *Rivers of Memory.* Boulder, Colo.: Pruett Publishing Co, 1993.

Montgomery, M. R. *Many Rivers to Cross: Of Good Running Water, Native Trout, and the Remnants of Wilderness.* New York: Touchstone/Simon & Schuster, 1996.

Moore, Kathleen Dean. *Riverwalking: Reflections on Moving Water.* New York: Lyons & Burford, 1995.

Morris, Jan. *Pleasures of a Tangled Life.* New York: Vintage Books, 1989.

Neihardt, John G. *The River and I.* Lincoln: University of Nebraska Press, 1997.

Newby, Eric. *Slowly Down the Ganges: An Enthralling and Hilarious Voyage Down India's Sacred River.* New York: Viking Penguin, 1966.

Nichols, Gary C. *River Runner's Guide to Utah and Adjacent Areas.* Salt Lake City: University of Utah Press, 1986.

Niemi, Judith, and Barbara Wieser, eds. *Rivers Running Free: A Century of Women's Canoeing Adventures.* Seattle: Adventura Books, 1992, 1997.

Norman, Seth. *Meanderings of a Fly Fisherman.* Gallatin Gateway, Mont.: Wilderness Adventures Press, 1996.

Nugent, Rory. *Drums Along the Congo: On the Trail of Mokele-Mbembe, The Last Living Dinosaur.* New York: Houghton Mifflin, 1993.

Offutt, Chris. *The Same River Twice: A Memoir.* New York: Simon & Schuster, Inc., 1993; Penguin Books, 1994.

O'Hanlon, Redmond. *In Trouble Again: A Journey Between the*

Orinoco and the Amazon. New York: Vintage
Departures/Random House, 1988.

Palmer, Tim. *America by Rivers.* Washington, D.C.: Island Press,
1996.

Palmer, Tim. *Endangered Rivers and the Conservation Movement.*
Berkeley: University of California Press, 1986.

Palmer, Tim. *Lifelines: The Case for River Conservation.* Washington,
D.C.: Island Press, 1994.

Palmer, Tim. *The Snake River: Window to the West.* Washington,
D.C.: Island Press, 1991.

Patterson, R. M. *Dangerous River.* Toronto: Stoddart Publishing,
1990.

Perkins, Robert. *Into the Great Solitude: An Arctic Journey.* New
York: Dell Publishing, 1992.

Peterson, Brenda. *Living by Water: True Stories of Nature and Spirit.*
New York: Ballantine Books, 1994.

Pritchett, V. S. *At Home and Abroad.* New York: North Point
Press, 1989.

Quammen, David. *Wild Thoughts from Wild Places.* New York:
Scribner Books, 1998.

Roche, Judith, and Meg McHutchison, eds. *First Fish, First
People: Salmon Tales of the North Pacific Rim.* Seattle: University
of Washington Press, 1998.

Rosenblum, Mort. *The Secret Life of the Seine.* Reading, Pa.:
Addison-Wesley, 1994.

Russell, Andy. *The Life of a River.* Stillwater, Minn.: Voyageur
Press, 1987.

Ryan, Kathleen Jo, ed. *Writing Down the River: Into the Heart of the
Grand Canyon.* Flagstaff, Ariz.: Northland, 1998.

Ryden, Hope. *Lily Pond: Four Years with a Family of Beavers.* New
York: William Morrow and Company, 1989.

Schwenk, Theodor. *Sensitive Chaos: The Creation of Flowing Forms in Water and Air.* London: Rudolf Steiner Press, 1996.

Schwiebert, Ernest. *Remembrances of Rivers Past.* San Francisco: Donald S. Ellis/Creative Arts, 1984.

Semken, Steven H. *River Tips and Tree Trunks: Notes and Reflections on Water and Wood.* North Liberty, Iowa: Ice Cube Press, 1996.

Smith, Annick, ed. *Headwaters: Montana Writers on Water and Wilderness.* Missoula, Mont.: Hellgate Writers, 1996.

Snyder, Gary. *The Practice of the Wild.* San Francisco: North Point Press, 1990.

Spurr, Daniel. *River of Forgotten Days: A Journey Down the Mississippi in Search of La Salle.* New York: Henry Holt, 1998.

Stanton, Richard L. *Potomac Journey.* Washington, D.C.: Smithsonian Institution Press, 1993.

Stafford, Kim. *Having Everything Right: Essays of Place.* Seattle: Sasquatch Books, 1986.

Stegner, Page, ed. *Call of the River: Writings and Photographs.* New York: Tehabi Books/Harcourt Brace, 1996.

Stegner, Wallace. *The Sound of Mountain Water.* Lincoln: University of Nebraska Press, 1985.

Stovall, Linny, ed. *Head/Waters.* Hillsboro, Oreg.: Blue Heron Publishing, 1994.

Stutz, Bruce. *Natural Lives, Modern Times: People and Places of the Delaware River.* New York: Crown Publishing, 1992.

Teal, Louise. *Breaking Into the Current: Boatwoman on the Grand Canyon.* Tucson: University of Arizona Press, 1994.

Thesiger, Wilfred. *The Marsh Arabs.* London: Penguin Books, 1964.

Thomas, Bill. *American Rivers: A Natural History.* New York: W. W. Norton and Co., 1978.

Thoreau, Henry David. *A Week on the Concord and Merrimack Rivers*. New York: Thomas Y. Crowell, 1981.

Twain, Mark. *Life on the Mississippi*. New York: The New American Library of World Literature, Inc., 1961.

Van Beek, Steve. *The Chao Praya: River in Transition*. Oxford: Oxford University Press, 1995.

Wallace, David Raines. *The Untamed Garden and Other Personal Essays*. Columbus: Ohio State University Press, 1986.

Wallach, Jeff. *What the River Says*. Hillsboro, Oreg.: Blue Heron Publishing, 1996.

Walton, Izaak. *The Compleat Angler*. Hopewell, N.J.: Ecco Press, 1995.

Western Writers of America. *Water Trails West*. New York: Avon Books, 1978.

Wheat, Doug. *The Floater's Guide to Colorado*. Helena, Mont.: Falcon Press, 1984.

Wilkinson, Alec. *The Riverkeeper*. New York: Alfred A. Knopf, Inc., 1990.

Williams, Terry Tempest. *An Unspoken Hunger: Stories from the Field*. New York: Vintage, 1994.

Willamette Kayak and Canoe Club. *Soggy Sneakers: A Guide to Oregon Rivers*. Seattle: The Mountaineers, 1994.

Winchester, Simon. *The River at the Center of the World: A Journey Up the Yangtze and Back in Chinese Time*. New York: Henry Holt, 1996.

Winternitz, Helen. *East Along the Equator: A Journey Up the Congo and Into Zaire*. New York: Atlantic Monthly Press, 1987.

Worster, Donald. *Rivers of Empire: Water, Aridity and the Growth of the American West*. New York: Pantheon, 1985.

Worster, Donald. *An Unsettled Country: Changing Landscapes of the American West*. Albuquerque: University of New Mexico Press, 1994.

Zalis, Paul. *Who is the River?* New York: Atheneum, 1986.

Zwinger, Ann H. *Downcanyon*. Tuscon: University of Arizona Press, 1995.

Zwinger, Ann H. *Run, River, Run*. Tuscon: University of Arizona Press, 1984.

River Organizations

U.S.-based groups:

American Rivers
1025 Vermont Avenue, NW, Suite 720
Washington, DC 20005
USA
Phone: 202-347-7550
Fax: 202-347-9250
E-mail: mbowman@amrivers.org

Anacostia Watershed Society
(The Anacostia is Washington, D.C.'s *other* river.)
4302 Baltimore Avenue
Bladensburg, MD 20710-1031
Phone: 301-699-6204
Fax: 301-699-3317
Email: REBh20@aol.com
WWW: http:www.anacostiaws.org

Friends of the River (California river focus)
915 20th Street
Sacramento, CA 95814
USA
Phone: 916-442-3155
Fax: 916-442-3398
E-mail: chare@friendsoftheriver.org
WWW: http://www.friendsoftheriver.org

International Rivers Network
1847 Berkeley Way

Berkeley, CA 94703
USA
Phone: 510-848-1155
Fax: 510-848-1008
E-mail: irn@irn.org
WWW: http://www.irn.irn.org

International Rivers Network (IRN) is the only organization in the world devoted to protecting rivers on an international scale, from the Amazon to the Zambezi. IRN envisions a world in which the connection between environmental integrity and human rights is universally understood and respected, and supports local communities working to protect their rivers and watersheds in the U.S. and abroad.

The National Organization for Rivers
212 West Cheyenne Mountain
Colorado Springs, CO 80906
USA
Phone: 719-579-8759
Fax: 719-576-6238
E-mail: nors@rmi.net
WWW: http://www.nationalrivers.org

River Alliance of Wisconsin (Wisconsin river focus)
122 State St., Suite 202
Madison, WI 53703-2500
USA
Phone: 608-257-2424
Fax: 608-251-1655
E-mail: wisrivers@wisconsinrivers.org
WWW: http://www.wisconsinrivers.org

River Network
520 SW 6th Avenue #1130
Portland, OR 97204
USA
Phone: 503-241-3506 or 1-800-423-6747

Fax: 503-241-9256
E-mail: info@rivernetwork.org
WWW: http://www.rivernetwork.org

River of Words Project
PO Box 4000-J
Berkeley, CA 94704
USA
Phone: 510-848-1155
Fax: 510-848-1008
E-mail: row@irn.org
WWW: http://www.irn.org

River of Words (ROW) is an international children's art and
poetry project designed to nurture respect and understanding of
the natural world. By encouraging children to explore nature,
local watersheds, and their own imaginations, River of Words
helps young people to develop a sense of belonging to their communities and the to the web of life. ROW conducts extensive
teacher training and curriculum development and administers a
free annual worldwide art and poetry contest that is co-sponsored
by The Library of Congress and International Rivers Network.

Trout Unlimited
1500 Wilson Boulevard; Suite 310
Arlington, VA 22209-2404
USA
Phone: 703-522-0200
Fax: 703-284-9400
E-mail: trout@tu.org
WWW: http://www.tu.org

Groups in other parts of the world:

European Rivers Network
8 Rue Crozatier
F-43000 Le Puy

FRANCE
Phone: +33 (16) 471055788
Fax:+33 (16) 471026099
E-mail: ern@globenet.gn.apc.org or ern@rivernet.org

Center for Water Policy/ICDRP
c/o Dr. N Bhattachary,
50D/AD Block,
Shalimar Bagh,
Delhi 110 052
INDIA
Fax: +91 11 713 4654
E-mail: cwaterp@del3.vsnl.net.in

Environmental Monitoring Group
PO Box 18977
Wynberg 7824,
Cape Town
SOUTH AFRICA
Phone: +27 21 761 0549
Fax: +27 21 762 2238

Help the River Volga
P.O. Box 34
Sol Kolpakova E.
Nizag Novgorod 603163
RUSSIA
Phone: +7 8312 30 28 81
Fax: +7 8312 39 11 91
E-mail: dront@glas.apc.org

Meinung People's Association
12 Fu-An Street
Meinung 843, Kaohsiung
TAIWAN
Phone: +886 7 6810467 or +886 7 6810371
Fax:+886 7 6810201

E-mail: mpa@listserv.nsysu.edu.tw
E-mail: soongtindoong@pcmail.com.tw

Movimento dos Atingidos por Barragens
Rua 7 de abril, 264
sala 723
01014-000 Sao Paulo, SP
BRAZIL
Phone/fax: +55 11 256 0839

Narmada Bachao Andolan (NBA)
B-13, Shivam Flats
Ellora Park
Baroda 390 007
INDIA
Phone/fax: +91 265 382232
E-mail: nba@lwbdq.lwbbs.net

Rivers! Japan
670, Takakura, Fujisawa-shi
Kanagawa-ken 252-0802
JAPAN
Phone: 81 466 44 8517
Fax: 81 466 46 3309
email: tniikura@gb3.so-net.ne.jp

SEK Klub Gaja
PO Box 261
43-301 Bielsko-Biala 1
POLAND
Phone/fax: 00 48 33 8 12 36 94
E-mail: klub@gaja.most.org.pl

Sobrevivencia
25 de Mayo 1618
Casilla de Correos 1380
Asunción
PARAGUAY

Phone: +595 21 480182 / 224427
Fax: +595 21 550451
E-mail: survive@sviven.una.py

Southeast Asia Rivers Network - Thailand Chapter
25/5 Moo 2
Soi Sukha-pibarn 27
Changkien-Chedyod Rd
Tambol Chang Phuek Muang
Chiang Mai 50300
THAILAND
Phone: 053 221157 (h)
E-mail: ethnet@chmai.loxinfo.co.th

SUNGI Development Foundation
House No. 17, Street 67, Sector G-6/4
Islamabad
PAKISTAN
Phone: +92 51 273272, 276579, 276589
Fax:+92 51 823559
E-mail: mishka@sungi.sdnpk.undp.org

Index

Index of Contributors

Acknowledgments

Heartfelt thanks to the folks at Travelers' Tales: James O'Reilly, Wenda O'Reilly, Sean O'Reilly, Tim O'Reilly, Lisa Bach, Jennifer Leo, Deborah Greco, Susan Brady, Tara Weaver, Natanya Pearlman, Cynthia Lamb, Patty Holden, Judy Johnson, Trisha Schwartz, and especially to Larry Habegger.

To my friends and colleagues at International Rivers Network: Monti Aguirre, Elizabeth Brink, Aleta Brown George, Selma Barros de Oliveira, Lorena Cassady, Yvonne Cuellar, Annie Ducmanis, Dzhennet Eschekova, Ignacio Fernandez, Mary Houghteling, Aviva Imhof, Patrick McCully, Lori Pottinger, Steve Rothert, Elyse Shafarman, Doris Shen, Glenn Switkes, Susanne Wong, and Petra Yee.

About the Editor

In her youth, Pamela Michael crossed the United States several times, by thumb, rail, bus and car, sometimes with her infant son in tow (and often her Irish wolfhound, as well). She didn't leave the continent until she was over forty, but has made up for lost time, visiting over twenty-five countries in the last decade.

Michael has published articles in the *San Francisco Examiner*, *Odyssey*, *Shape*, *Salon.com*, *Maiden Voyages*, and many other newspapers and magazines, as well as contributing stories to several books in the Travelers' Tales Series.

Her books include *A Woman's Passion for Travel: More True Stories from A Woman's World*, *A Mother's World: Journeys of the Heart* (both with Marybeth Bond), *ROWing Partners: 101 Ways to Community Partnerships*, and *The Whole World is Watching: Media Involvement in Education*.

She also hosts a travel show on public radio, and wrote and produced a nationally-broadcast four-part series on Buddhism in the United States, narrated by Richard Gere. She is director and co-founder (with Robert Hass) of River of Words, an international children's environmental poetry and art project.

After spending her "wonder years" in the suburbs of Washington, D.C., doing a brief stint as a child-bride in

Manhattan (well, she was eighteen), struggling as a single welfare mother/novice political activist in Cambridge, Massachusetts, she finally arrived in California just in time for the "Summer of Love" and decided to stay until she found it. Still looking and now a grandmother, she lives in Berkeley with her Tibetan Terrier, Yeti.

TRAVELERS' TALES GUIDES
LOOK FOR THESE TITLES IN THE SERIES

FOOTSTEPS: THE SOUL OF TRAVEL
A NEW IMPRINT FROM TRAVELERS' TALES GUIDES

An imprint of Travelers' Tales Guides, the Footsteps series unveils new works by first-time authors, established writers, and reprints of works whose time has come…again. Each book will fire your imagination, disturb your sleep, and feed your soul.

KITE STRINGS OF THE SOUTHERN CROSS
A Woman's Travel Odyssey
By Laurie Gough
ISBN 1-885211-30-9
400 pages, $24.00, Hardcover

THE SWORD OF HEAVEN
A Five Continent Odyssey to Save the World
By Mikkel Aaland
ISBN 1-885211-44-9
350 pages, $24.00, Hardcover

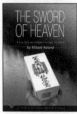

STORM
A Motorcycle Journey of Love, Endurance, and Transformation
By Allen Noren
ISBN 1-885211-45-7
360 pages, $24.00, Hardcover

ᦏPECIAL INTEREST

THE FEARLESS SHOPPER:
How to Get the Best Deals on the Planet
By Kathy Borrus
ISBN 1-885211-39-2, 200 pages, $12.95

◊PECIAL INTEREST

THE GIFT OF RIVERS:
True Stories of Life on the Water
Edited by Pamela Michael
Introduction by Robert Hass
ISBN 1-885211-42-2, 256 pages, $14.95

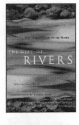

SHITTING PRETTY:
How to Stay Clean and Healthy While Traveling
By Dr. Jane Wilson-Howarth
ISBN 1-885211-47-3, 200 pages, $12.95

THE GIFT OF BIRDS:
True Encounters with Avian Spirits
Edited by Larry Habegger & Amy G. Carlson
ISBN 1-885211-41-4, 352 pages, $17.95

TESTOSTERONE PLANET:
True Stories from a Man's World
Edited by Sean O'Reilly, Larry Habegger & James O'Reilly
ISBN 1-885211-43-0, 300 pages, $17.95

THE PENNY PINCHER'S PASSPORT TO LUXURY TRAVEL:
The Art of Cultivating Preferred Customer Status
By Joel L. Widzer
ISBN 1-885211-31-7, 253 pages, $12.95

✐PECIAL INTEREST

DANGER!
True Stories of Trouble and Survival
Edited by James O'Reilly, Larry Habegger & Sean O'Reilly
ISBN 1-885211-32-5, 336 pages, $17.95

FAMILY TRAVEL:
The Farther You Go, the Closer You Get
Edited by Laura Manske
ISBN 1-885211-33-3, 368 pages, $17.95

THE GIFT OF TRAVEL:
The Best of Travelers' Tales
Edited by Larry Habegger, James O'Reilly & Sean O'Reilly
ISBN 1-885211-25-2, 240 pages, $14.95

THERE'S NO TOILET PAPER...ON THE ROAD LESS TRAVELED:
The Best of Travel Humor and Misadventure
Edited by Doug Lansky
ISBN 1-885211-27-9, 207 pages, $12.95

A DOG'S WORLD:
True Stories of Man's Best Friend on the Road
Edited by Christine Hunsicker
ISBN 1-885211-23-6, 257 pages, $12.95

$\mathscr{W}$OMEN'S TRAVEL

A WOMAN'S PATH:
Women's Best Spiritual Travel Writing
Edited by Lucy McCauley, Amy G. Carlson, and Jennifer Leo
ISBN 1-885211-48-1, 320 pages, $16.95

A WOMAN'S PASSION FOR TRAVEL:
More True Stories from A Woman's World
Edited by Marybeth Bond & Pamela Michael
ISBN 1-885211-36-8, 375 pages, $17.95

SAFETY AND SECURITY FOR WOMEN WHO TRAVEL
By Sheila Swan & Peter Laufer
ISBN 1-885211-29-5, 159 pages, $12.95

WOMEN IN THE WILD:
True Stories of Adventure and Connection
Edited by Lucy McCauley
ISBN 1-885211-21-X, 307 pages, $17.95

A MOTHER'S WORLD:
Journeys of the Heart
Edited by Marybeth Bond & Pamela Michael
ISBN 1-885211-26-0, 233 pages, $14.95

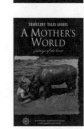

$\mathcal{W}$OMEN'S TRAVEL

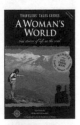

A WOMAN'S WORLD:
True Stories of Life on the Road
Edited by Marybeth Bond
Introduction by Dervla Murphy
ISBN 1-885211-06-6
475 pages, $17.95

Winner of the Lowell
Thomas Award for Best
Travel Book—Society of
American Travel Writers

GUTSY WOMEN:
Travel Tips and Wisdom for the Road
By Marybeth Bond
ISBN 1-885211-15-5, 123 pages, $7.95

GUTSY MAMAS:
Travel Tips and Wisdom
for Mothers on the Road
By Marybeth Bond
ISBN 1-885211-20-1, 139 pages, $7.95

$\mathcal{B}$ODY & SOUL

THE ULTIMATE JOURNEY:
Inspiring Stories of Living and Dying
James O'Reilly, Larry Habegger & Richard Sterling
ISBN 1-885211-38-4
336 pages, $17.95

ADVENTURE OF FOOD:
True Stories of Eating Everything
Edited by Richard Sterling
ISBN 1-885211-37-6
336 pages, $17.95

ℬODY & SOUL

THE ROAD WITHIN:
True Stories of Transformation and the Soul
*Edited by Sean O'Reilly, James O'Reilly
& Tim O'Reilly*
ISBN 1-885211-19-8, 459 pages, $17.95

LOVE & ROMANCE:
True Stories of Passion on the Road
Edited by Judith Babcock Wylie
ISBN 1-885211-18-X, 319 pages, $17.95

FOOD:
A Taste of the Road
*Edited by Richard Sterling
Introduction by Margo True
ISBN 1-885211-09-0
467 pages, $17.95*

THE FEARLESS DINER:
Travel Tips and Wisdom for Eating around the World
By Richard Sterling
ISBN 1-885211-22-8, 139 pages, $7.95

ℭOUNTRY GUIDES

IRELAND
True Stories of Life on the Emerald Isle
Edited by James O'Reilly, Larry Habegger, and Sean O'Reilly
ISBN 1-885211-46-5, 368 pages, $17.95

COUNTRY GUIDES

AUSTRALIA
True Stories of Life Down Under
Edited by Larry Habegger
ISBN 1-885211-40-6, 375 pages, $17.95

AMERICA
Edited by Fred Setterberg
ISBN 1-885211-28-7, 550 pages, $19.95

JAPAN
Edited by Donald W. George
& Amy Greimann Carlson
ISBN 1-885211-04-X, 437 pages, $17.95

ITALY
Edited by Anne Calcagno
Introduction by Jan Morris
ISBN 1-885211-16-3, 463 pages, $17.95

INDIA
Edited by James O'Reilly & Larry Habegger
ISBN 1-885211-01-5, 538 pages, $17.95

COUNTRY GUIDES

FRANCE

Edited by James O'Reilly, Larry Habegger
& Sean O'Reilly
ISBN 1-885211-02-3, 517 pages, $17.95

MEXICO

Edited by James O'Reilly & Larry Habegger
ISBN 1-885211-00-7, 463 pages, $17.95

────── ★*★* ──────

Winner of the Lowell
Thomas Award for Best
Travel Book – Society of
American Travel Writers

THAILAND

Edited by James O'Reilly
& Larry Habegger
ISBN 1-885211-05-8
483 pages, $17.95

SPAIN

Edited by Lucy McCauley
ISBN 1-885211-07-4, 495 pages, $17.95

NEPAL

Edited by Rajendra S. Khadka
ISBN 1-885211-14-7, 423 pages, $17.95

COUNTRY GUIDES

BRAZIL
Edited by Annette Haddad & Scott Doggett
Introduction by Alex Shoumatoff
ISBN 1-885211-11-2
452 pages, $17.95

— ★★★ —
Benjamin Franklin
Award Winner

CITY GUIDES

HONG KONG
Edited by James O'Reilly, Larry Habegger & Sean O'Reilly
ISBN 1-885211-03-1, 439 pages, $17.95

PARIS
Edited by James O'Reilly, Larry Habegger & Sean O'Reilly
ISBN 1-885211-10-4, 417 pages, $17.95

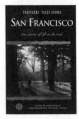

SAN FRANCISCO
Edited by James O'Reilly, Larry Habegger & Sean O'Reilly
ISBN 1-885211-08-2, 491 pages, $17.95

ℛEGIONAL GUIDES

SUBMIT YOUR OWN TRAVEL TALE

Do you have a tale of your own that you would like to submit to Travelers' Tales? We highly recommend that you first read one or more of our books to get a feel for the kind of story we're looking for. For submission guidelines and a list of titles in the works, send a SASE to:

Travelers' Tales Submission Guidelines
330 Townsend Street, Suite 208, San Francisco, CA 94107

or send email to ***guidelines@travelerstales.com***
or visit our Web site at **www.travelerstales.com**

You can send your story to the address above or via email to ***submit@travelerstales.com***. On the outside of the envelope, ***please indicate what country/topic your story is about***. If your story is selected for one of our titles, we will contact you about rights and payment.

We hope to hear from you. In the meantime, enjoy the stories!